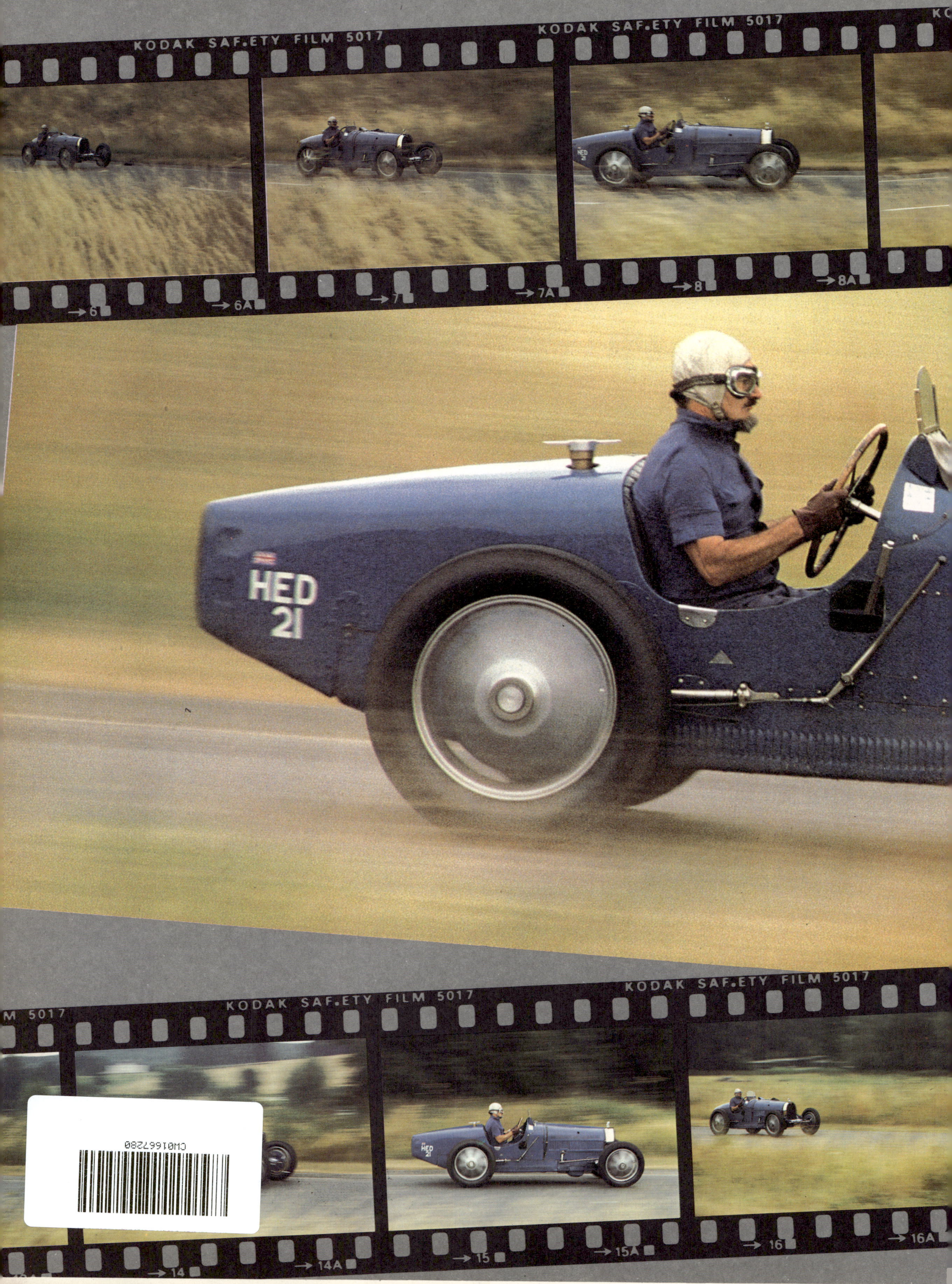
KODAK SAF.ETY FILM 5017
6
6A
7
7A
8
8A
HED 21
14
14A
15
15A
16
16A

GREAT MARQUES
BUGATTI

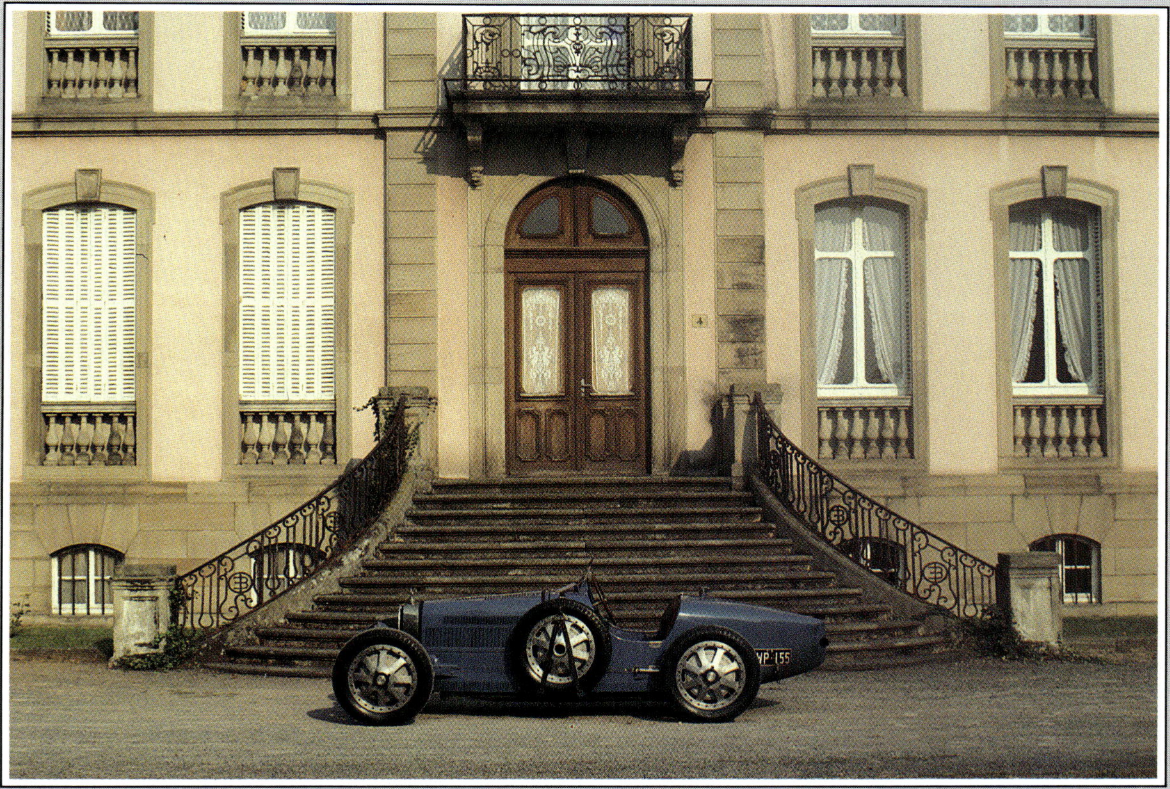

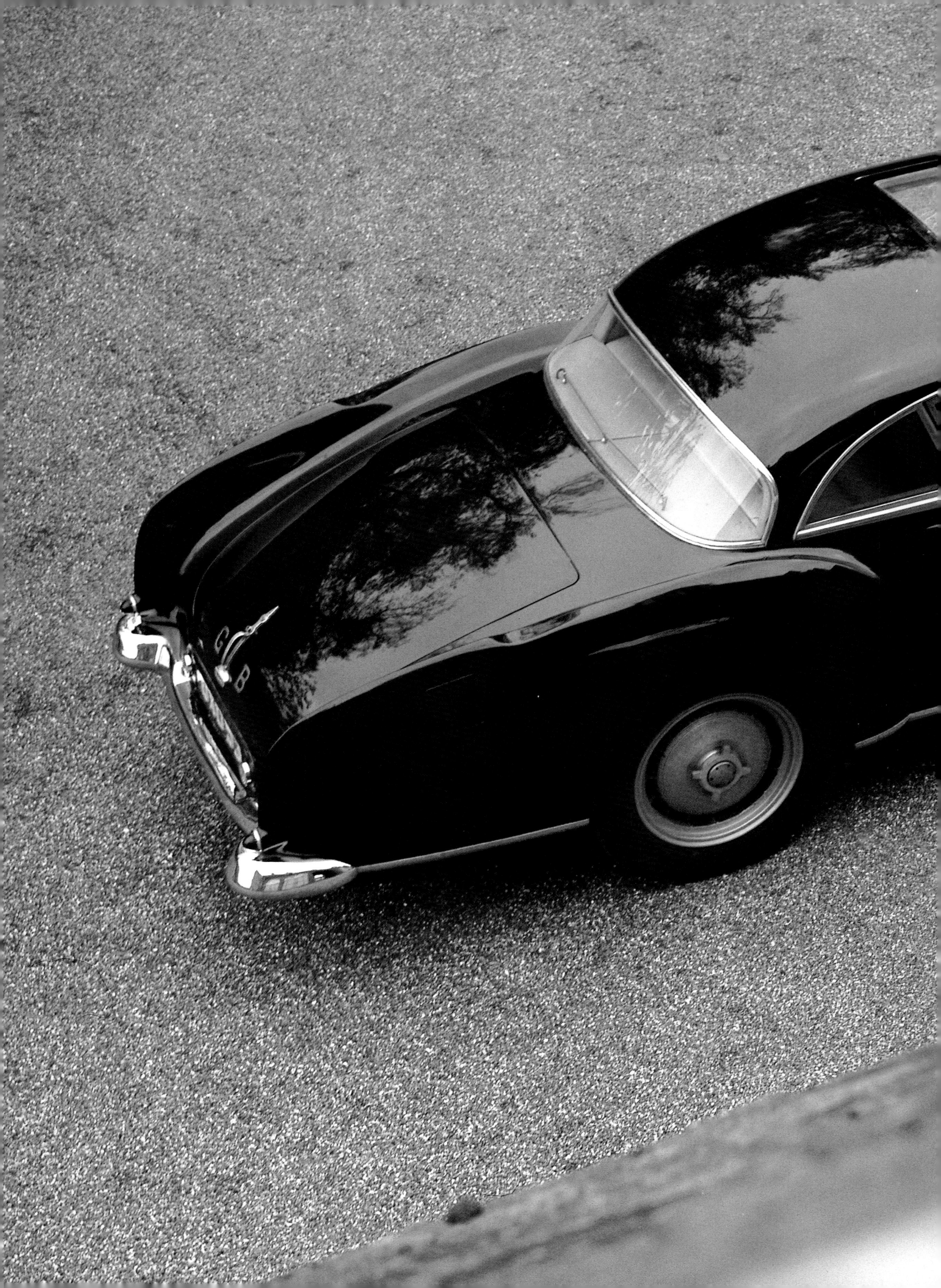
GB

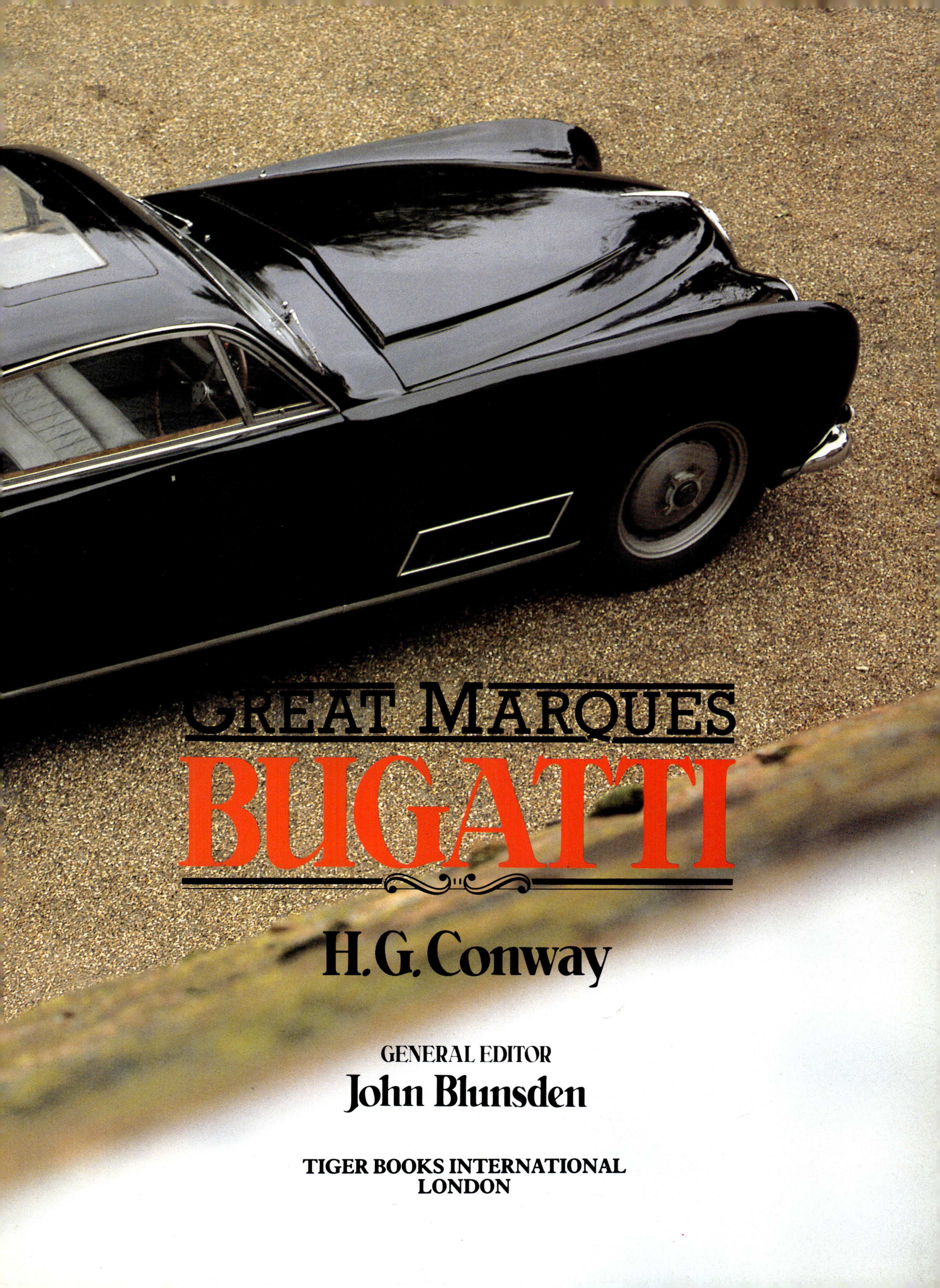

GREAT MARQUES
BUGATTI

H.G. Conway

GENERAL EDITOR
John Blunsden

TIGER BOOKS INTERNATIONAL
LONDON

Author's note

Ettore Bugatti was one of the more remarkable car manufacturers in the history of the automobile, already noteworthy for a wide range of talented designers and successful – and not so successful – entrepreneurs. The designing and building of a car whose licence he sold before he was 21 years old was astonishing enough; to produce a further eight designs before he was 30 was equally noteworthy. To set up a factory to produce successfully cars bearing his own name was a tribute to his own skill as a designer and constructor.

His name will for ever be associated with racing cars, especially the brilliant 1924 Type 35, and perhaps some of his departures from common sense, such as the monster Royale or the four-wheel-drive racing car, serve more to heighten interest in him than to detract from his reputation.

This book can only deal with his main and most interesting car productions: he was a man of many talents, a compulsive designer and sketcher of boats, railcars, steam engines, boilers, horse-drawn coaches, even his personal apparel.

His was an amazing, indeed uniquely talented family. The furniture of his father Carlo, and the animal sculpture of his brother Rembrandt, are just as renowned in their own fields as Ettore's cars.

Where possible, owners and custodians of the cars, at the time of photographing, are mentioned in the captions to the illustrations.

We would particularly like to thank Jean-Claude Derlerm and Patrick Garnier of the Musée National de l'Automobile de Mulhouse in France for their co-operation and for allowing us to photograph some of the Bugattis in this magnificent collection.

H.G. Conway

ENDPAPERS Mr I. Preston's 1929 Type 35B.

PAGE 1 A Type 35 in front of the Bugatti Château St Jean at Molsheim.

PAGES 2 AND 3 A Type 50 with Saoutchik bodywork. From a private collection in England.

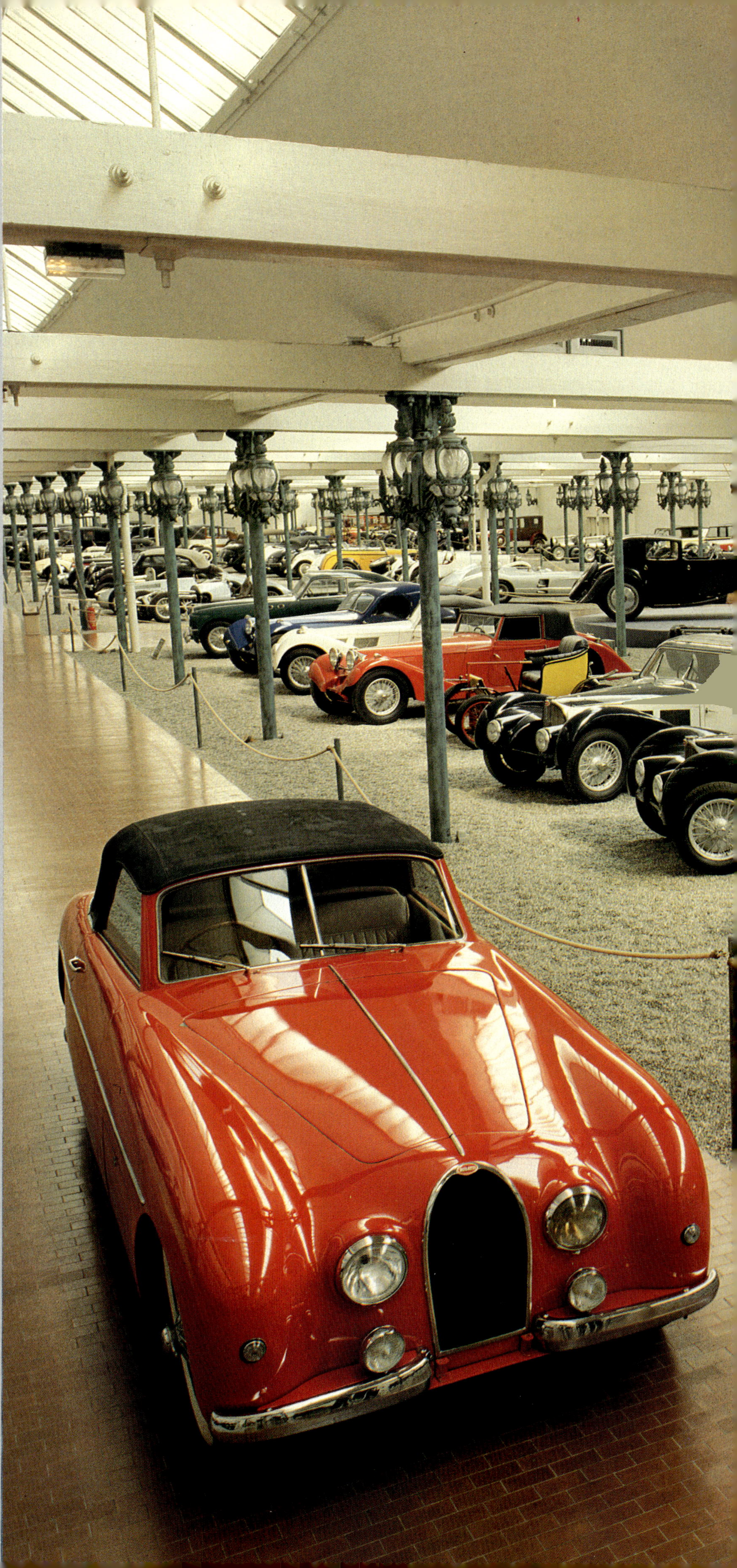

THESE PAGES Some of the Bugattis at the Musée National de l'Automobile, Mulhouse. In the foreground is the Type 101 by Gangloff.

Special photography:
Chris Linton, Ian Dawson, Jean-Paul Caron and **Laurie Caddell**

First published in Great Britain in 1984 by Octopus Books Limited

This edition published in 1989 by Tiger Books International PLC, London

ISBN 1 870461 97 5

Produced by Mandarin Offset
Printed and bound in Hong Kong

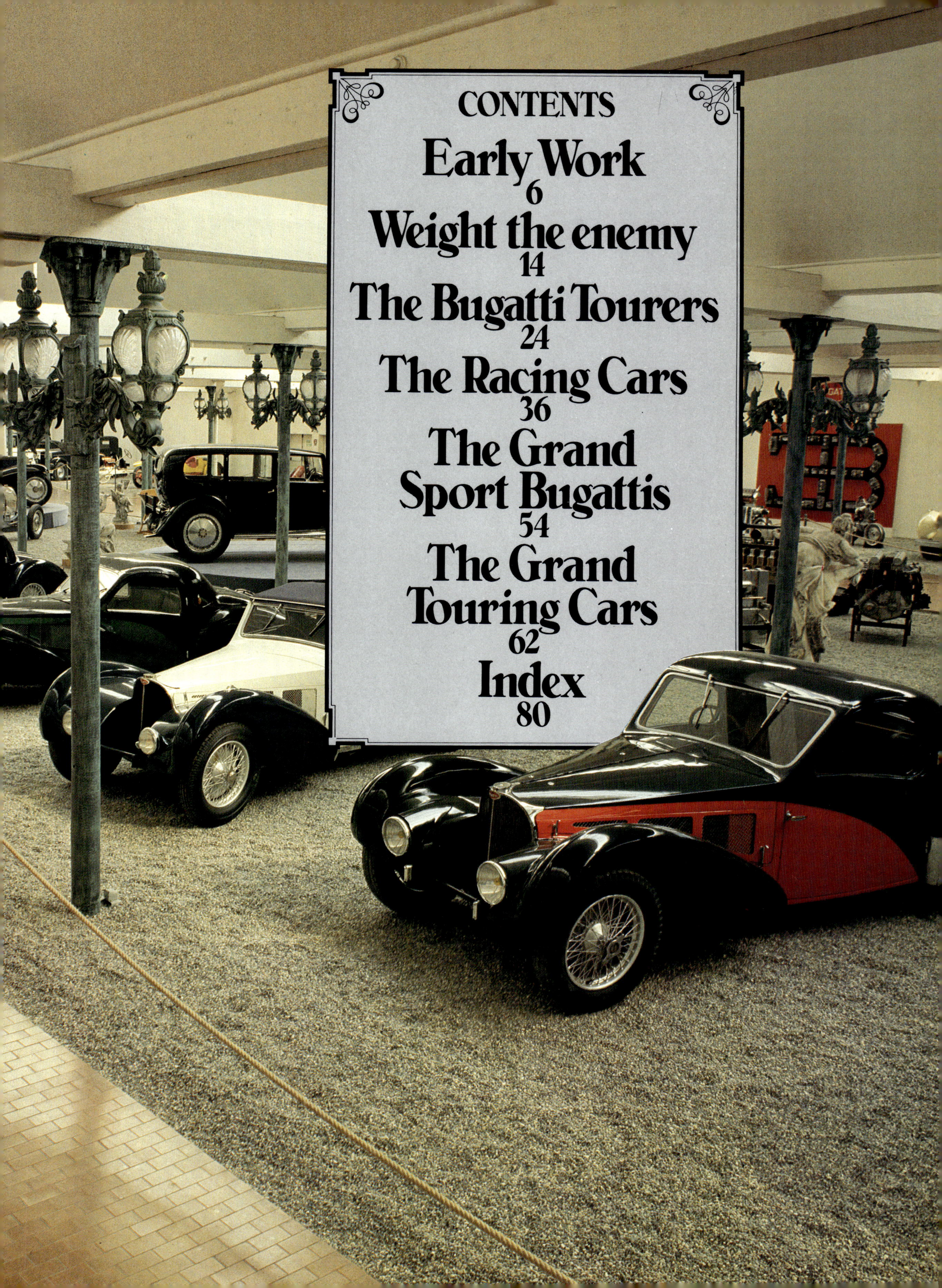

CONTENTS

RIGHT By the time he was 27, in 1908, Bugatti was achieving the quality of engine and chassis design exemplified by this Type 8 Deutz car, the last chain-driven version he was to produce.

BELOW A year later came the splendid little 1.2-litre Type 10 produced as a 'private venture', a prototype that sparked off manufacture of the Bugatti marque at Molsheim in Alsace in 1910.

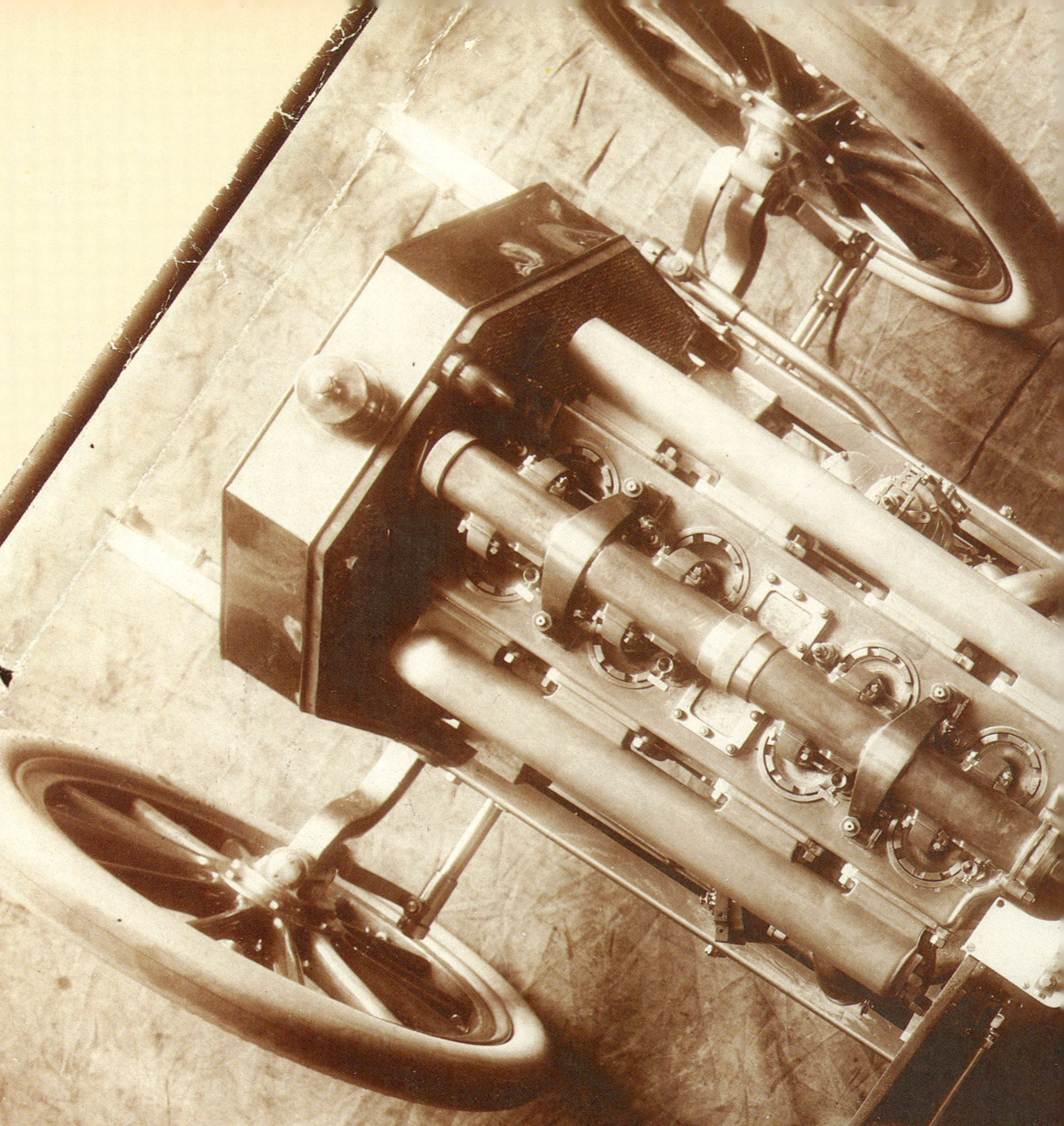

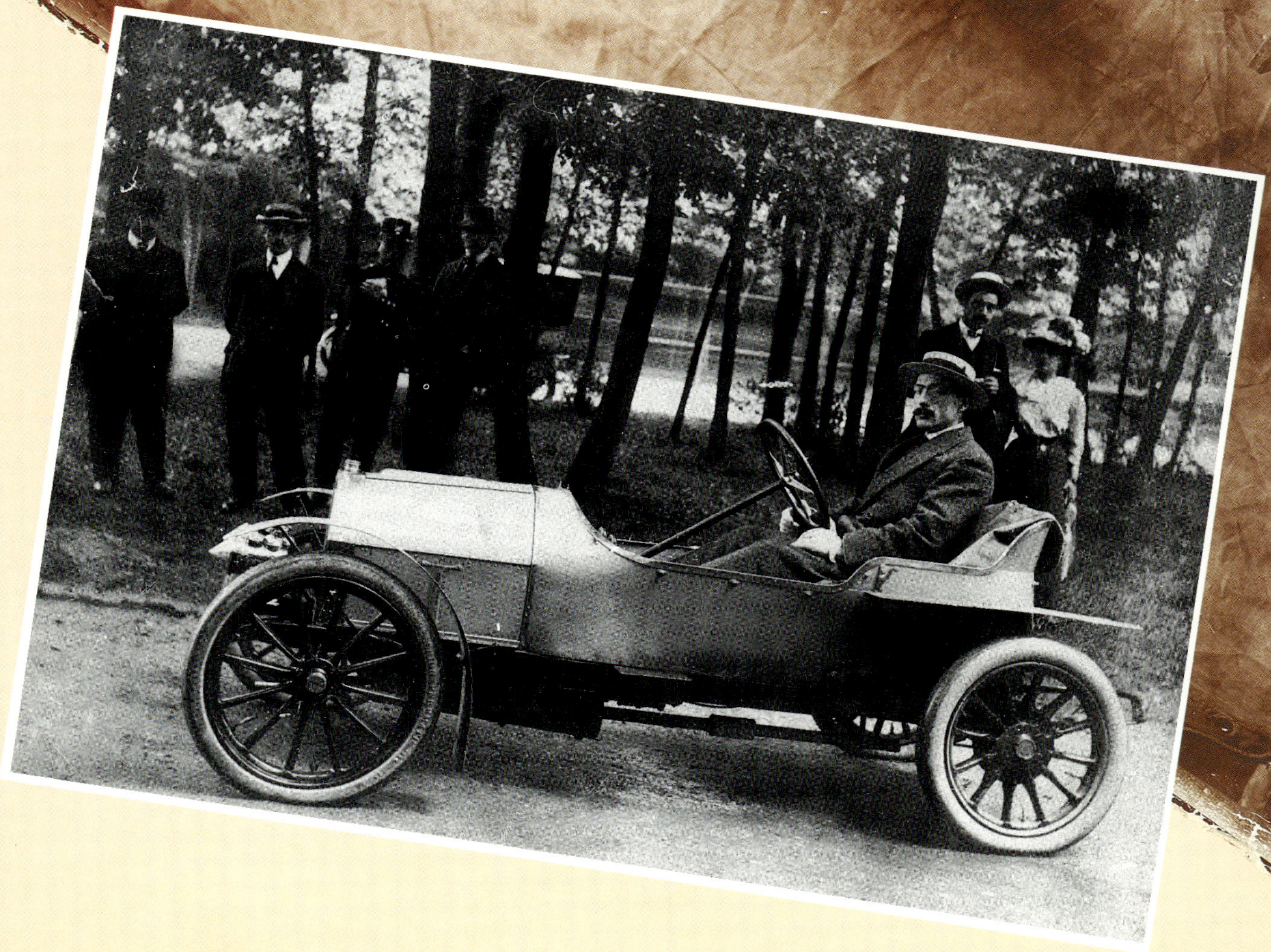

Early Work

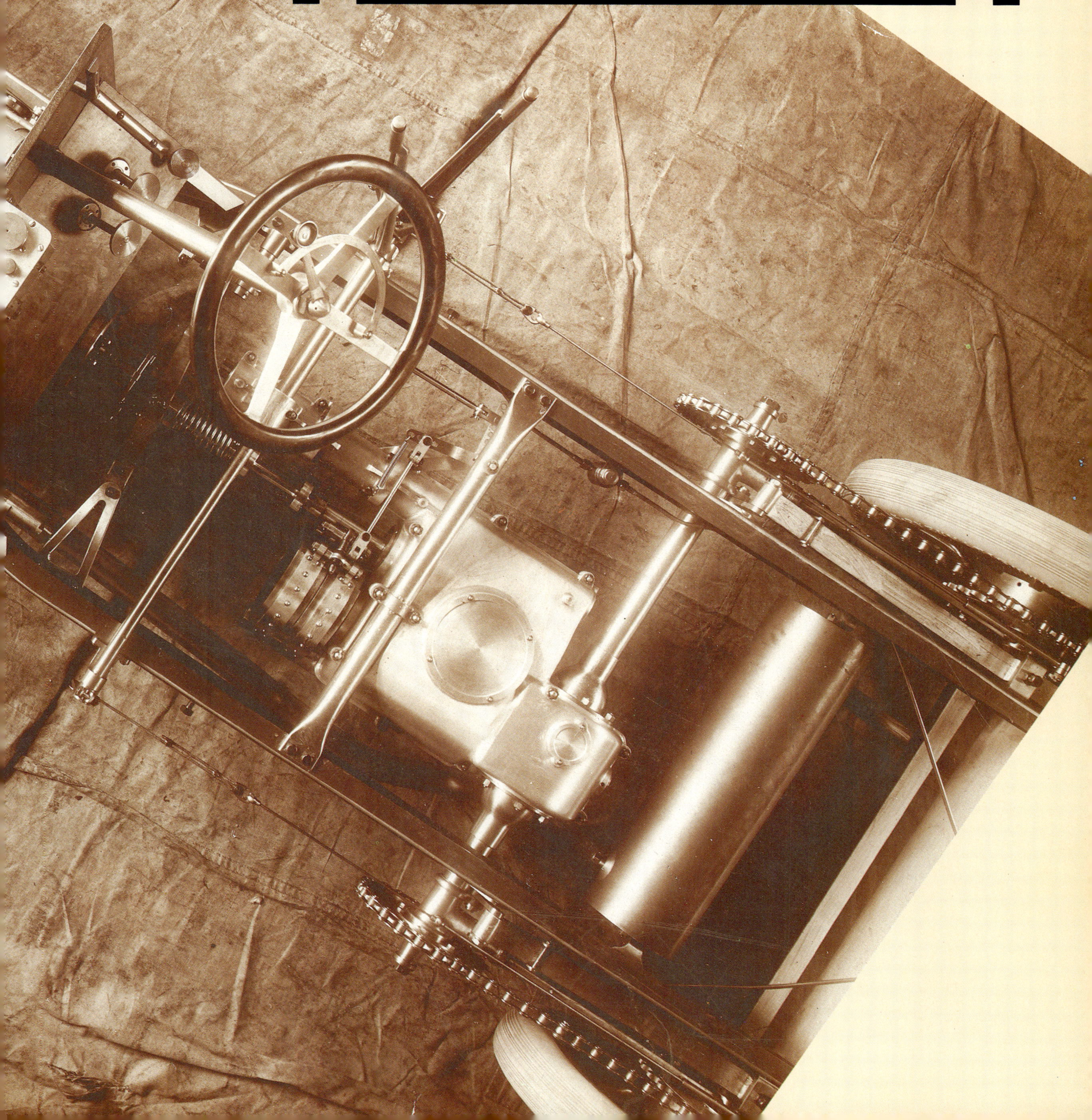

IN the north of Italy, between the Alps and the Apennines along the Mediterranean coast, lies the plain of Lombardy. To the west are Turin and Milan, industrial cities with long traditions of metalwork and art; to the east is Venice, famous too for its craftsmen in all manner of material. In the centre is Brescia where the origins of the Bugatti family can be found. Carlo Bugatti (1856–1940) lived in Milan during his early years, becoming a remarkable designer and maker of furniture, strange to the modern eye and now much sought after by the museums of the world; in 1880 he married Thérèse Lorioli and they had a daughter Deanice in 1880 and two sons, Ettore in 1881 and Rembrandt in 1885.

The two boys were brought up in a household where art and craft went hand in hand, and where skill with brush, clay or wood was taught and practised. Soon it was noticed that Rembrandt the younger son had a remarkable natural talent with clay: later he was to develop into an internationally honoured *animalier*, or sculptor of animals (sadly he ended his own life in despair in 1916).

The elder son Ettore soon became more interested in the mechanical arts of engines and machines, bicycles and, inevitably, the new road vehicles that the internal combustion engine had spawned – a development taking place in northern Italy as well as France and Germany during his adolescence.

It was natural enough for Ettore to be apprenticed to a local cycle maker, Prinetti & Stucchi, where he learned the mechanical skills of the workshop, and evidently gained much knowledge of normal machine processes which were later of importance to him when designing his own cars and setting up factories. His schooling, however, was traditional, lacking technical instruction; throughout his life his cars were designed by eye and an instinct developed by observation, rather than by theoretical knowledge. Draughtsmanship was a natural skill in the family, and Ettore soon became competent on an engineering drawing board. While at Prinetti & Stucchi he was allowed to motorize one of the firm's tricycles with a single-cylinder de Dion engine, and later seems to have produced one with two engines. When he was 18 or 19 he also took part in several of the road races that were run at the end of the century between the towns of northern Italy; Verona to Mantua and Pinerolo to Turin were typical wins. These gave him a taste for speed.

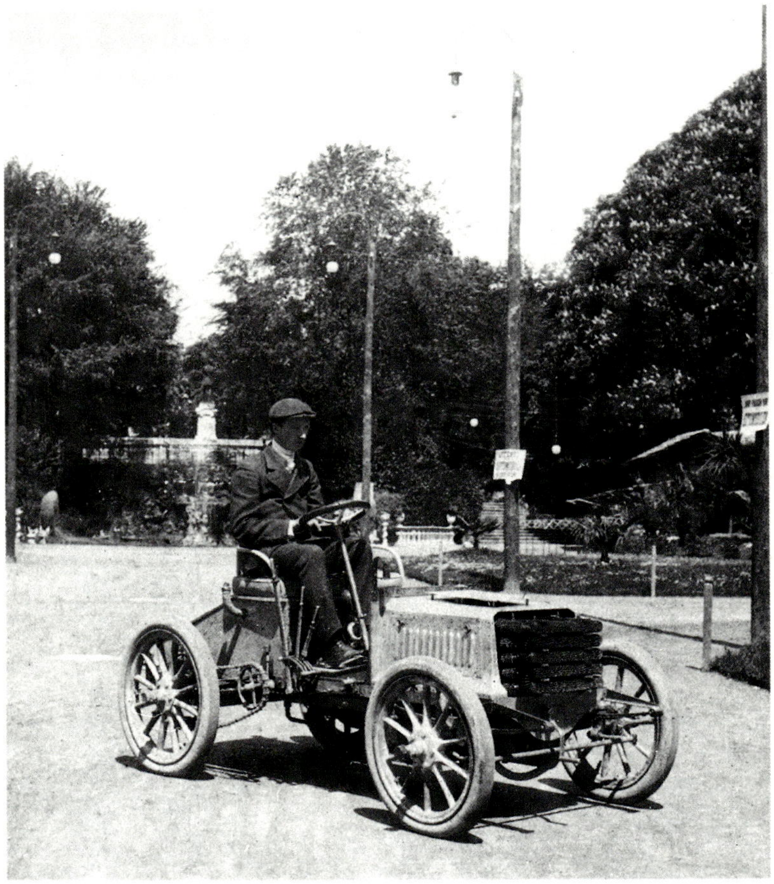

BELOW De Dietrich displayed cars designed by Bugatti and others at early Paris Automobile Salons. Here, probably in 1903, the company showed the first Ettore Bugatti design (in the centre) alongside models from Turcat-Méry. The short man seen on the left is L.T. Delaney, from England, who was later associated with Lea-Francis.

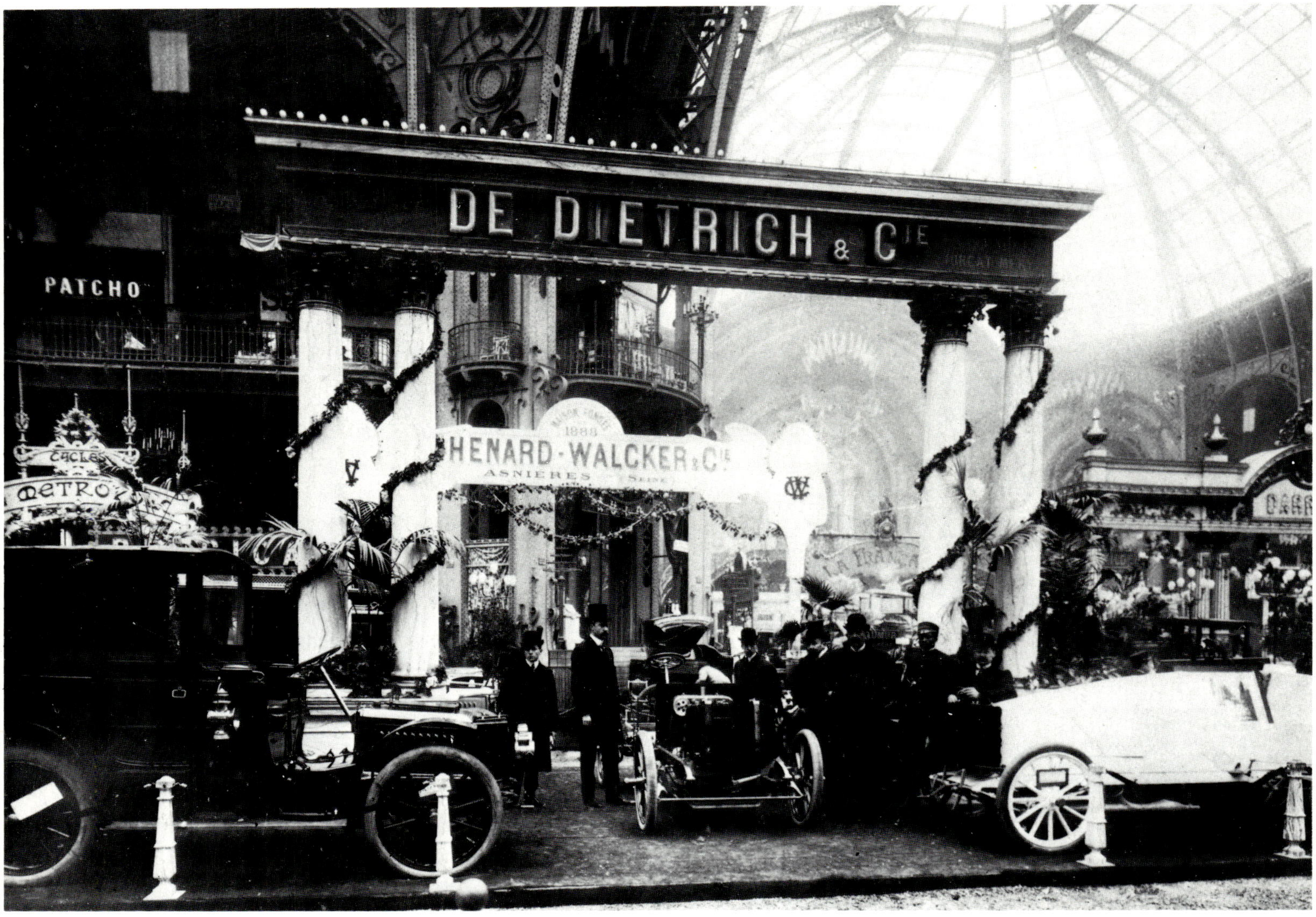

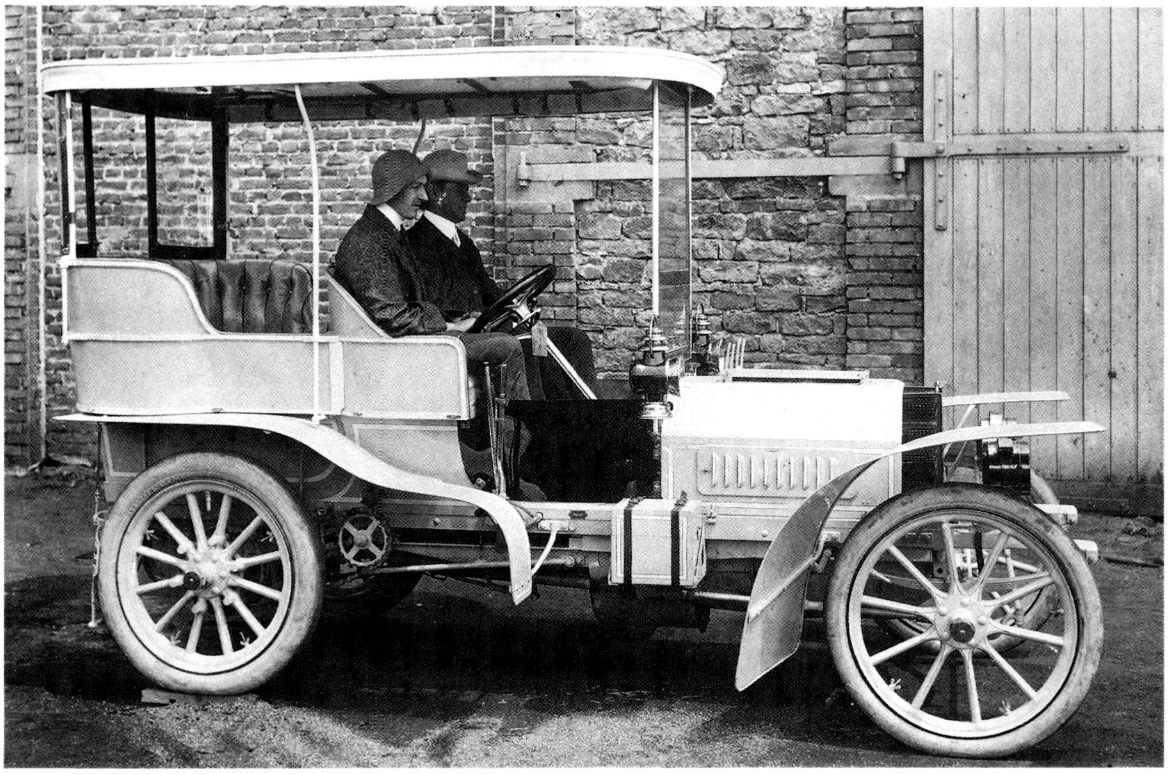

LEFT Ettore Bugatti in his prototype four-cylinder car, which he called Type 2, in 1901. For a young man not yet 21 this was a remarkable tour de force. *It was this car that led Baron de Dietrich to engage Bugatti to design a series of models for him at his factory at Niederbronn in Alsace. This was to set Bugatti on course as a vehicle designer, and later manufacturer, unique in the annals of the automobile.*

RIGHT Ettore and his friend Emil Mathis in an early de Dietrich car. Ettore designed them and Mathis sold them, but we know from documents still in existence that Bugatti, like many a designer after him, was more interested in new ideas and models than in eliminating the faults of his early designs; and racing was yet another distraction! Nevertheless, there was soon a following of ardent admirers anxious to buy his latest productions.

In 1898 or '99 he produced a four-wheel vehicle with four engines, two at the front and two at the rear. Various historical references differ on the detail of this machine, but it is certainly what he later called his Type 1. Prinetti & Stucchi, however, did not want to continue with motorized cycles or vehicles and Bugatti left.

In 1900 two brothers, the Counts Gulinelli, who were friends of his father Carlo, offered to finance a new project which Ettore set about designing at home. This was a four-cylinder (90 × 120 mm bore and stroke) car which was ready for the road in 1901. It is not known exactly how and where the car was built, but there was already a large component industry in the Milan–Turin area by that time and it would not have been difficult to get castings made, frames bent up, gears cut and so on. Nevertheless, for one so young and inexperienced to produce a car that worked is a most remarkable example of ability.

The de Dietrich licence

The car (the Type 2) was shown at an International Exhibition in Milan in 1901 and was awarded one of the major prizes. Many industrialists interested in the new, developing industry of motor car production saw the vehicle. Among them was Baron de Dietrich from the company bearing his name at Niederbronn in Alsace, at that time part of Germany. He was already producing motor vehicles, particularly buses and trucks, and was searching for a car to manufacture; consequently he offered to engage this obviously talented young designer to scheme out a range of vehicles for Niederbronn to make. The Type 2, itself too small, was excellent in conception and worked well enough. What was wanted were larger versions on the same lines. So it was agreed with Carlo and his under-age son that a licence would be prepared. Although the agreement itself was signed by Carlo in June 1902 (Ettore's 21st birthday was on 15 September 1902), it is likely that Ettore had already spent several months on the required series of cars. In the event his work at Niederbronn from 1902 to 1904 covered Types 3 to 5 (but the sequence is not certain).

	Horsepower	Bore and stroke
Type 3	16	114 × 130 mm – 5.3 litres
Type 4	24	130 × 140 mm – 7.4 litres
Type 5	60 (racer)	160 × 160 mm – 12.9 litres

All three versions had four cylinders, with overhead valves operated by a pair of camshafts in the crankcase – one of the earliest, if not the first, overhead-valve designs. The valves were operated by *pull* rods rather than by pushrods with rockers used in today's familiar arrangement to reverse the direction of motion from low-mounted camshafts: a fine example of original, or 'lateral', thinking by Ettore. The cylinders were cast in pairs and the water jackets were created by surrounding the cylinders with copper (later aluminium) 'cans'. A curious feature of the cylinder block was that the exhaust ports were taken down a cast duct from the overhead ports to the bottom of the block to cool the gases or heat the water! Today we may do this to heat the inlet passages, but what Ettore had in mind is not clear.

The two camshafts were driven by gears at the front of the engine, exposed and unprotected and, it may be suspected, subject to noise and wear. The pull rods operated the valves by L-shaped offset brackets, an interesting but not very happy solution, which Ettore was to abandon on later designs as speeds increased.

Ignition used a coil, probably of the vibrator type, for each cylinder; the spark was distributed by a rotating wiper arm to the appropriate cylinder in turn, instead of the single coil and multiple contact breaker which produces a spark from a single coil in turn to each cylinder, the system we use today. But Bugatti had to make his own, and had no Bosch to help him!

As far as we can see from available information and drawings, the engine bearings were lubricated by 'drip' from a tank, as there was no oil pump. The whole engine and clutch assembly was mounted on a subframe carried below the main frame at the front. The transmission was through a gearbox fixed to the frame, with the output shaft above the input and the driver sitting rather high on top of the casing. The gearbox had four speeds, changed in sequence, a pair of bevels and differential driving chain sprockets to the rear wheels.

A small number of de Dietrich cars was produced, certainly many fewer than 100. The two touring cars were very similar, but the racer was significantly different, with the driver initially seated at the rear! Bugatti first produced a version of the touring car on these lines and raced it at Frankfurt in September 1902; perhaps he had worked on it in the months before the licence was signed. Then he designed and made at Niederbronn what we call Type 5, a much larger four-cylinder, 160 × 160 mm, of no less than 12.9 litres, intended for Bugatti to drive in the infamous Paris-Madrid race in 1903; in fact this event was stopped by the French authorities at Bordeaux as many fatal accidents had occurred (including to Marcel Renault, one of the founders of the famous French car company). Although several de Dietrich cars from other designers were entered and run, the new Bugatti was refused permission to start, because of the rearward position of the driver and the lack of forward vision. Bugatti then moved the driver forward to a more normal, if higher, position and he used the car in at least one racing event in 1904.

A contemporary de Dietrich catalogue lists two engine sizes (18–22 hp and 30–34 hp), and two chassis sizes: 'normal', track and wheelbase 1.25 m × 2.4 m (4 ft 1¼ in × 7 ft 10½ in) and 'limousine', 1.35 m × 2.85 m (4 ft 5 in × 9 ft 4¼ in) – these dimensions are seen many times on later Bugatti cars made at Molsheim.

The touring cars achieved some modest sales success, helped perhaps by Bugatti's racing appearances. One was exhibited at shows in Berlin and Vienna (1903), and in London in the following year under the name Burlington. However much we may wonder how reliable such a new and untried design might have been, it is significant that Bugatti at this early age was able to extract glowing testimonials from some of his customers. *Automobile Welt* in 1904 carried this paragraph:

> The excellent features of de Dietrich – Licence E. Bugatti cars have resulted already in many recognitions and all owners of these cars have expressed their greatest satisfaction. A new, very valuable, proof of the first-class quality of Bugatti cars is expressed in a letter from the well-known General McCoskry Butt, who is noted in American sporting circles and who bought a 24 PS de Dietrich – Licence Bugatti car during his stay in Europe. As the gentleman concerned already owns cars and boats, this verdict from an expert is very valuable. He wrote to Mr E.E.C. Mathis, General Agent for de Dietrich cars:
>
> 'In reply to your letter of 22 August in which you inquire if I am satisfied with the de Dietrich – Licence Bugatti car which you delivered to me on 15.4.1904, I wish to say that it is in my opinion impossible to design a better machine. I drove the car from Strassburg [Strasbourg] via Frankfurt to Dresden and used it daily during the months of April, May, June, July and August for journeys of about 150 km each. There were also longer journeys, including one which led me through the French and Swabian Jura over Nuremberg to the southern part of the Vogesen [Vosges], over Belfort to Gray and Besançon; also a single journey from Gray to Amiens (440 km in 11 hours); from Amiens to Metz over Sedan through the Ardennes and afterwards through the northern part of the Vogesen [Vosges] over Bitsch to Strassburg [Strasbourg].
>
> During these hard journeys in the hills, the machine never missed a stroke and during the period I have been the owner of this car, I never had any trouble. The machine is, as you could see, in the same condition as when I bought it. For this reason I am prepared to buy one of your new 40 PS "Hermes" Licence Bugatti cars, because the engine has the unique advantage of being suitable for an automobile-boat: i.e. during the period in which I am unable to use the car.
>
> Yours sincerely,
> McCoskry Butt, Brig. Gen.'

But all was not well between de Dietrich and Bugatti; it has been said that the former wished to withdraw from car manufacture as it was unprofitable. It is more likely that the youthful Bugatti was spending too much of the company's money and his own time on racing cars at the expense of dealing with customer complaints about the touring cars. The licence was terminated by a lawyer's letter of 3 February 1904, but the personal relations between the baron and Ettore remained cordial for some years.

The move to Mathis

The scene now moved from Niederbronn to the nearby city of Strasbourg. Emil Mathis was the agent for de Dietrich cars there and was the same age as Bugatti. The two became friends. It was natural enough, when de Dietrich no longer wanted to use Bugatti, for Mathis to propose a joint project to design and make cars for Mathis to sell.

Thus a few weeks later, on 1 April 1904, Mathis signed a licence with Bugatti to design a new car for him, the licence being for an initial period of two years. The car was to be known as the Hermes, and would be built by the Société Alsacienne de Construction Mécanique (SACM) at Illkirch-Graffenstaden, near Strasbourg. Bugatti at once set up a drawing office in an attic in the Hôtel de Paris, in the Rue de la Nuée Bleue, Strasbourg, a building that belonged to Mathis's father. He was soon assisted by one of Mathis's mechanics, Ernest Friderich, who remained his faithful aide for many years, finally becoming the Bugatti agent in Nice.

The new car owed much to the de Dietrich design but was improved in many important areas. Now only the inlet valves were overhead and operated by the same pull-rod system; the exhaust valves were at the side, below the inlets and operated by normal tappets from a single camshaft, the driving gear of which was within the crankcase and was stated to have been made of fibre. An oil pump was now fitted but still supplied oil to small jets, and a magneto replaced the coils.

The clutch was much improved, with a single disc on the gearbox shaft clamped between moving parts of the flywheel, thus lightening the gear change. The gearbox now had its output shaft below the engine axis to lower the seating on the chassis; and a great improvement, attributed to

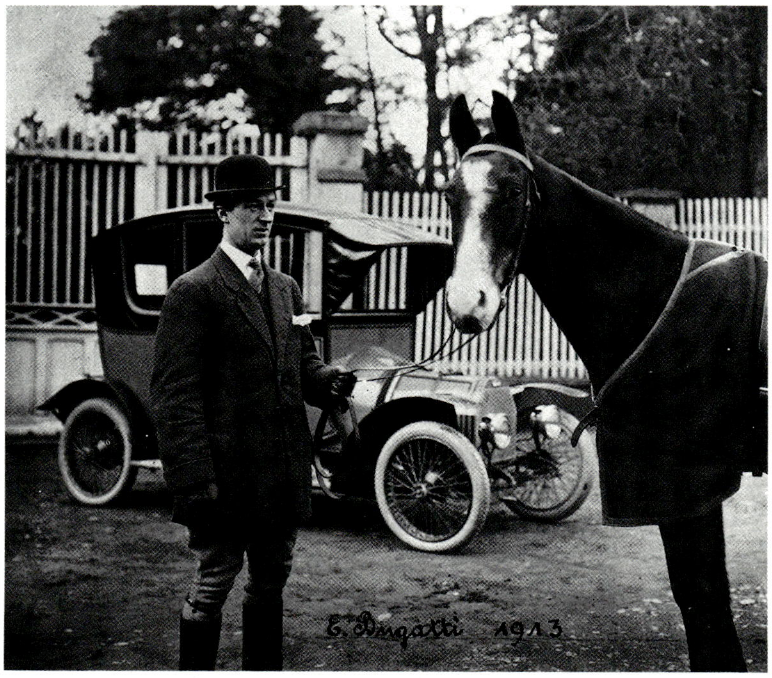

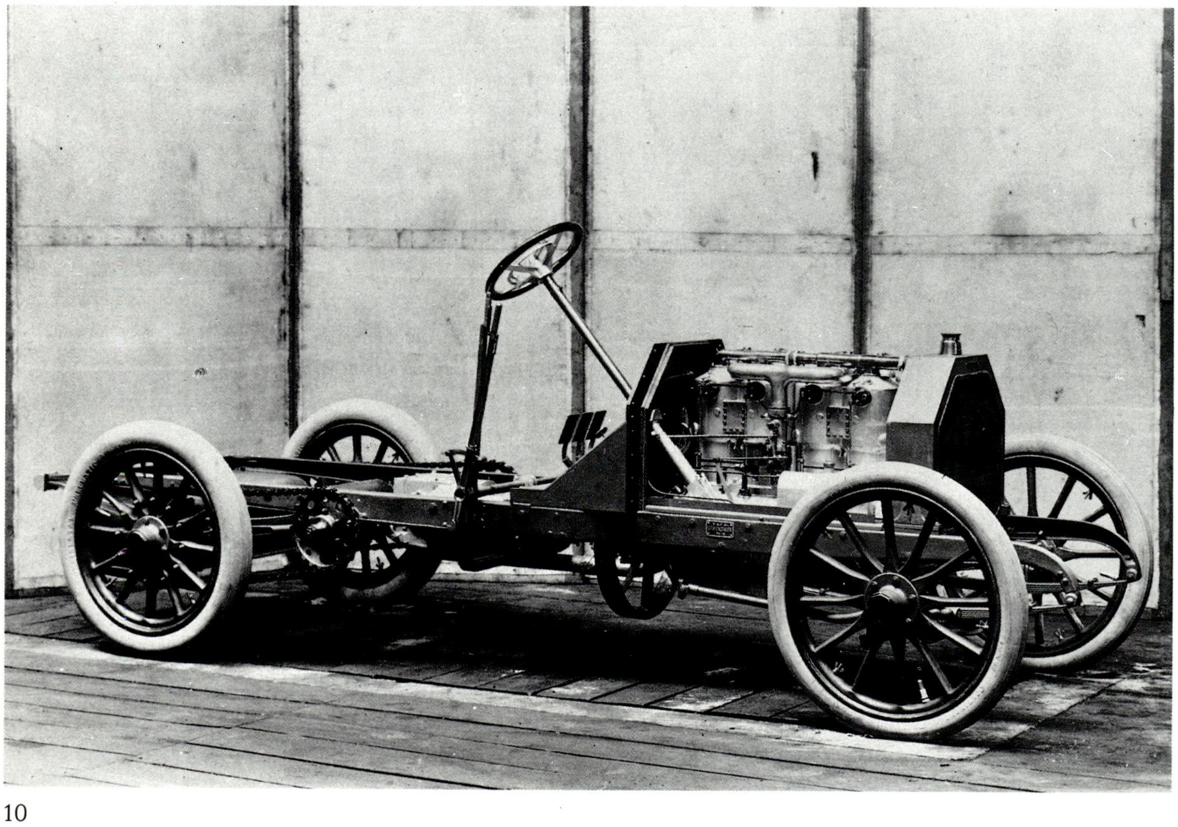

ABOVE Ettore Bugatti at the age of 32 at Molsheim, already interested in horses. In the background is the Type 15 that Mme Bugatti used, the chassis of which is now in the Hampton Collection in Britain, while the body still exists in France!

LEFT A new Bugatti-designed Mathis Hermes chassis at the factory in Graffenstaden, about 1905. The engine was improved and now had overhead inlet and side exhaust valves operated by a single camshaft. Transmission was still by chain, but the gearbox layout now allowed a lower floor to the body. Cylinders were cast in pairs and the flywheel seems to have fan blade spokes.

RIGHT Ettore Bugatti regularly took part in competitive trials or rallies in his cars, although he avoided racing proper. Here he is at the wheel of a Deutz car with Emil Mathis as passenger in the 1909 Prince Henry trials in southern Germany. The elliptical radiator badge reads 'Deutz': Bugatti was soon to adopt a similar one reading 'Bugatti' for all Molsheim cars.

the 'Système Mercedes', was to use sliding selector rods for gear changing to avoid having to go successively through the gears as was the case with the earlier de Dietrich design. As before, the drive to the rear wheels was by chain and the chassis frame was a straightforward design without an engine subframe.

Bugatti allocated Types 6 and 7 to the Mathis series, although the first Mathis catalogue listed:

Horsepower	Bore and stroke
50	136 × 150 mm
60	140 × 150 mm
90	160 × 160 mm

From other references it is certain that Type 6 relates to the first two, and Type 7 to the 90 hp version. Mathis's 1906 catalogue, however, seems to have inflated the hp figures since it listed 50, 80 and 120 hp models!

The car achieved some success, the first chassis (No.351) being delivered on 15 April 1905 to 'Burlington', no doubt the London agent who never received the de Dietrich version publicized the year before. The British chassis was used successfully and indeed was driven at least once at the Southport sand races by L. T. Delaney.

However, only a few of these cars were produced; according to available records a total of 15 was made up to 1907, the licence agreement having expired in March 1906, and the arrangement continuing informally. There is certainly evidence of customer complaints and a lack of attention to them by Ettore, which no doubt disillusioned Mathis and led to the dissolution of the partnership.

Deutz in Cologne

Whatever the precise reasons for the break with Mathis we do know that in early 1907 Bugatti had discussions with the Gasmotoren Fabrik Deutz company of Cologne in Germany. This powerful concern, famous for the engines originated by its designer Nicolaus August Otto, now wanted to enter into car production; no doubt the Deutz technical director Adolf Langen knew Bugatti and appreciated his talents from his experience with two Mathis cars. Work by Bugatti on a new car started in March 1907 and a formal licence agreement was signed on 1 September 1907 with a duration of five years.

Bugatti produced two basic four-cylinder designs for Deutz, the Types 8 and 9, each listed with various engine sizes. The first type retained chain drive and the second now had Bugatti's first shaft and bevel gear back axle. Whatever the commercial success the company achieved, Bugatti's designs themselves were excellent.

The engine now had two overhead valves in a cast-iron cylinder monobloc, with cast water jackets. The camshaft was overhead driven by a vertical shaft and bevel gearing. Motion between cam and valve was via a curved arc-shaped follower with rollers on each end, the progenitor of the later and famous 'banana' tappets used on the 1910–25 8- and 16-valve Bugatti cars made at Molsheim.

The clutch on this car now used the multi-plate system standardized by Bugatti on all his cars up to 1932. In this the several iron and steel plates, running in oil, were pressed together by a linkage or toggle system, which when forced into an 'on-centre' position by a spring, created a great pressure on the plates (the action is similar to a toggle lock on a trunk or suitcase). A highly ingenious remote control was used to operate the clutch to release it: a steel tube full of short dumb-bell-like rollers, capable of following a curve, pushed at one end and projected at the other. The transmission was still by chain, but the input and output shafts now lay side by side and the gears were moved by three selectors.

The frame and overall chassis layout were excellent and typical of what was to follow at Molsheim. Brakes in that period were on rear wheels and the transmission, but the design looks effective.

The Type 9 and the break with Deutz

It is not known how many Type 8 cars were produced, but in 1909 an improved version came out. This now had – for the first time from Bugatti's drawing board – a propeller shaft and normal gear axle with its crown wheel and pinion. Few cars by that time had chain drive and Bugatti clearly responded to pressure from the market place.

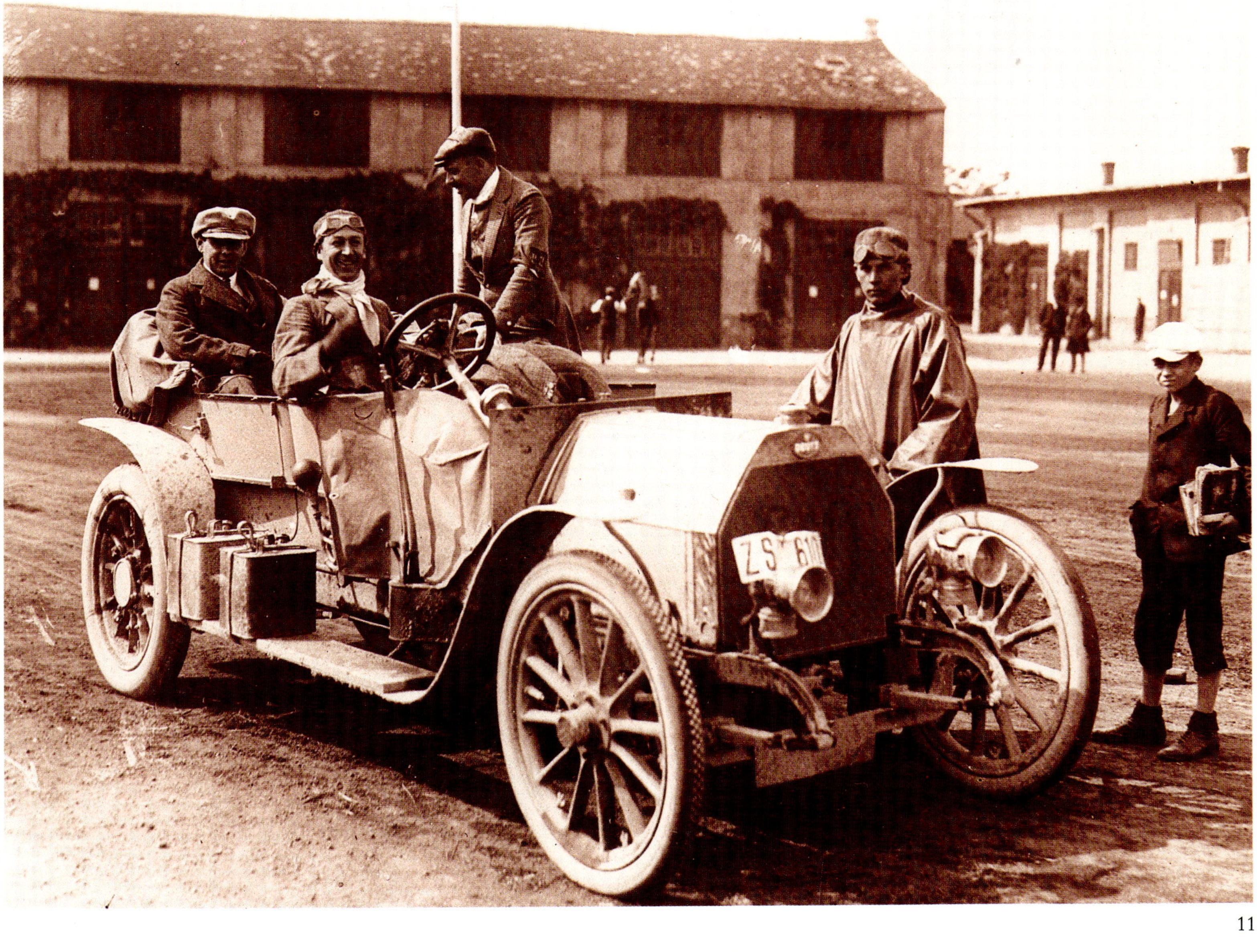

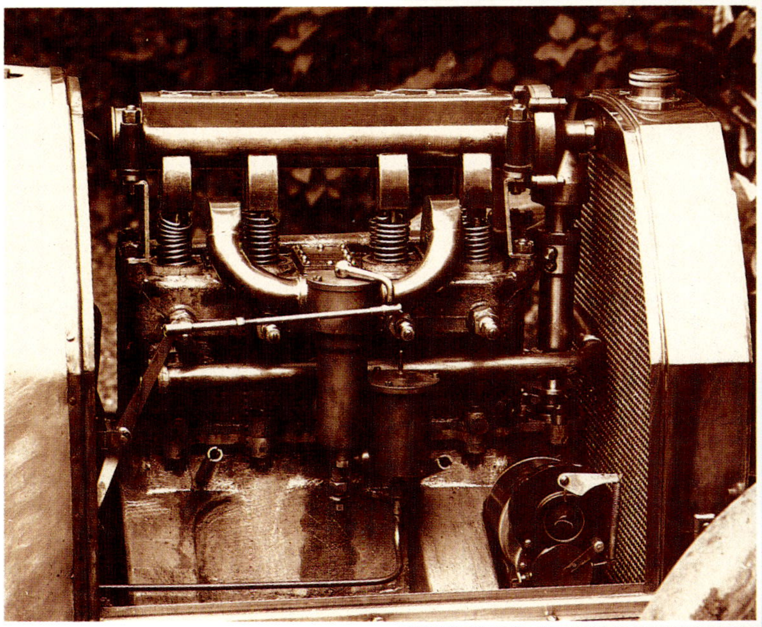

The prototype Type 10 built at Cologne in 1909 remained a prize possession at Molsheim until 1940, when it moved with the family and many of the factory workers to Bordeaux, in southwest France, ahead of the advancing German army. By some unexplained circumstance it was left behind by Ettore when he moved back to Paris in 1941; it later turned up in Marseille, to be sold to Belgium and then to the Harrah Automobile Museum in Reno, Nevada. The engine owes a great deal to the much larger Deutz design, its valves being exposed and operated by curved tappets in guides from a single overhead camshaft. The body was known affectionately at the factory as the Baignoire *('Bathtub').*

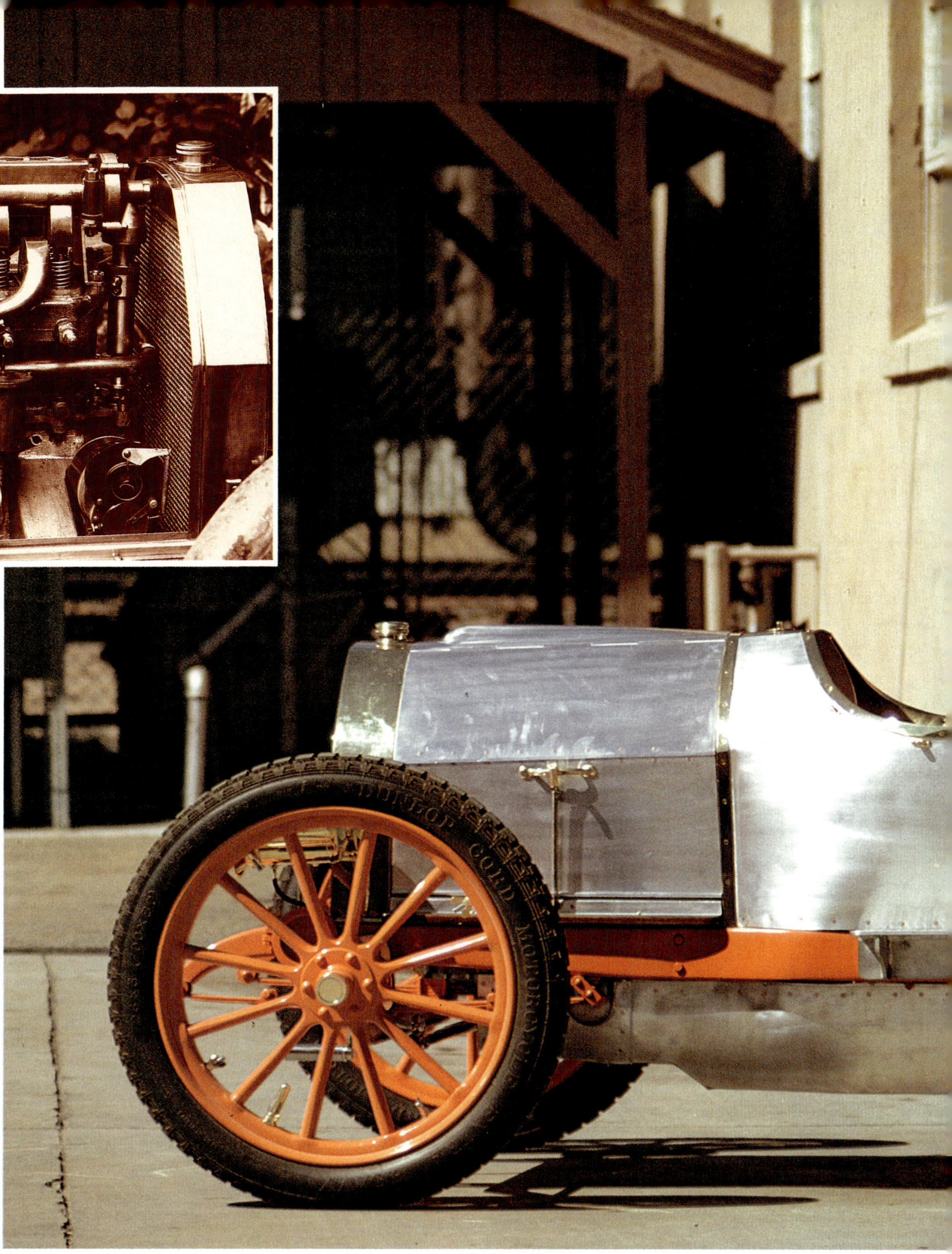

The whole transmission, gearbox, propeller shaft and rear axle, has a layout familiar to anyone who has seen Molsheim products up to 1930–2, illustrating how once Bugatti had achieved a good design he remained with it, enlarging or reinforcing as necessary.

The gearbox casing straddled the chassis and was attached at three points (later cars used four points to help stiffen the frame). The gear layout used what is known to the expert as a 'high-speed' layshaft, or countershaft, meaning that the constant-mesh gears which a gearbox requires were at the rear driving the layshaft faster than the propeller shaft. The sliding gears are on the input or engine shaft. Thus when changing gear the layshaft does not have to change speed, only the cluster of sliding gears; this reduction of inertia considerably lightens the gear change in comparison with the conventional box used then – and indeed today – on most cars. No doubt the high layshaft speed led other designers to concentrate on what is now the conventional layout, but the easy gear change was to remain a feature of Bugatti cars for years.

All was not well between Bugatti and Deutz, although we do not know the details. In a letter of 16 November 1909, the company terminated the licence agreement of 1907, as from 15 December. Production of the car went on for a time, but this famous engine-making firm had difficulty penetrating the automobile market, already dominated by great names in their own right. Car production ceased in 1911.

The small car and Molsheim

Bugatti's arrangement with Deutz allowed him a design office in his house at Cologne, led by Felix Kortz, who was to work with him on car production until he was killed in a road accident in 1926.

Around the time he was designing the Type 9 Ettore became interested in a light car of less than 1½ litres capacity, in contrast to his earlier designs of 4 to 12 litres. It is not known exactly what set him on this course, but the circumstances can be deduced with reasonable certainty.

In Bugatti's home town of Milan was Isotta-Fraschini, another car company that had connections with de Dietrich and had produced a fine-looking little voiturette intended for the 1908 Grand Prix des Voiturettes to be run at Dieppe. This car was described in detail in the Italian journal *Motori, Cicli, Sport* of 1 September 1908. It had a four-cylinder engine (62 × 100 mm, 1.2 litres), an overhead camshaft driven by a shaft and bevel gears, a separate gearbox with four speeds, a normal-type rear axle and four half-elliptic springs on a simple frame. It looked splendid, and although not successful in the race it was much commented on!

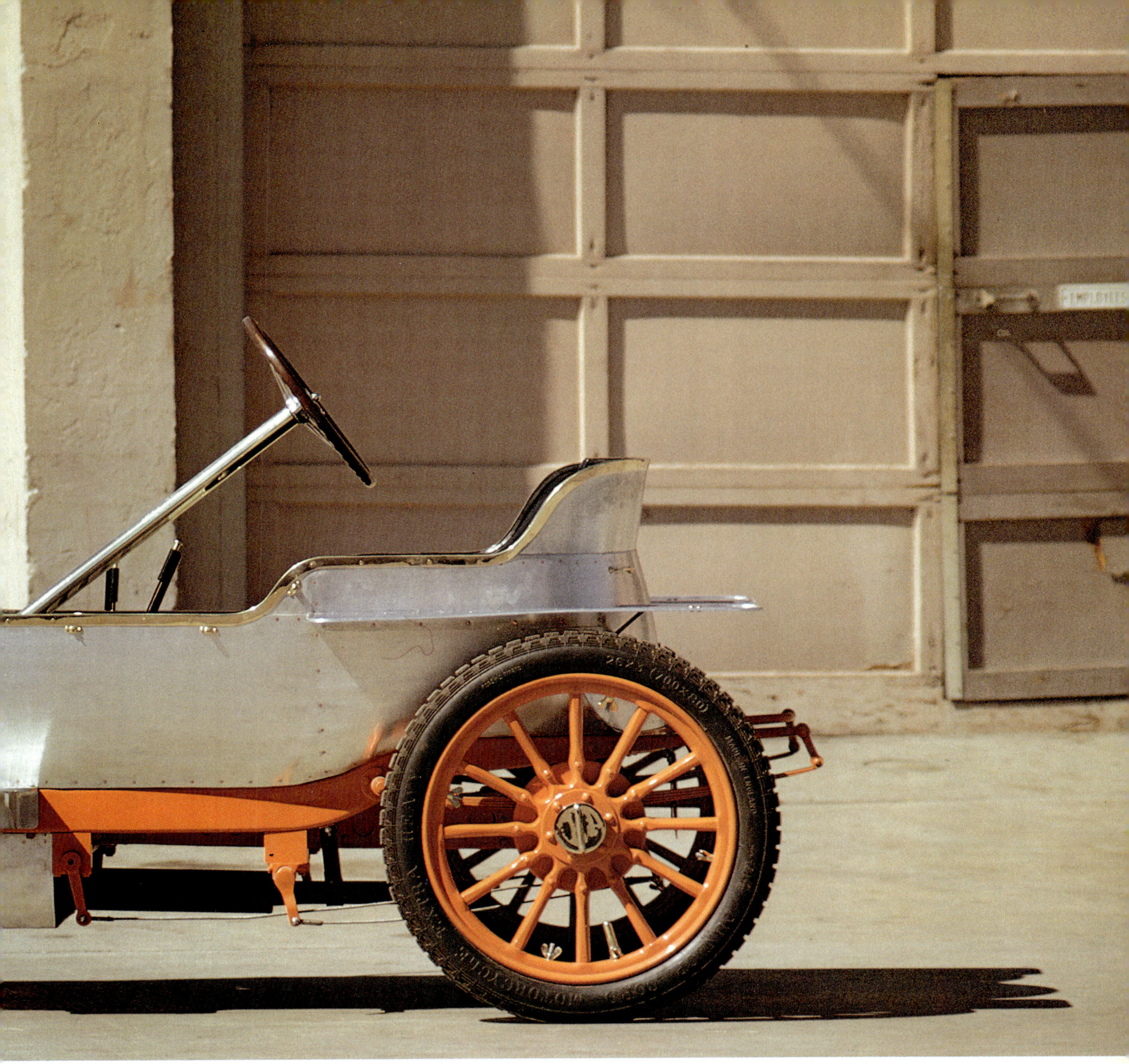

It is safe to assume that Ettore, who might not necessarily have seen the car, but must have read the journal, was struck by the potential of a light car of this type, and may indeed have been stimulated by the thought of another Italian helping de Dietrich. In any event he set out to design his Type 10 for himself, and in fact produced it in his own premises. We have a letter from Ettore to his friend Emil Mathis in April 1909, telling him that 'the little car is finished and is marvellous!'.

The superficial similarity between the Isotta car and Bugatti's Type 10 and the later Type 13 is so close that some have suggested Bugatti may have designed the Isotta. This is not so, as Stefanini at the Isotta works was entirely responsible. An examination of original drawings still in existence makes it very clear that two different designers were at work.

Bugatti's car owes much to the conceptual detail of the Type 9 Deutz that he was designing at the same time, although its dimensions matched the small Isotta. It had a four-cylinder, 62 × 100 mm, 1200 cc engine, with overhead valves in a cast-iron block, the valves operated by the Deutz-like 'banana' tappets. The clutch used the Deutz multi-disc, toggle operation system, and the gearbox was of the same layout; so was the back axle, although much lighter. The frame and suspension were scaled-down versions of the Type 9. The result was a delightful lightweight car of excellent performance, much admired by all who drove it and teaching Bugatti that, as he was able to state in his publicity later: 'le poid c'est l'ennemi!' (weight is the enemy). This car can be seen today in the Harrah Automobile Museum in Reno, Nevada.

The next few months were critical to the future of Bugatti. He was a better master than a servant; designing for others was a way of life to be changed. Now in his 28th year he wanted to be independent, and had connections and friends who could help. One was the Spanish banker de Vizcaya who owned a hunting lodge in Alsace and had associations with the Darmstadt bank that had helped finance the Type 8 taken up by Deutz. He was enthusiastic about the new little car. At the end of 1909 Bugatti moved back to Alsace from Cologne, with his faithful colleagues Kortz and Friderich (just back from his national service), into an old dye works at Molsheim, a small town a few kilometres west of Strasbourg.

So 1 January 1910 saw Automobiles Ettore Bugatti established as an independent manufacturer, with plans to produce the 1200 cc car, with some minor changes, as the Type 13, the first Bugatti car. As a lover of horses, what Ettore wanted to do was to produce a 'thoroughbred' little car, and we can now see in his thinking, and in his publicity, the concept of a pure-blood or *pur-sang* vehicle.

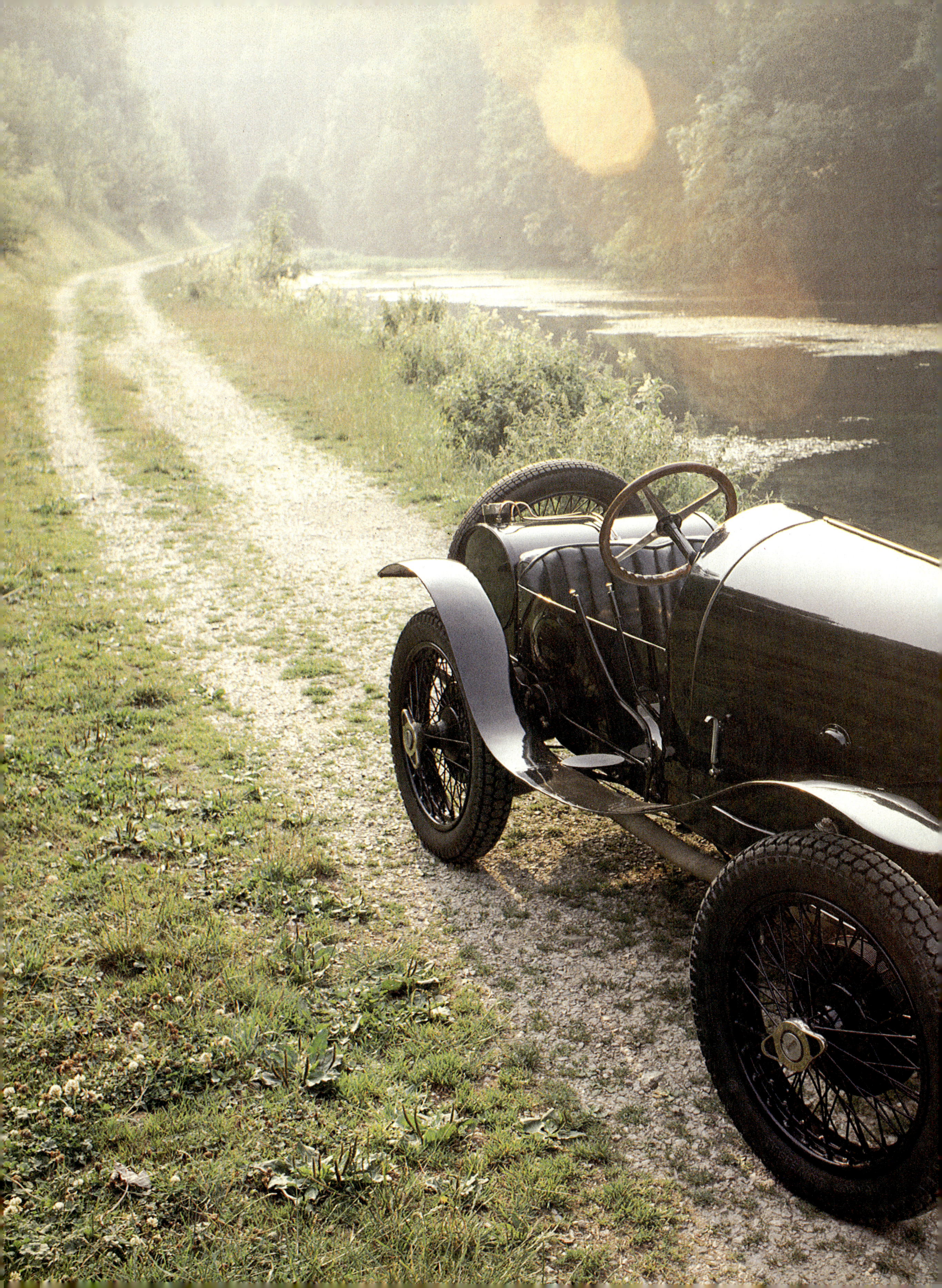

Weight the enemy

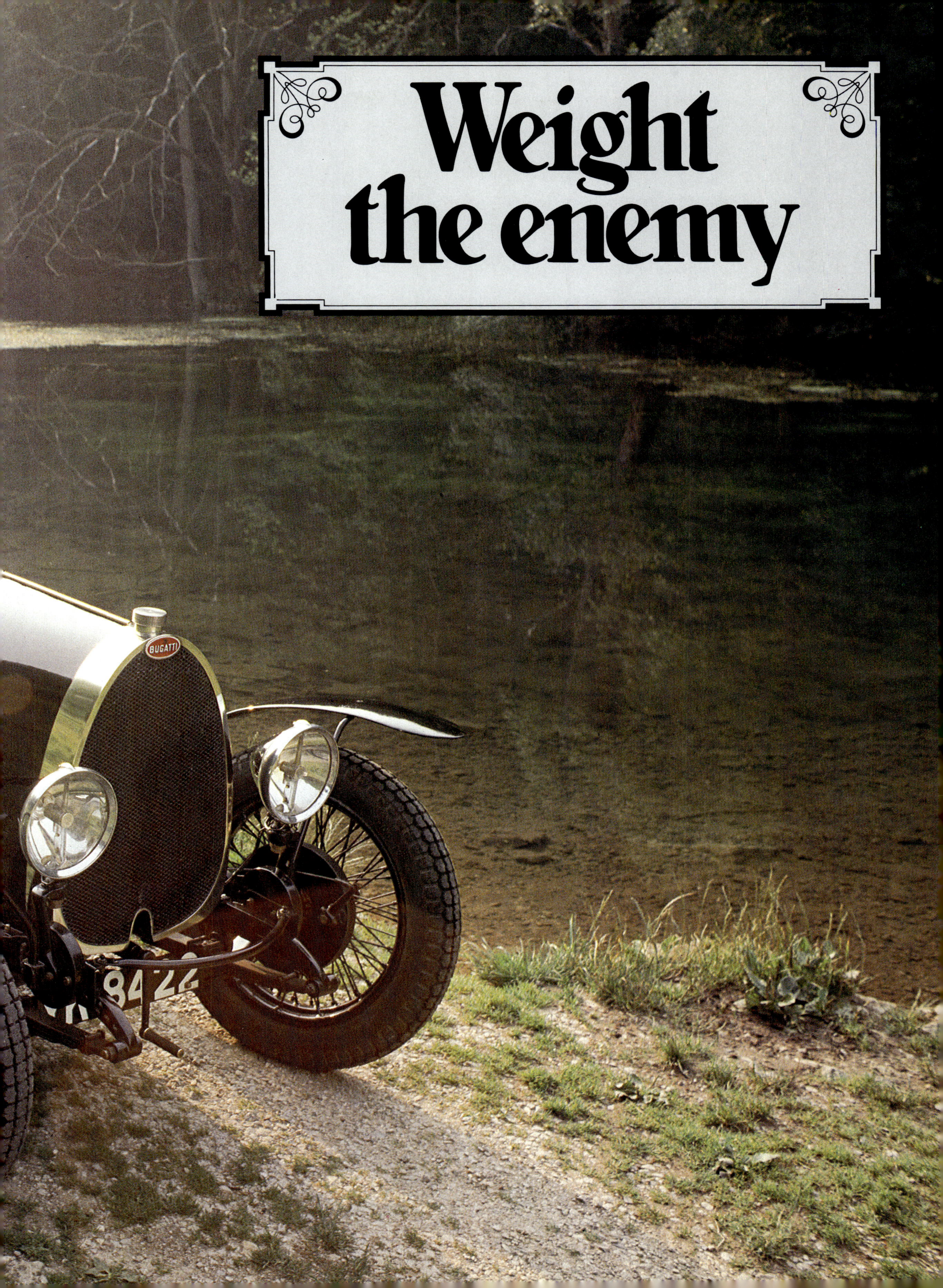

THE little car, the Type 10, attracted all who saw it and tested it. Now the production version, the Type 13, with some improvements, was launched early in 1910 as the first car to bear the name Bugatti.

It is not known what happened to Bugatti's designations Types 11 and 12. They may have been left for Deutz, or more likely simply do not exist. Then in 1910 he allocated Types 15 and 17 to longer-wheelbase versions of the Type 13.

	Wheelbase
Type 13	2.0 m (6 ft 6¾ in)
Type 15	2.4 m (7 ft 10½ in)
Type 17	2.55 m (8 ft 4½ in) (double rear springs)

Five chassis were produced in 1910, followed by 75 in 1911, reaching a total of about 350 when war intervened in August 1914.

The engine was increased in size to 65 × 100 mm, 1327 cc, and the valve mechanism was enclosed in a casing bearing Ettore Bugatti's signature cast on it. The four-cylinder block was in one piece with integral cylinder head; the exhaust valves were seated on the casting and the inlet valves were carried on separate cages screwed in from above, a feature retained from the earlier designs. The engine was later known as the 'eight-valve' (*huit soupapes*) to distinguish it from the later four-valve head or 'sixteen-valve' (*seize soupapes*).

The cylinder block was closed at the top by a bronze casing carrying the camshaft, the cams in this early period being separate and pinned to the shaft proper. The cams operated the valves through curved (banana-shaped) followers sliding in housings lined with white metal. The camshaft was driven by bevel gears through a vertical shaft at the front of the engine, in turn driven by the crankshaft.

The block sat on an aluminium alloy crankcase, split on the crank axis, and straddling the frame on four arms bolted to the frame, the crank having three split bronze bearings.

Eight-valve Types 13–23
Years made 1910–20
No. made 435

ENGINE	
Type	Monobloc, overhead valve
No. of cylinders	4
Bore/stroke mm	65 × 100
Displacement cc	1327
Valve operation	Curved tappets
Sparkplugs/cyl.	1
Supercharged	No
Carburettor	1 Zenith
BHP approx.	20
DRIVE TRAIN	
Clutch	Multi-plate, wet
Transmission	4-speed and reverse, gate change
CHASSIS	
Wheelbase	T13: 2.0 m (6 ft 6¾ in) T15,22: 2.4 m (7 ft 10½ in) T17,23: 2.55 m (8 ft 4½ in)
Track	1.15 m (3 ft 9¼ in)
Suspension – front	½ elliptic
Suspension – rear	1910–13 ½ elliptic; 1913 reversed ¼ elliptic
Brakes	Drum at rear by hand, transmission by foot
Tyre size	710 × 90 etc
Wheels	Originally wood, later Rudge
PERFORMANCE	
Maximum speed	100 km/h (62 mph)

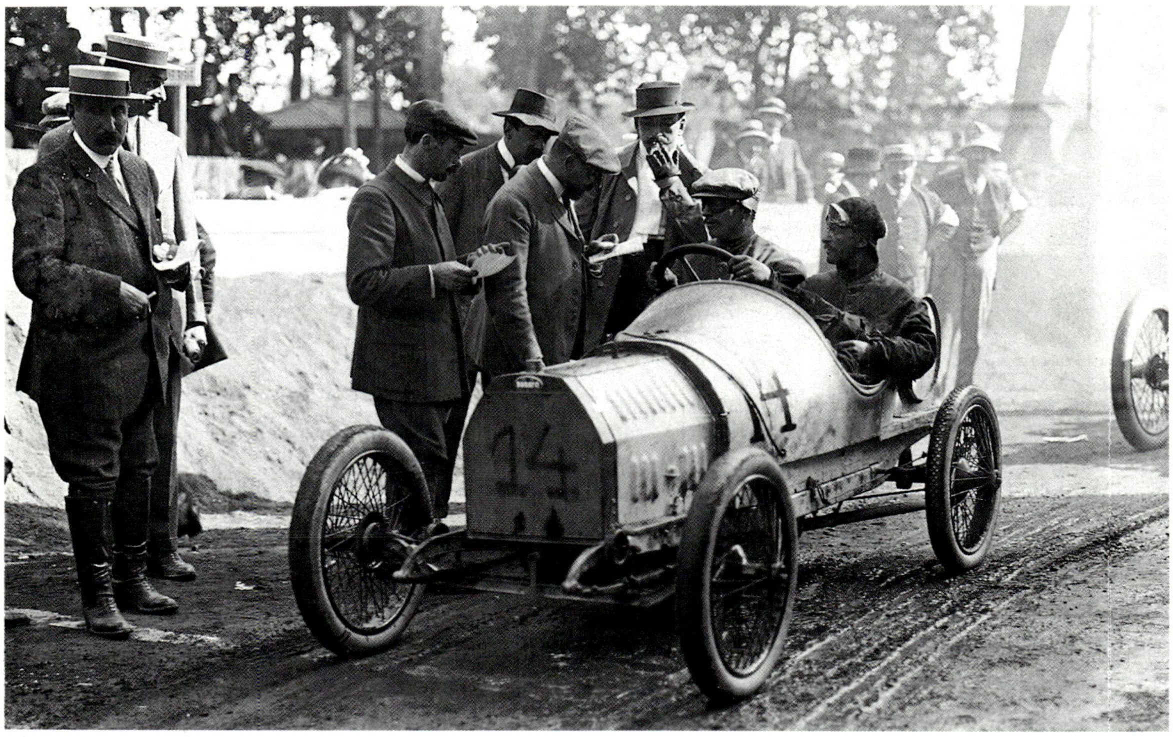

A pair of skew gears drove a cross shaft at the front of the engine from the vertical drive shaft, with a Bosch magneto on the right and a water pump on the left. There was no oil pump on the early cars, the cambox being filled and the bearings lubricated by drip feed from a dash tank, the system used on the typical lathe in Bugatti's workshop.

The clutch was multi-disc, with alternate steel and cast-iron discs, running in an oil–paraffin bath. It was operated by the toggle mechanism Bugatti had designed for Deutz – and then used up to 1932!

The gearbox had a cast aluminium casing straddling the frame and attached at three points on these early cars, later at four for greater rigidity. The internal mechanism was as on the Type 10, with four speeds. There was a drum brake operated from the brake pedal behind the gearbox, and a propeller shaft connected the drive to the rear axle.

The chassis frame was waisted at the front with semi-elliptic springs and a normal H-section front axle, and the rear springs also were semi-elliptic; the rear reversed semi-elliptics so familiar on Bugattis came later. The hand

ABOVE Ettore Bugatti's mechanic Ernest Friderich drove a Type 13 in the small car class in the 1911 French Grand Prix at Le Mans and finished second to Hémery in a large Fiat, after all the other cars had dropped out.

RIGHT This splendid 8-valve Type 15 is the second oldest Bugatti in existence; it originally carried a 'razor-edge' body and was used by Mme Bugatti. It was imported into England in chassis form in 1912 by Col. Dawson of Lowestoft who kept it until 1938, when it passed to the present owner. It still runs perfectly. Provided by C.W.P. Hampton Collection.

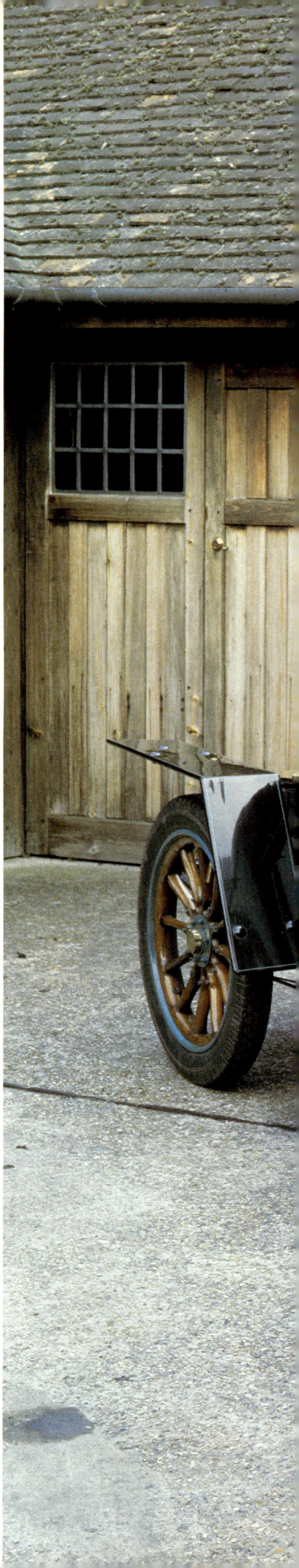

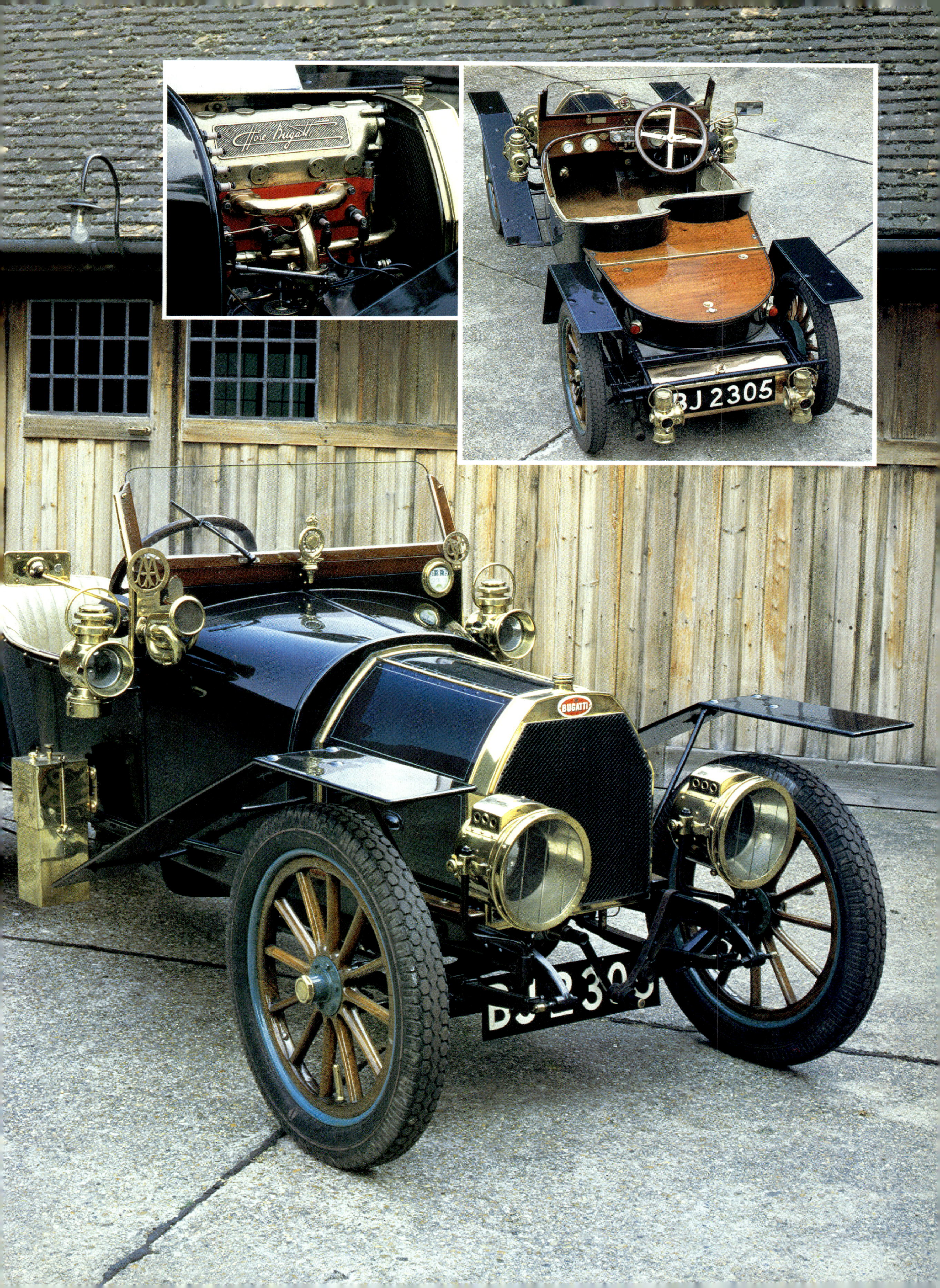
Ettore Bugatti
BJ 2305

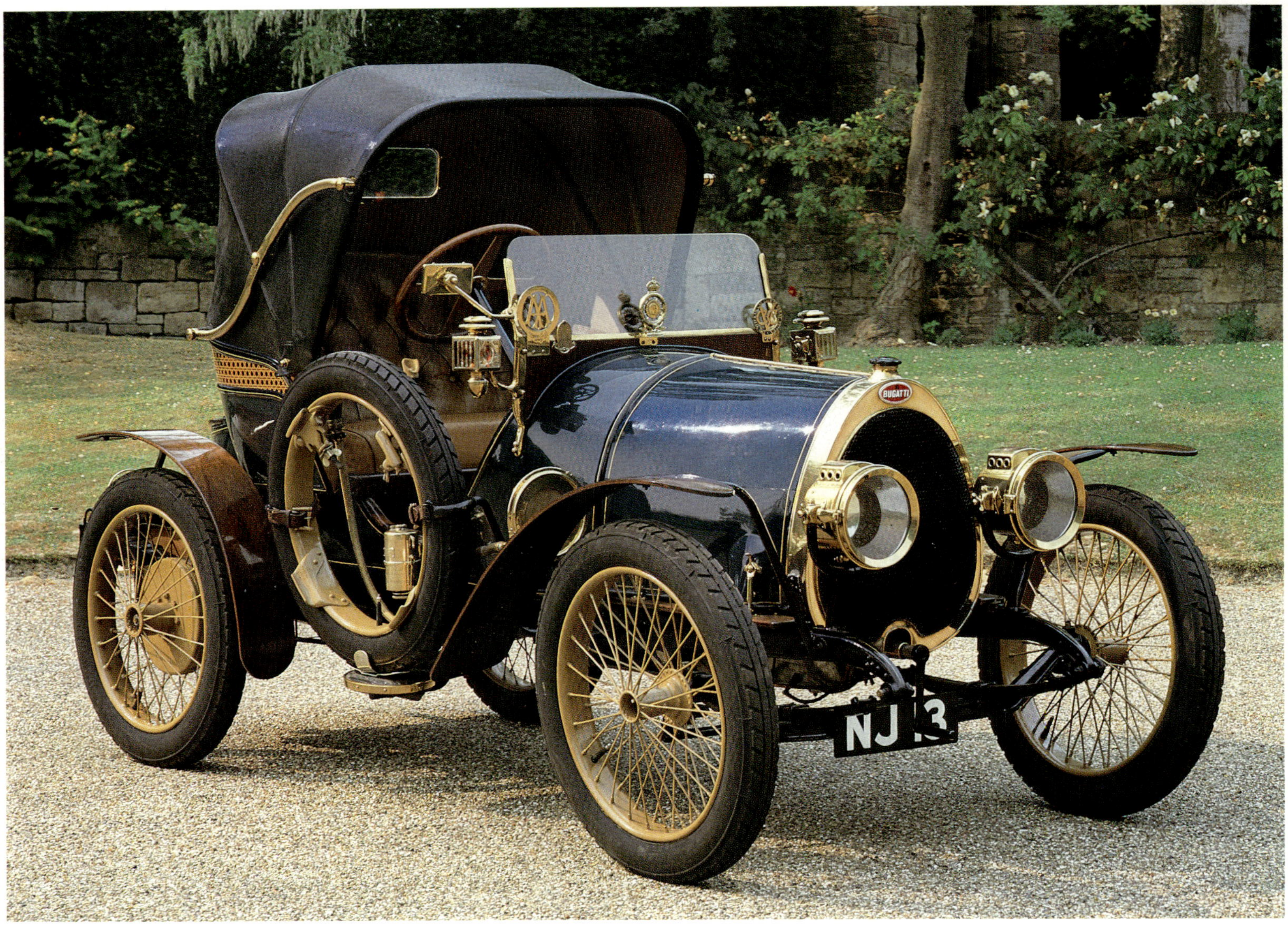

brake on the car operated the rear brakes with cast-iron shoes running direct on the drums.

The engine probably produced about 15 hp and would certainly revolve up to about 3000 rpm, a very high speed for the period. Bugatti claimed a top speed of 100 km/h (62 mph), which was no doubt attainable.

The car was exhibited at the December 1910 Paris Automobile Salon in a modest display in the gallery and created some interest, helped by good results a few weeks earlier at the Gaillon hill climb. The *Motor* account of the event was followed by a road test in Paris by its correspondent W. F. Bradley, extracts from the article being quoted by Bugatti in his first catalogue for the Salon. ('Its upkeep is a mere trifle' became '*effectivement une plaisanterie*': a joke being not quite the same thing!)

According to factory records the first chassis delivered were No. 361 and 362, perhaps as demonstrators. Chassis 363 went to de Vizcaya, Ettore's banker, and 365 went to Prince Hohenlohe (this is now in the Prague technical museum as the oldest existing Bugatti). Chassis 366, dated December 1910, went to the Paris Salon with a coachbuilt saloon body, was then used by Madame Bugatti, and was finally sold in 1912 to Colonel C. P. Dawson, who replaced the body with a light two-seater, which it still carries in the collection of the present owner.

From time to time a car took part in sprints or hill climbs at Gaillon, Mont Ventoux and elsewhere in France, building up successes in the light car classes, and then Ettore audaciously entered it in the voiturette class in the French Grand Prix at Le Mans in 1911. The little car came in second, although in truth only the winner, Victor Hémery in a Fiat, actually finished the race, and the Bugatti was flagged off. A contemporary account noted that the Bugatti seemed to be a 'mouse trotting after an elephant – one failure of the elephant and the mouse might win. Alas it could not be because the police closed the race off at 12 o'clock and the little mouse had just finished its 10th lap out of 12!' Even so, 12 laps were 648 km (403 miles) and Hémery had taken 7 hours 6 minutes.

In 1913 the model was improved by the addition of an oil pump at the front of the cambox to increase the supply to the crankshaft, rods, and to the cambox.

Two other important changes were also made in 1913; for the first time Bugatti fitted his chassis with reversed quarter elliptic springs at the rear – a scheme he had devised the year before for the Bébé car he had designed under contract for the French Peugeot company. The system had the advantage of extending the chassis frame rearwards and improving the support for coachwork. The other change was to replace the square-cut radiator with an oval or egg-shaped one, a basic shape he adopted from this point onwards. Now he used the designations Type 22 and 23 to replace the earlier Type 15 and 17, but retained T13 for the short-wheelbase model.

Bugatti's opinion that weight was the enemy proved correct. The car, in spite of its small size and modest capacity, had a lively performance and a good turn of speed. It handled well on corners and was surprisingly comfortable. The gear change was a delight, the low inertia of the gear trains allowing simple gear changing without any modern synchronizing device. 'What more can a man want of his car in the way of speed than to be able to hold practically any other car he may meet outside of Brooklands', wrote the *Automotor Journal* on 7 February 1914. Magazines and pressmen extolled its virtues in France and Germany as well as in Britain. American journals took note of it, all feeding the Bugatti mystique which Ettore's earlier designs, and indeed his own personality, had engendered.

In the summer of 1914, with war clouds approaching, Bugatti produced a new 69 mm bore cylinder block and cambox for the top half of the engine, with four valves per cylinder to improve the breathing. This engine is correctly known as Type 27, but the chassis retained the designations T13, 22 and 23. This *seize soupapes* engine was intended for the Grand Prix des Voitures Légères due to be run at Clermont-Ferrand in France on 23 August 1914 and two or three cars were prepared. In the event the race was cancelled as war came on 4 August. The engines (or possibly the cylinder blocks and camshaft housings) were buried, and Ettore left Molsheim for Italy, then neutral.

After the war, in 1919, the parts were dug up and three chassis were prepared once more for racing when Bugatti had recovered his factory. Meanwhile he had spent the First World War, for a short time in Italy and

LEFT In 1913 Bugatti improved the lubrication system of the 8-valve car, introducing for the first time an oval radiator, and reversed quarter elliptical springing at the rear – both features he was to retain for many years. This 1914 chassis, actually catalogued as a Type 22, passed through many hands, and was used for racing before World War 2. It was salvaged, rebuilt and fitted with a contemporary-style replica body by the present owner in 1967. Provided by C.W.P. Hampton Collection.

RIGHT The 16-valve Type 13 racing team with Ettore at the rear, after success in the 1920 Voiturette Grand Prix for 1.4-litre cars at Le Mans. The winner Friderich is on the right, de Vizcaya on the left and Baccoli, Bugatti's Milan agent, in the centre. Baccoli finished fifth. It was 50 years before it became generally known that de Vizcaya's engine had thrown a connecting rod; to keep news of this from press and public, Ettore got the car disqualified by 'inadvertently' starting to add water when it came into the pits.

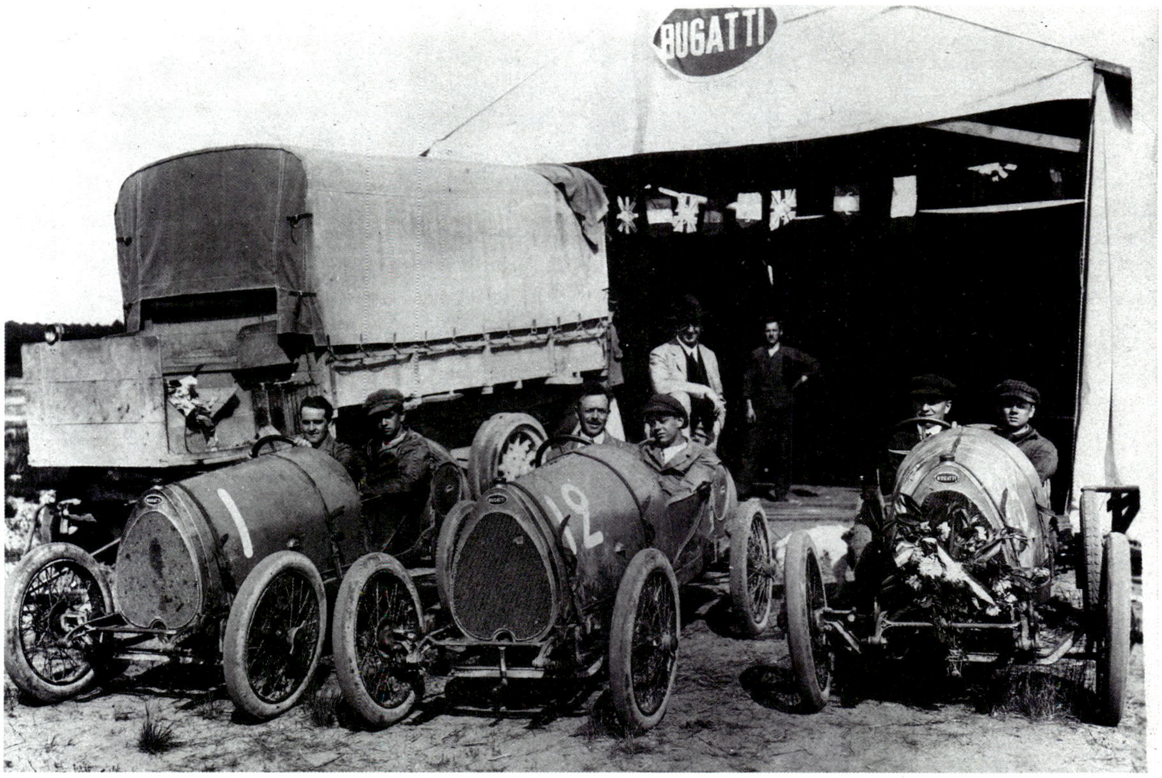

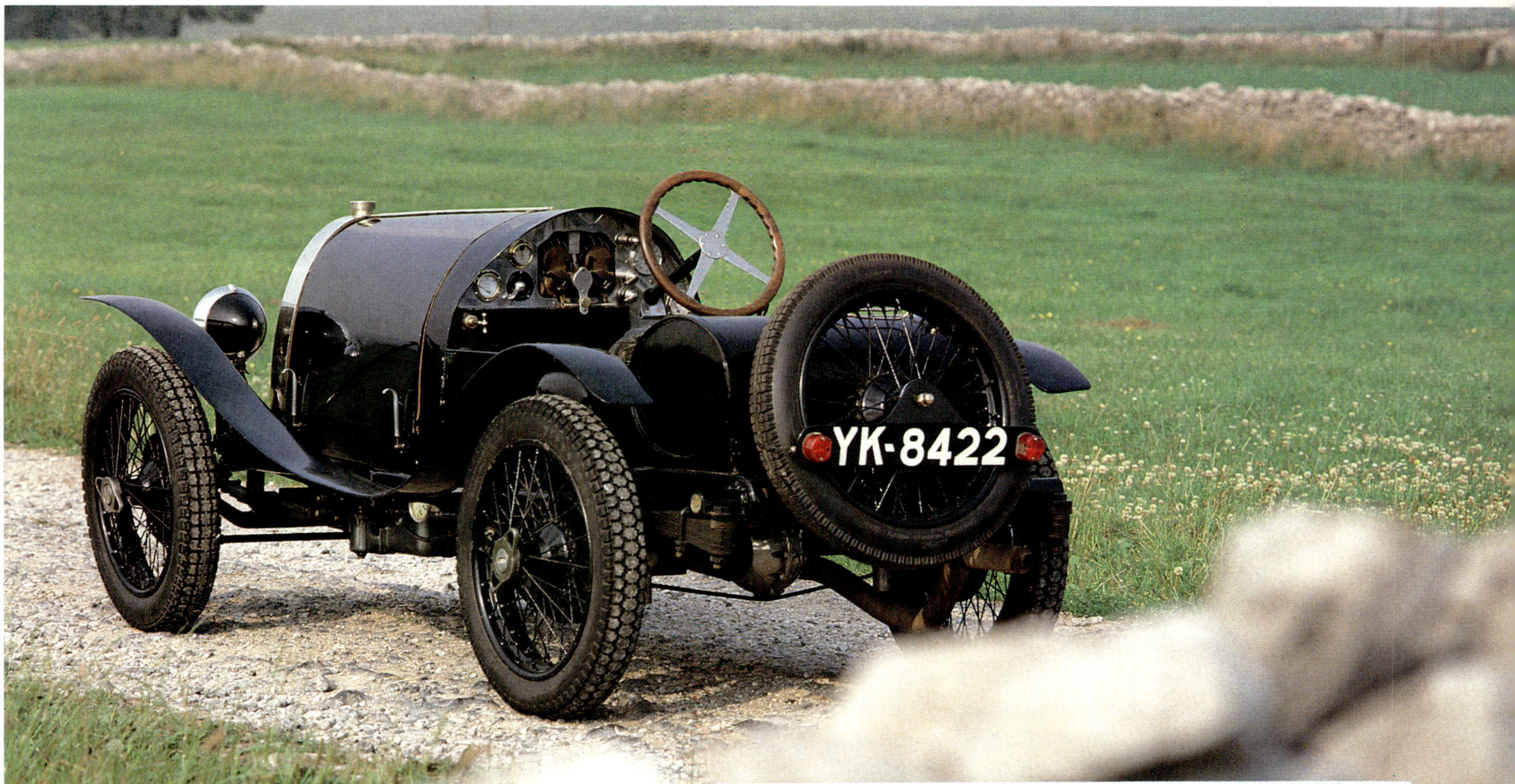

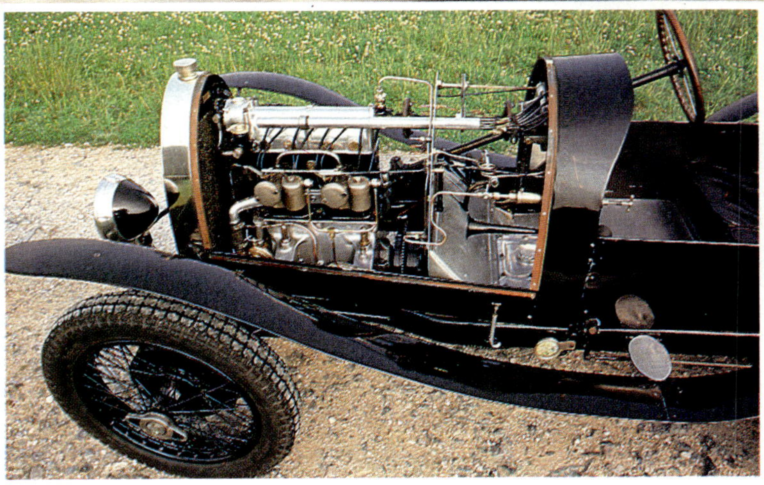

PAGES 14-15 AND ABOVE This superb 1925 Type 13 'bolster tank' racing Bugatti has been built as exactly as possible with original Bugatti parts on a replica frame. These later Type 13s had the crankshaft carried on ball bearings and the steering box on top of the crankcase mounting arm. They retained the twin magnetos and the sparse bodywork, but now had front-wheel brakes. Performance was exciting: in their day few cars could hold them on the road or on hill climbs. Provided by Mr D.R. Marsh.

then in Paris, designing 8- and 16-cylinder aero engines for Diatto and Delaunay, and finally a 16-cylinder unit that was adopted by the US government for manufacture by the Duesenberg factory in New Jersey. The story of Bugatti's developing interest in 8-cylinder cars comes later.

Production of the eight-valve car was resumed at Molsheim in 1919, chassis 738 to 843 (July 1920) with 66 mm bores being completed before the new 16-valve series could get into full production in the autumn of 1920, initially with 68 mm bore, later 69 mm. Licences were sold to Diatto in Italy, and later Rabag in Germany and Crossley in Manchester. But although the financial payments were helpful, as was the publicity, no great production was achieved by any of the licensees.

The outstanding event of 1920, however, was the success of the 16-valve car at the Voiturette Grand Prix at Le Mans, Friderich winning at 92.7 km/h (57.6 mph) and Baccoli in another car coming fifth. Even more sensational was the result at Brescia in 1921, when Bugatti filled the first four places with Friderich in the lead again at a sensational 116 km/h (72 mph). These cars were Type 13s with roller bearing crankshafts, and big ends, and the model thereafter became known as the Brescia. Production deliveries of the Type 13 racing car retained the roller bearings on the main bearings, but reverted to white metal on the rods; the touring Types 22 and 23 then were similarly changed, and received other modifications and became the 'Brescia modifiée', with the steering box on the crankcase, to move the driver forward.

Some 40 'full' Brescias (as they were known), with their short chassis, twin magnetos in the dash, and bolster tank bodies, were sold for racing. An earlier 1920 Le Mans car had been delivered to Henry Segrave for Brooklands, but Raymond Mays had the later model and achieved remarkable success in hill climbs in Britain in 1922–4 in his *Cordon Rouge*, later in *Cordon Bleu*. The model could lap Brooklands at around 160 km/h (100 mph), and Leon Cushman took a second place in the Junior Car Club 200-mile race in 1922 at 146 km/h (91 mph)!

These successes in competition cemented the prestige and reputation of Bugatti sports cars, overcoming the problems of bad braking, oiling plugs, and the general rough behaviour of the occasional touring car that had not been well looked after!

A typical press report on the 16-valve car is this extract from *Light Car*.

There is not a shadow of doubt that, to one who can appreciate the charms of a highly strung, mettlesome sporting car, the Bugatti is very fascinating to handle. With a four-speed close-ratio gearbox, a fairly low-speed but very powerful 1½-litre 16-valve engine, the car gets over the road in a most remarkable fashion, and withal, has that trait for answering immediately to the movement of any control that reminds one vividly of the pleasurable sensations of real motoring obtained when driving a much bigger high-class sports model – say, a Bentley or a 30-98 hp Vauxhall car which are out of the reach of the average light carist's purse in these times of tribulation. In traffic the Bugatti does not shine any more than does any other car. Most of its very low speed work is done on bottom gear (on which, incidentally, 20 mph can be reached with wheel-spinning acceleration in next to no time), for second speed is 6 to 1 only. Travelling steadily, top can be engaged at 20 mph, but the engine does not show up well at the time. But at 30 mph let any other car try to pass. Double-clutch, snick in second, tread on the accelerator and the car ceases to be ordinary and becomes a Bugatti. The engine picks up its speed wondrously quickly, with the low boom of its exhaust note rising pleasantly and clear as the car shoots away. On second 40 mph is easily possible, third gear gives over 50 mph and we timed the car over the flying mile at Brooklands at 62.5 mph with two up and a slight but almost negligible wind astern.

Undoubtedly, however, the beauty of the 'Bug' is the way it holds the road. The steering is as nigh perfect as any we have ever handled on cars small or large. The rear springs – reversed quarter-elliptics – do not dither on road waves, neither do they 'float' sullenly over undulations; instead at all times they appear to be flexible, rapid in action and always prepared to take up the shock between axle and chassis, at the same time controlling the movements of the driving wheels so that they are pressed firmly against the road surface and held down to their job properly. The result is a car that can be taken round corners in compass-drawn curves without fear of slip or steering lag – a car that always goes where its driver wants.

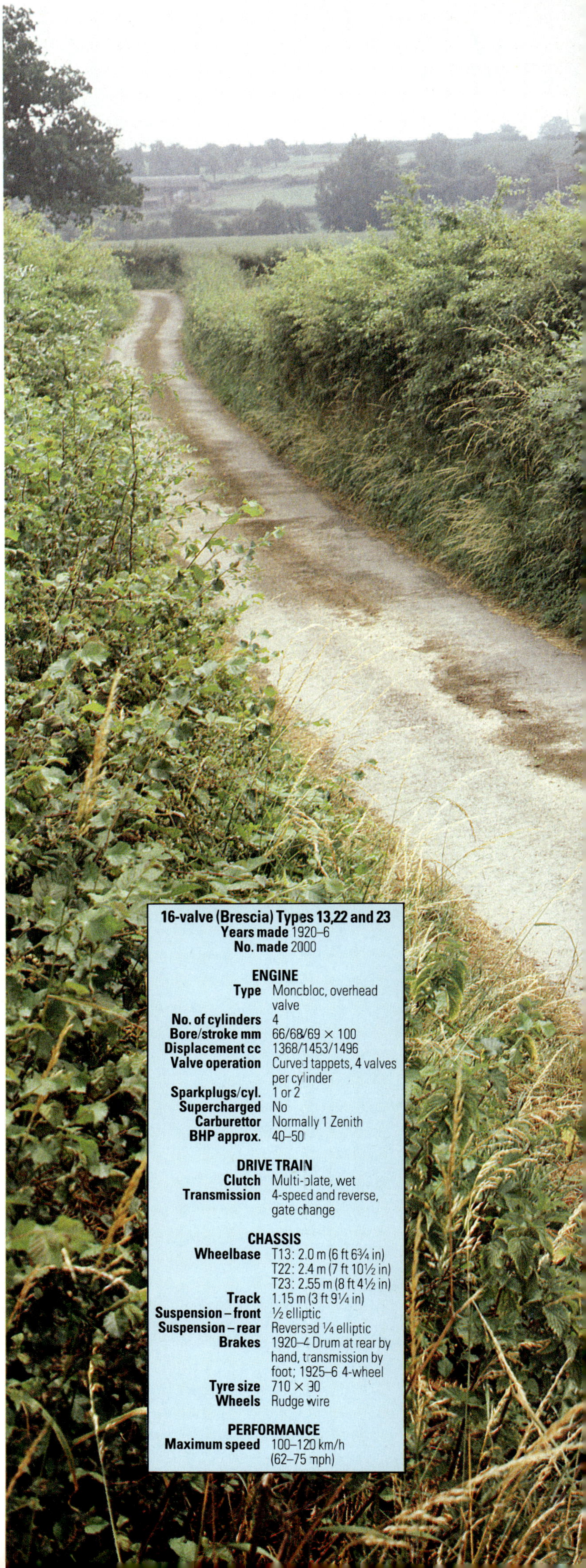

16-valve (Brescia) Types 13,22 and 23
Years made 1920–6
No. made 2000

ENGINE

Type	Moncbloc, overhead valve
No. of cylinders	4
Bore/stroke mm	66/68/69 × 100
Displacement cc	1368/1453/1496
Valve operation	Curved tappets, 4 valves per cylinder
Sparkplugs/cyl.	1 or 2
Supercharged	No
Carburettor	Normally 1 Zenith
BHP approx.	40–50

DRIVE TRAIN

Clutch	Multi-plate, wet
Transmission	4-speed and reverse, gate change

CHASSIS

Wheelbase	T13: 2.0 m (6 ft 6¾ in) T22: 2.4 m (7 ft 10½ in) T23: 2.55 m (8 ft 4½ in)
Track	1.15 m (3 ft 9¼ in)
Suspension – front	½ elliptic
Suspension – rear	Reversed ¼ elliptic
Brakes	1920–4 Drum at rear by hand, transmission by foot; 1925–6 4-wheel
Tyre size	710 × 30
Wheels	Rudge wire

PERFORMANCE

Maximum speed	100–120 km/h (62–75 mph)

A longer-wheelbase Type 23 'Brescia modifiée, delivered to the banker Leo d'Erlanger in 1925 and used by him in Tunisia. It had many owners in England before being rebuilt with a replica period four-seat body in 1961. The later touring Brescias combined performance with comfort. Provided by Mr & Mrs J. White.

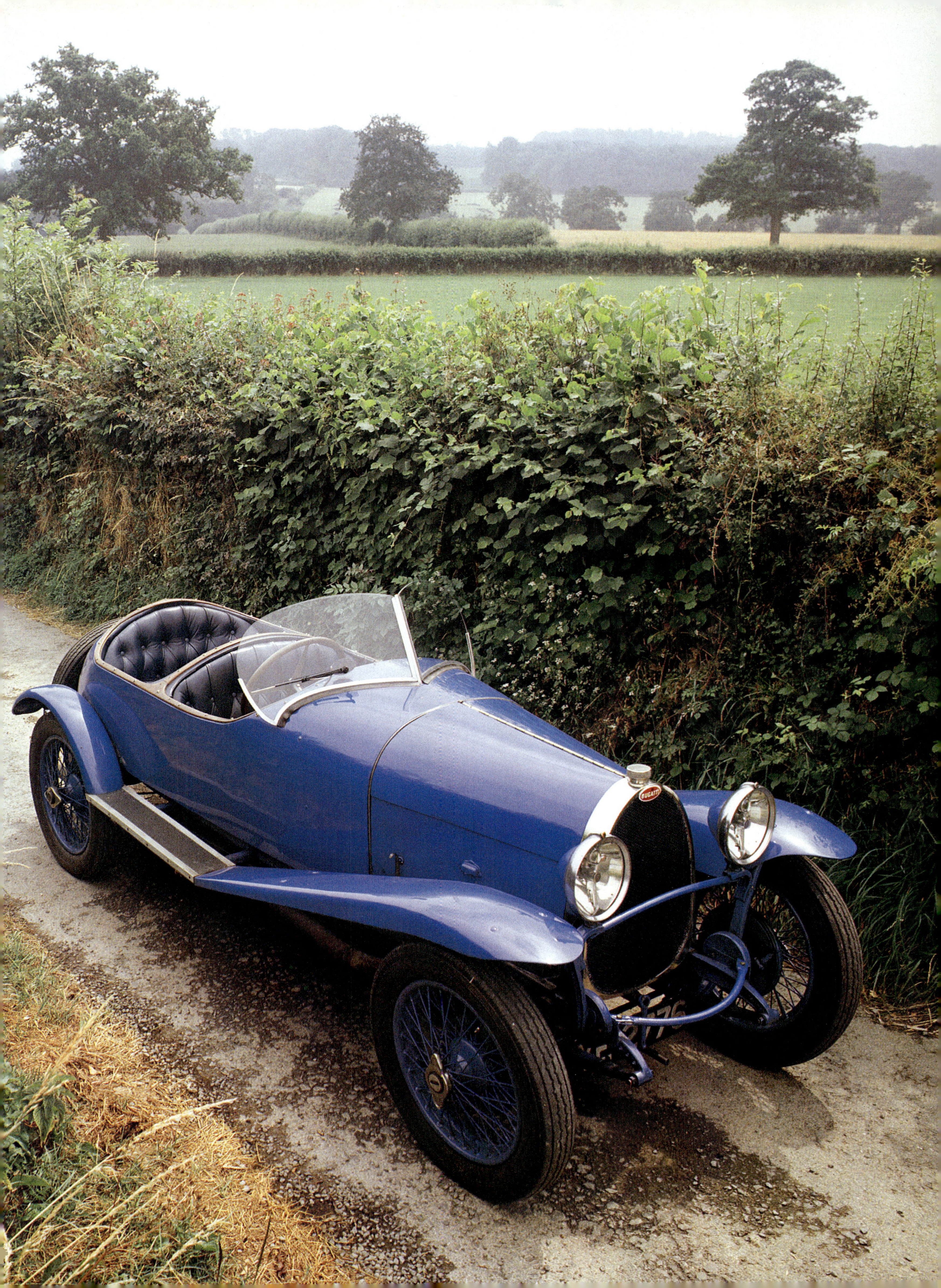

Another account, this time from *The Autocar* in 1923, helps to show how in spite of its faults, the reputation of the car increased.

> Like every other car, it makes the enthusiast sigh for an interview with the designer, part of which would be spent in almost fulsome praise, and part on somewhat searching questions, to which the heckled engineer would doubtless return prompt and contemptuous replies. But before I complete my panegyric and switch off into semi-criticism, let me admit frankly that I have never handled an engine commending more wholesale and unreserved reverence. It is a beauty, if ever there was one.
>
> This marvellous engine, perennially cool, eternally willing, and quite konkproof, is backed up by the most automatic gear change imaginable. I believe Bugatti experts hold that it is well to make a tiny pause or even to double-clutch when passing up from first to second gear; but the kind of driver with no dodges up his sleeve to cope with every awkward change and who hates scrunching pinions in public or private will find the Bugatti gears tacitly respond to a lightning flick of his forefinger under all conditions. No stunts are requisite. Though there is no clutch-stop, you merely tip in whatever gear you want at any road or engine speed, and nothing but the altered beat of the exhaust indicates that you have just performed what might rank as something of a feat in gear changing on many cars.
>
> The indirect gears are not quiet, but the French laugh at such hypercriticism. If your engine is running as it should, say they, the roar of the exhaust will smother any gear hum there may be.
>
> There are notoriously two schools of fast drivers. The one drives on the brakes and follows modern French fashion in demanding a stopping device on all four wheels, so that the car can be pinned down to rest within a few yards, however speedy the gait. The other school holds that a real driver should need no brakes. It believes that brakes are the last resource of the inefficient motorist, who should blush whenever he applies them, driving rather on his throttle and exhausting his impetus to a nicety. To this school M. Bugatti undoubtedly belongs, unless it be that brakes are the Achilles' heel of his genius, and he simply is not interested in them.

No doubt criticism such as this of the lack of front brakes and the retention of a transmission brake helped to get the Brescia's stopping power brought up to date.

Nevertheless, the Brescia Bugatti in its various models was the most successful Bugatti in terms of production, some 2000 being made between 1920 and mid-1926. The last few years' production was much improved and civilized, with proper electric equipment, excellent four-wheel brakes and a few minor improvements to the engine.

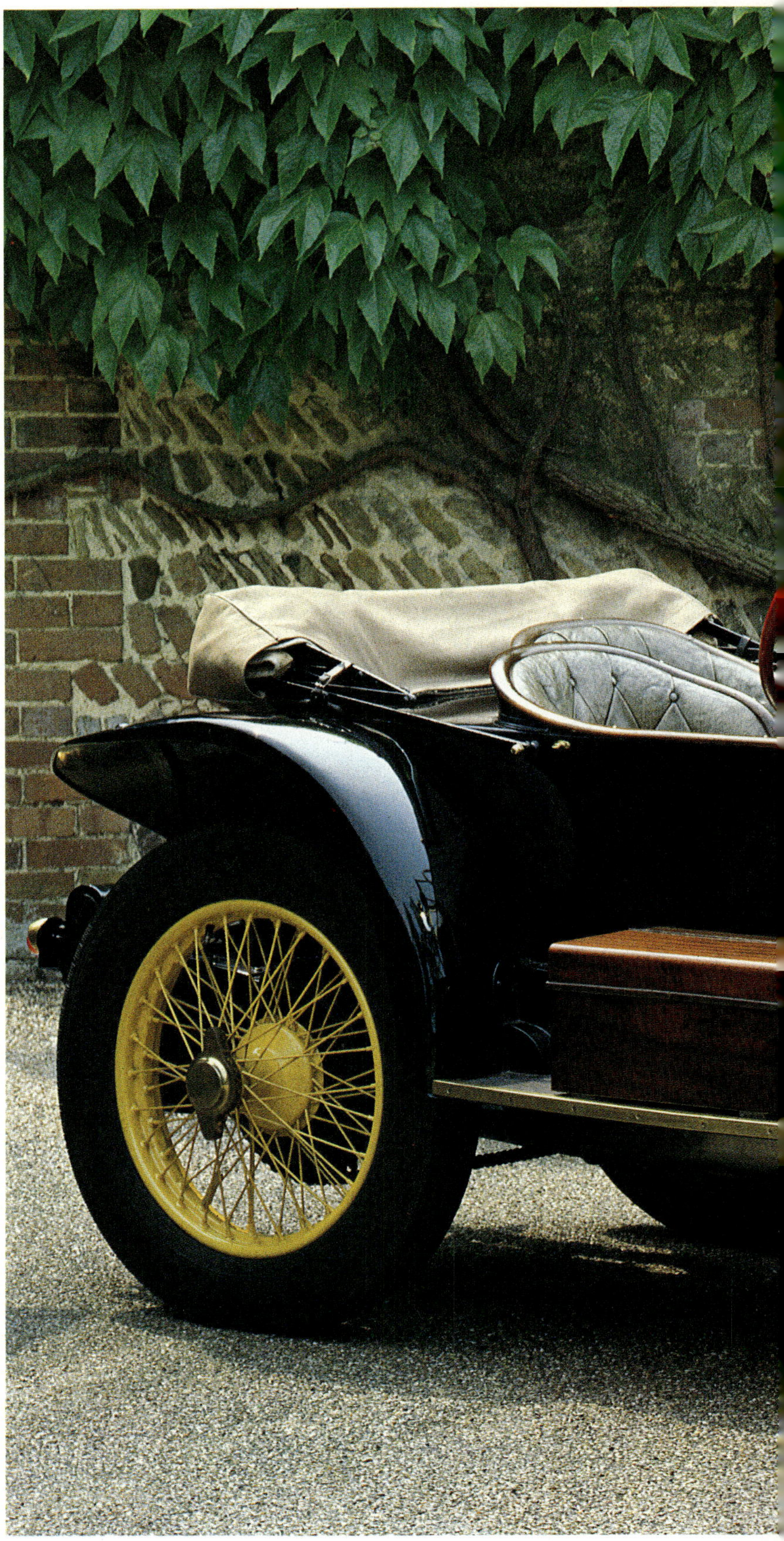

Molsheim experiments

Bugatti's interest in eight-cylinder engines seems to have stemmed from an experimental chassis built about 1912 which had two eight-valve, four-cylinder engines in tandem! Little is known of the results but his first aero engine, designed in 1915 for Diatto, was a straight-eight that performed well on test. It was inevitable that Bugatti would soon design an eight-cylinder car, which he did as soon as the war was over and he had managed to restart at Molsheim in 1919. The story of the eight-cylinder cars is recounted in the next chapter.

An important activity at Molsheim before 1914 was the production of a few large chain-driven 5-litre cars for competition. The prototype chassis of this design was a Deutz which Ettore used in high-speed Prince Henry trials in 1909 and 1910. The first model built at Molsheim carries the chassis number 471 of 1912 and is the car Ettore himself used in various events and hill climbs, including Mont Ventoux. It may be that the chassis and transmission were Deutz or Deutz-related, and that only the engine (evidently the Type 16) was new. One of these cars was sold to the famous French aviator Roland Garros (chassis 474) who became a good friend of Ettore. Garros had several exploits to his name before the First World War, including the first flight across the Mediterranean. During the war he was shot down and imprisoned, but escaped to fly again and then sadly was killed in an aerial battle three weeks before the Armistice. The 'Garros' car came to England and, rebodied, is still in good hands and fine condition. Three more of these chain-driven *Rennwagen* were produced, evidently on the suggestion of Peugeot – and to be in competition for the 1912 season with Peugeot's own Grand Prix car, designed by that company's engineer Ernest Henry. It is said that Bugatti lost out on speed trials, achieving only 160 km/h (99 mph) to Peugeot's 185 km/h (115 mph), which is not surprising since the Peugeot's engine had 7.6 litres against Bugatti's 5.2. The anomaly in this tale is that the factory lists the three *Rennwagen* as produced in 1914, not 1912; a possible explanation is that Bugatti used a single, earlier car for the competition and produced the three cars in question later for his own purposes.

One chassis, with a normal rear axle, competed unsuccessfully in the 1914 Indianapolis 500-mile race, failing after 20 laps. The following year another went to the United States from Germany (not then at war with America) to compete in the race, again unsuccessfully, and later was much raced in California. The third car went with Bugatti to Italy when he left Molsheim in September 1914, and remained in chassis form in the family until sold in 1965 to the Schlumpf collection at Mulhouse in France.

Whatever the exact history of the 'Garros' model, the engine is of some historical importance as it was the first design to have three valves per cylinder, two inlet and a single exhaust, a construction that Bugatti was to use regularly up to 1930. The engine construction followed Bugatti lines,

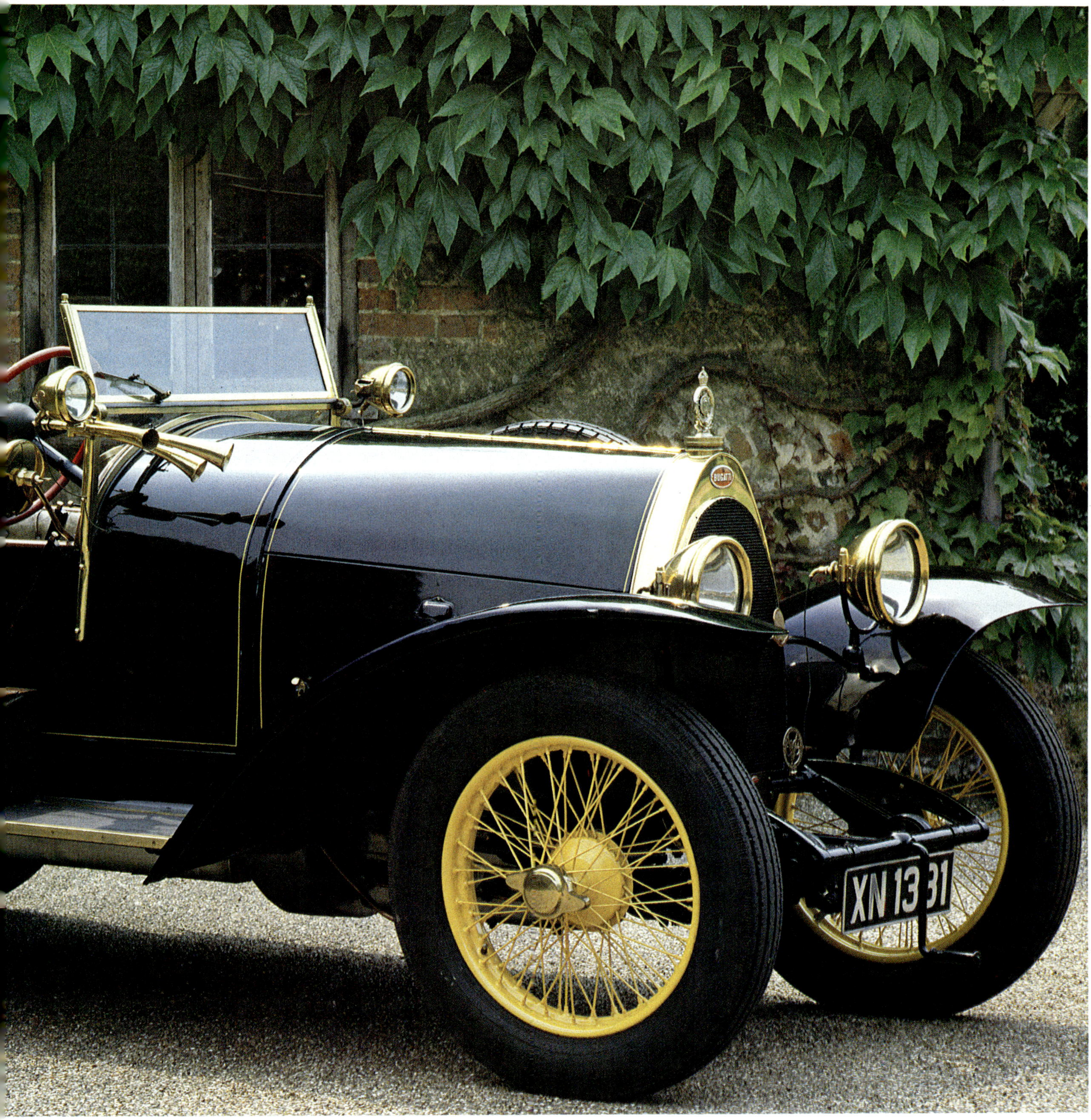

'Black Bess' is perhaps the most famous individual Bugatti. So named by one of its owners, Ivy Cummings, who raced it at Brooklands in the 1920s, it was originally delivered to the French aviator Roland Garros in September 1913 and is one of the two remaining 5-litre chain-driven pre-1914 cars. It passed from Garros' hands to the Sunbeam designer Louis Coatalen, then to the present owner in 1948. Provided by C.W.P. Hampton Collection.

with a split cast aluminium crankcase and a one-piece cylinder block with integral head. The valves were vertical and operated through hinged rockers from a single overhead camshaft driven by the usual bevels and vertical shaft at the front. Water pump and magneto were driven by a cross drive from the vertical shaft as on the smaller car, but the driven skew gear was elongated so that by sliding it sideways magneto timing could be varied. The crankshaft had five plain bearings on the earliest car (471) but only three on the one delivered to Garros (474). The early design had a very poor system for lubricating the bearings by drip (and hope!) and, fed by a camshaft-driven oil pump from a tank, the 'total loss' oil after milling around in the crankcase was rejected into a lateral reservoir on the side of the engine crankcase. A close-fitting crankcase helped pump out surplus oil. This system, perhaps typical of early Bugatti, was replaced on the later car by a supply through jets to crank and rods.

The car's clutch was a Bugatti multi-plate device and the gearbox and differential also seem similar, if not identical, to the assembly on the chain-driven Deutz (Type 8). The chassis had two pairs of front springs, and reversed quarter elliptics at the rear. Brakes were as on the Deutz, a foot brake on the rear of the gearbox and a hand brake for the rear wheels.

This 5-litre car had, and still has, a remarkable road performance, being able to cruise on a modern motorway at over 125 km/h (80 mph) with the engine rotating at about 1800 rpm. However, it must have been responsible for the apocryphal tale of Bugatti's reply to a critic of his car's brakes: 'I design my cars to go, not to stop!'

THE Bugatti Tourers

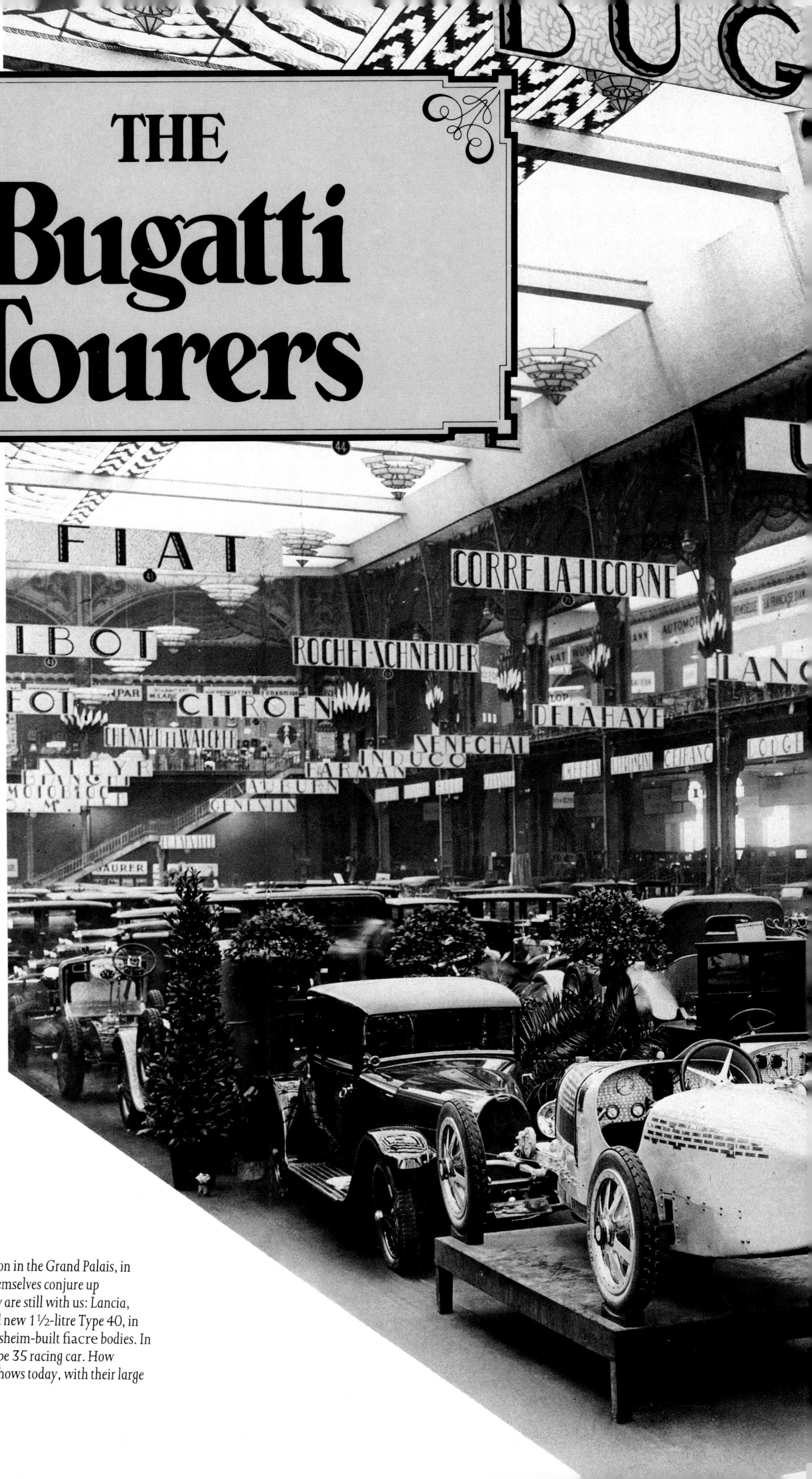

A typical Bugatti stand at the Paris Salon in the Grand Palais, in this case October 1926. The names themselves conjure up memories of forgotten makes, but a few are still with us: Lancia, Fiat, Citroën. Ettore shows his splendid new 1½-litre Type 40, in early short-chassis form, and with Molsheim-built fiacre bodies. In the foreground is a medal-bedecked Type 35 racing car. How different are the stands at automobile shows today, with their large spaces and hospitality rooms!

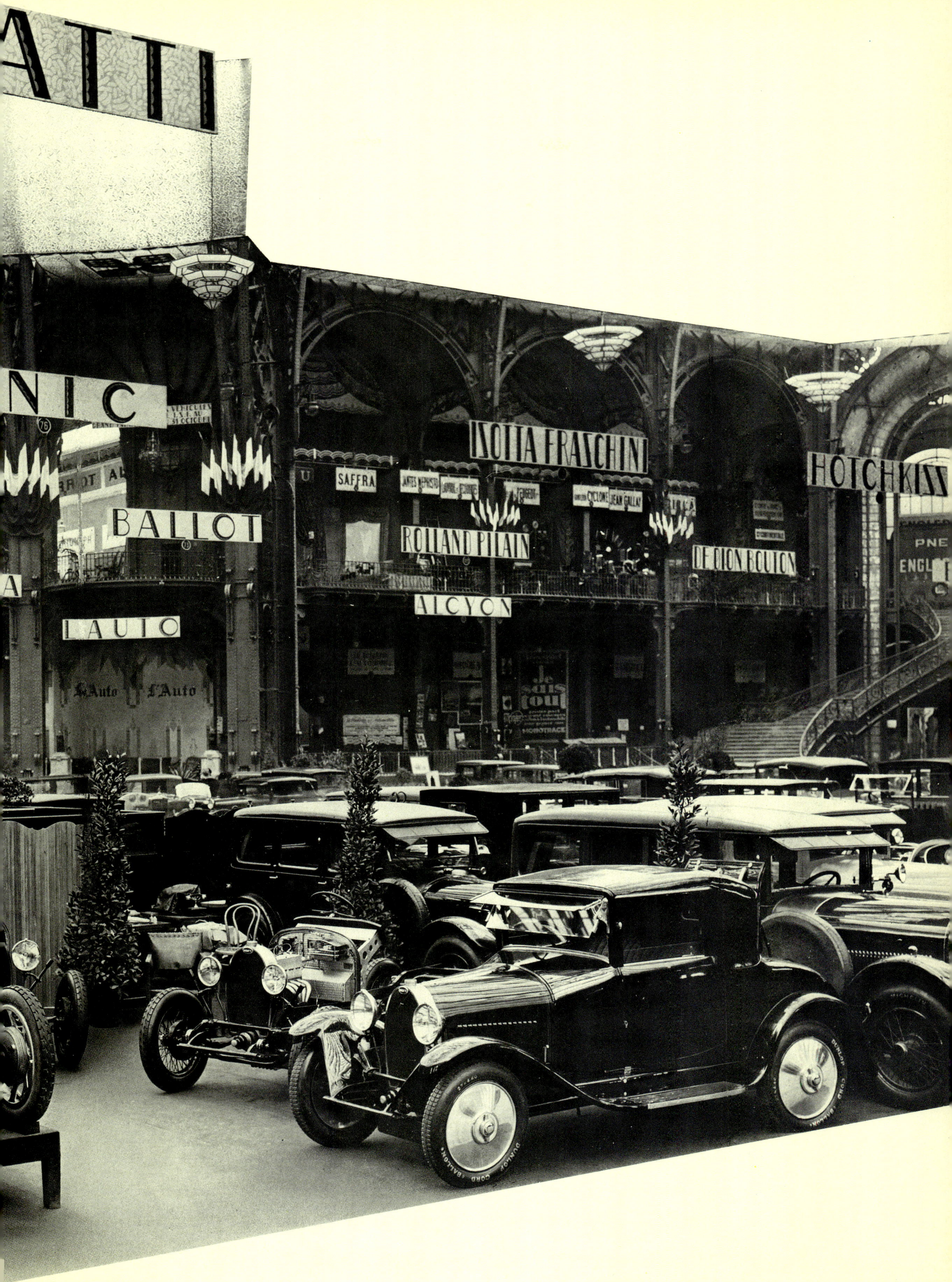
ATTI
NIC
BALLOT
L'AUTO
L'Auto
L'Auto
ISOTTA FRASCHINI
SAFFRA
ROLLAND PILAIN
ALCYON
DE DION BOUTON
HOTCHKISS
CYCLONE
JEAN GALLAY
PNE
ENGL
MONOTRACE
DUNLOP CORD BALLON

FROM his earliest days at Molsheim, Ettore dreamed of moving back into luxurious cars with the name Bugatti on their radiators. But he knew he did not then have the means. Wartime success – financial, if not in terms of production – with his aero engine helped to bolster his confidence, and when he opened up his factory at Molsheim again in 1919 he started the design of a 3-litre, 69 × 100 mm, eight-cylinder car with the type number 28 to follow the four-valve 1½-litre engine he had designed in 1914 as the Type 27.

Only one chassis was built and shown bare at Paris and in London in 1921. It bristled with design features, but his resources did not allow him to complete its development. The engine retained his three-valve cylinder head, with twin four-cylinder blocks, and a one-piece aluminium cambox for the overhead camshaft, bevel driven by a vertical shaft now between the two blocks. The crank was in two halves to allow the driving bevel to be placed centrally, and was carried on nine bearings.

The 'banana' tappets of the earlier four-cylinder engine were abandoned in favour of rows of *culbuteurs* or fingers levering up the cam lift by about 40 per cent at the valve. These rockers pivoted on a pair of long tubes fed by oil from the gear pump which was now used, and surplus oil splashed around in the cambox and dripped down on the camshaft journals.

A cross shaft in the centre drove a water pump on the left and the magneto on the right. The twin carburettors were of Bugatti design, but it is likely that they were never properly tested as Ettore soon standardized on Zenith or Solex.

The gearbox had only two forward speeds and was built into the rear axle, a design concept that Bugatti seems to have liked, perhaps because of the success he had had with the similar, chassis-mounted, device on his chain-driven cars. An intriguing chassis detail was the use of leather links on the steering rod connections, eliminating grease points and anticipating the modern use of plastics.

Bugatti no doubt had in mind that a 3-litre touring car could lead to a 3-litre racing car, as this was the standard capacity of the Grand Prix engine in 1920–1. But in 1922 the formula was reduced to 2 litres, which helped Bugatti to turn to a new touring-racing engine.

The eight-cylinder Type 30

The 2-litre solution made possible a new engine known at the factory as the Type 29/30, fitted to the longer wheelbase Brescia chassis, either the 2.4 m (7 ft 10½ in) Type 22 frame, or the 2.55 m (8 ft 4½ in) Type 23 one. However, a stronger, larger – 2.85 m (9 ft 4¼ in) wheelbase – frame soon appeared. There is evidence that the Type 29 designation related to a smaller, 1½-litre version of the 2-litre engine, but it did not materialize.

The engine showed major design improvements over the prototype Type 28. Bore and stroke were 60 × 88 mm, in two blocks of four, as before, with two inlet and one exhaust valve per cylinder. The camshaft had the same type of rockers or fingers as the 3-litre engine, but the bevel drive was at the front, as was the cross shaft driving the water pump on the left, and initially an oil pump on the right. The first cars were intended for racing and had twin magnetos carried in a cradle on the dash and driven from the end of the camshaft. The cradle contained a trio of gears giving a step-up of 2 to 1 from the camshaft half-speed, to run the magnetos at engine speed.

The crankshaft was now carried on three large double-row self-aligning ball bearings, the crank being in two halves to permit assembly of the centre bearing. Big ends were white-metalled, lubricated from jets squirting oil into grooves in the crank webs and then out to the rod journals.

The crank consisted of two four-cylinder cranks at right angles; impulses were regular at 90° intervals, but crank balance was defective with this arrangement. (It was not until 1929 that Bugatti adopted the better fully balanced layout.) The crankcase itself was a large one-piece aluminium casting with the crank fed in from one end, and bolted rigidly across the frame.

Carburation was from a pair of Zenith units, each feeding one cylinder block. The exhaust system was well engineered with each cylinder having a generous outlet pipe, clustering four at a time in 'bunch-of-banana' style.

The clutch and gearbox were from the 16-valve 1½-litre car, which seems to have managed the extra torque; later the gearbox was enlarged with wider gears, but retained the high-speed layshaft and reversed gear change with first and third backwards on the gear lever gate and second and top forwards. Also, the rear axle was similar to that on the smaller car, but the track was widened and the suspension had heavier springs, half elliptic at the front and reversed quarter elliptic at the rear as usual.

The brakes had large mechanically operated shoes at the rear and, in a new departure for Bugatti, smaller hydraulic brakes of his own design at the front; these were imperfectly designed in that the sealing of the master cylinder was not adequate and there was a risk that the brakes would only work with pumping. The hydraulic system was later replaced by the mechanical layout used on the later series Brescias.

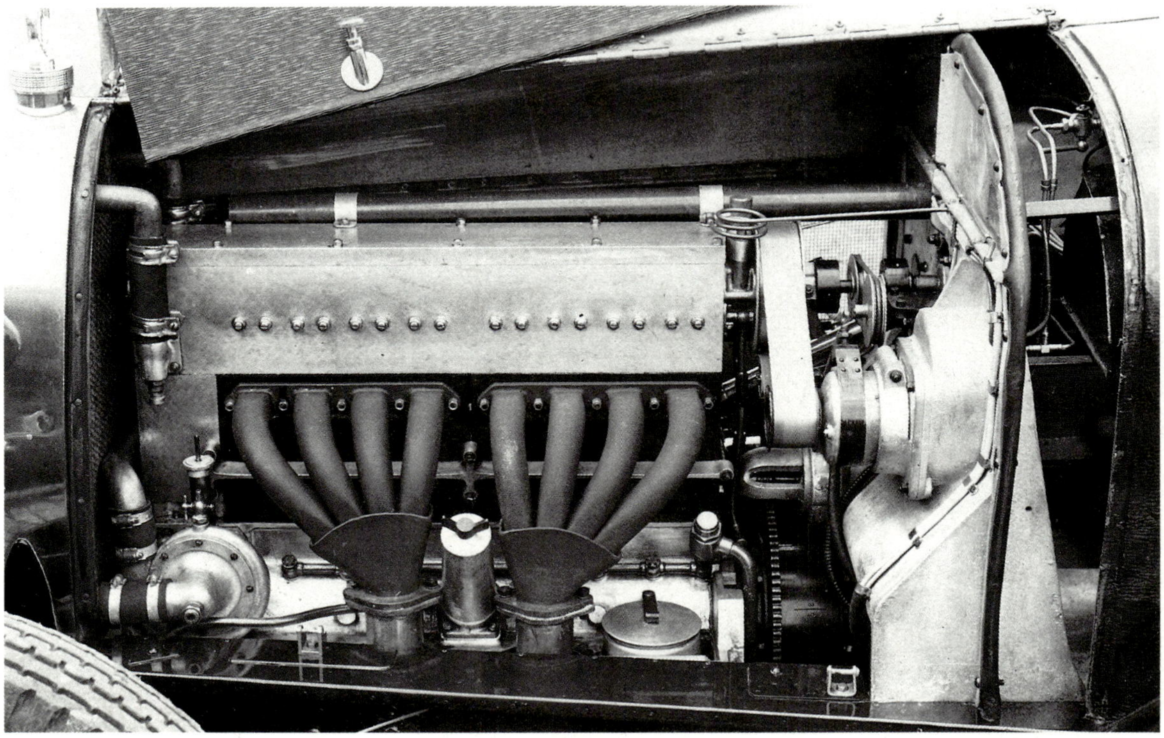

RIGHT The engine for the Type 30 shows the rectangular style of the eight-cylinder unit that Bugatti adopted between 1920 and 1932: twin four-cylinder blocks topped by a single cambox operating two inlet and one exhaust valve per cylinder. The excellent 'bunch of bananas' exhaust manifolds and the cast aluminium alloy crankcase bolted rigidly to the frame are typical features. The Type 30 also had a cast bulkhead, which carried the starter motor and dynamo.

The development of the car for racing is dealt with in the next chapter, but it is worth mentioning that the qualities of the touring model were well received by the motoring press and the first owners by the time the car got into proper production in 1923-4, after being shown at the Paris Salon in 1923. Three of the earliest cars came to Britain, one for Sir Robert Bird (MP for Solihull) and another for Lord Carnarvon, both of whom wrote eulogies of praise to Ettore – although later Bird became irritated when his bearings failed on the way to the south of France!

The Type 38: a limited success

The development problems with the racing cars and the improvements made in the engine for the 1924 Grand Prix at Lyon (in the T35) led Bugatti to design a replacement for the Type 30, which indeed had been much improved in 1924–5 with a heavier chassis frame and good four-wheel mechanical brakes.

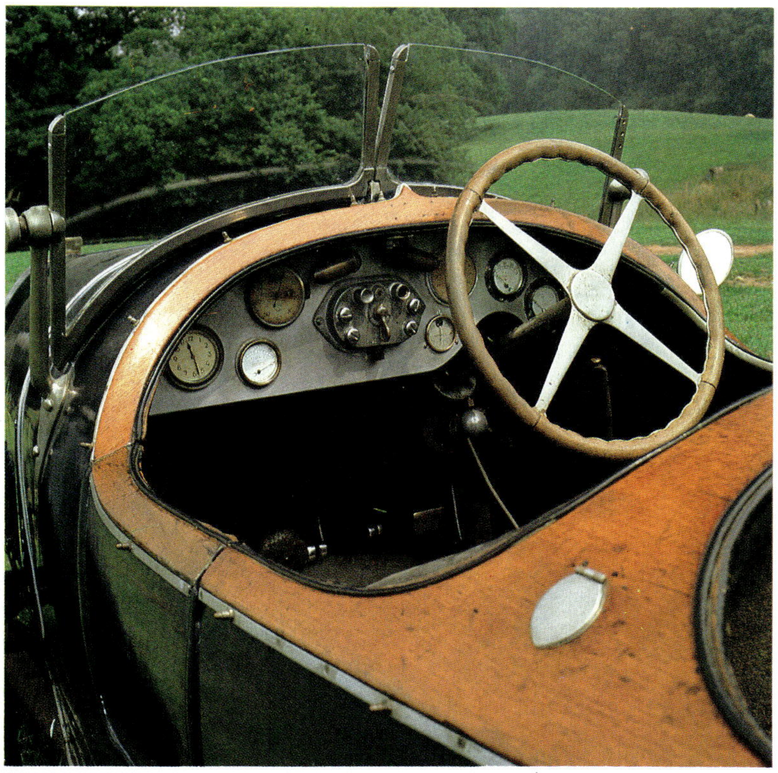

Type 30 Tourer	
Years made	1922–6
No. made	600
ENGINE	
Type	Two 4-cylinder monoblocs, overhead camshaft, roller bearing crankshaft, plain big ends
No. of cylinders	8
Bore/stroke mm	60 × 88
Displacement cc	1991
Valve operation	2 inlet, 1 exhaust per cylinder
Sparkplugs/cyl.	1
Supercharged	No
Carburettors	2 Zenith
BHP approx.	75 touring, 100 racing
DRIVE TRAIN	
Clutch	Multi-plate, wet
Transmission	4-speed and reverse, gate change
CHASSIS	
Wheelbase	2.55 m (8 ft 4½ in), 2.85 m (9 ft 4¼ in)
Track	1.2 m (3 ft 11¼ in)
Suspension – front	½ elliptic
Suspension – rear	Reversed ¼ elliptic
Brakes	1922–4 Front hydraulic, rear cable; 1925–6 cable
Tyre size	765 × 105, 820 × 120
Wheels	Rudge wire
PERFORMANCE	
Maximum speed	120–145 km/h (75–90 mph)

Bugatti's first eight-cylinder production car, the 2-litre Type 30 formed the basis of his brilliantly successful Type 35 Grand Prix model. The first Type 30s were used for racing and the early cars had very unreliable hydraulic front brakes. Later cable-operated brakes were fitted, but by the time the early model started production in May 1923 it proved in other respects a reliable fast touring car. The body, by Carrosserie Moderne of Strasbourg, is typical of the period, with four seats and mahogany decking around the edges. Provided by Mr M. Raahauge.

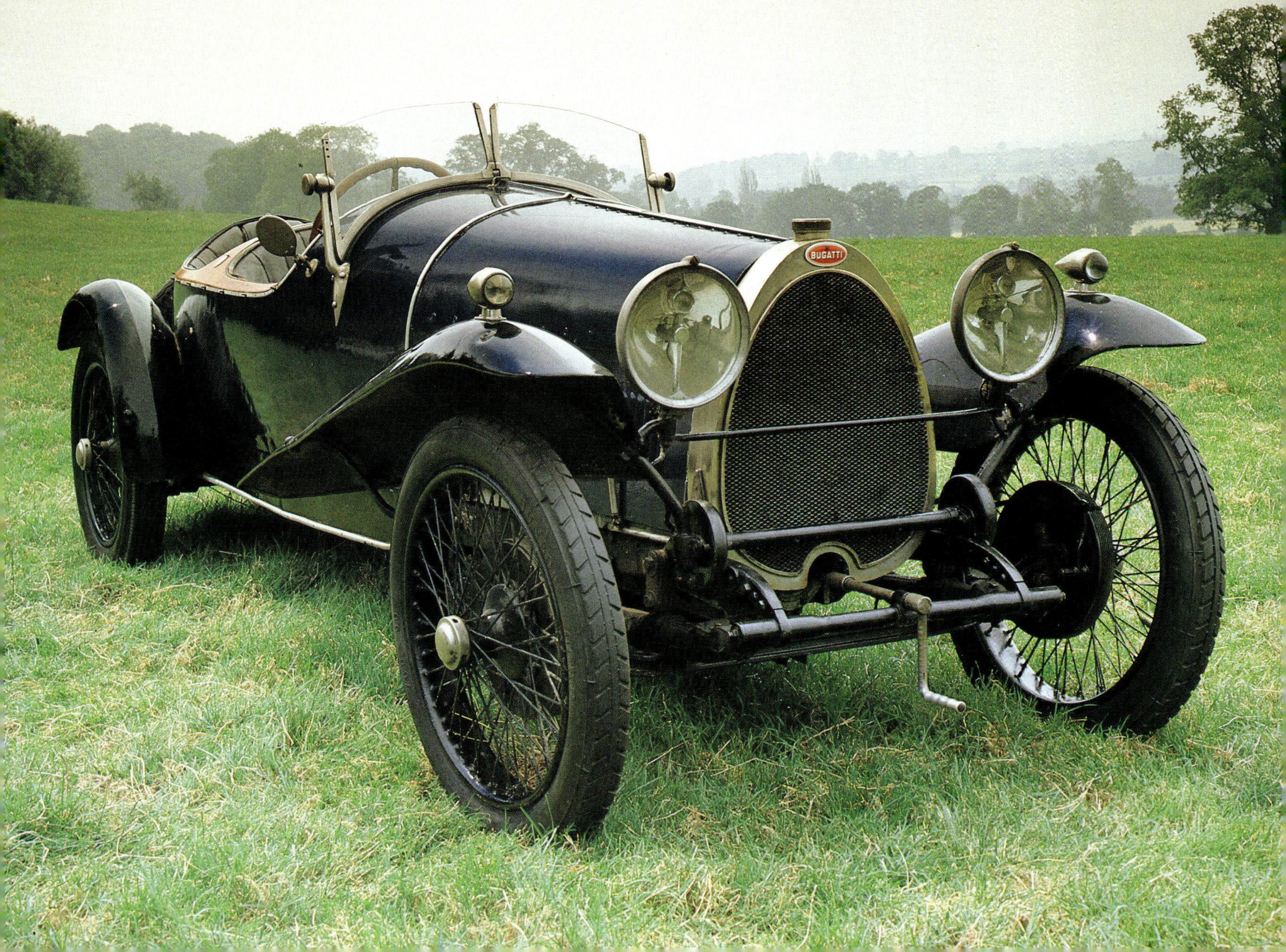

The Type 38 came out in the spring of 1926, and was new throughout except for the engine itself. The blocks, valve arrangements, crankshaft and bearings remained as on the Type 30. The crankcase now was split on the crank centre line like the racing T35, instead of being in one piece with the crank fed in from one end. Coil ignition replaced the magneto and a Delco distributor was driven from the rear of the camshaft. The oil pump was at the front of the engine and driven from a worm gear on the end of the crankshaft, a position to which it had already been moved on the later Type 30.

The chassis was all new, longer and heavier in section, still with the standard reversed quarter elliptic springs at the rear, but with a new solid, circular-sectioned and polished axle looking like that on the Grand Prix car. The brakes were large and the cable work to all four wheels was fully compensated and very well done – in what was to become the standard layout for many years. The front cables passed over the top of each kingpin at the front, and this allowed axle twist when the brakes were applied to give a degree of servo action.

A new gearbox had been designed, along normal 'low-speed layshaft' lines, giving a conventional gear change (first forward, top back) to a central lever. The gears, shafts and bearings were all heavier, and gone was the delightful feather-light gear change. This box was retained on several touring and sports models up to 1934.

The back axle used the central section, differential and bevel gears from the racing T35 and later T30 models, but the track was wider and the hubs and wheels larger. Hartford shock absorbers were now used, and the equipment included adequate electric starting and lighting, although this model introduced a dynamotor to the front of the engine, providing silent starting.

A road test in *The Motor* in August 1926 was friendly and extolled some virtues of the car, such as steering and brakes, and praised the gear change. Maximum speed was a modest 117 km/h (73 mph) at Brooklands and the report summarized the car as one 'for the real enthusiast who enjoys making full use of his gearbox to get rapid acceleration and fast hill-climbing'.

It was apparent that the chassis was too heavy for the 2-litre engine; it was to be transformed later with larger engines, but meanwhile in mid-1927 Bugatti added a supercharger, using his small unit from the four-cylinder racing Type 37A, and the drive arrangements from the racing Type 35B, all of which fitted the Type 38 engine perfectly. Power output and performance were improved but the crank and bearings were overloaded, resulting in a high mortality rate for the 38A, as this version was designated.

The total production of the Type 38 was about 385 cars over two years, of which 50 were supercharged; in many respects the car was one of Bugatti's least successful models and very few have survived.

The 3-litre Type 44: smooth, fast and reliable

The Paris Salon in October 1927 saw the Type 38 2-litre tourer replaced by a new 3-litre Type 44. Much of the chassis was the same, although the frame was longer, but the engine was new and the car transformed by the additional power and perhaps greater weight on the front end.

The engine, in conception, was a development of the 1920–1 prototype (Type 28) but greatly improved by the intervening experience. Cylinder dimensions were 69 × 100 mm, and the blocks and valve gears were the same as used on the Type 37, and on the touring Type 40 (see page 33), except that the water manifold was along the left not the right of the blocks. The water pump was driven on the left from the camshaft-driving vertical shaft between the blocks and, on the early cars, the oil pump was sandwiched between the block and the water pump and used a long suction pipe from the sump. This occasionally failed to suck up and was

RIGHT A contemporary picture of the new Type 30 shows the superb paintwork achieved with many coats of brushed lacquer and a final layer of varnish. The beaded-edge tyres, battery box on the running board and the V-screen without wiper are typical of the period around 1923.

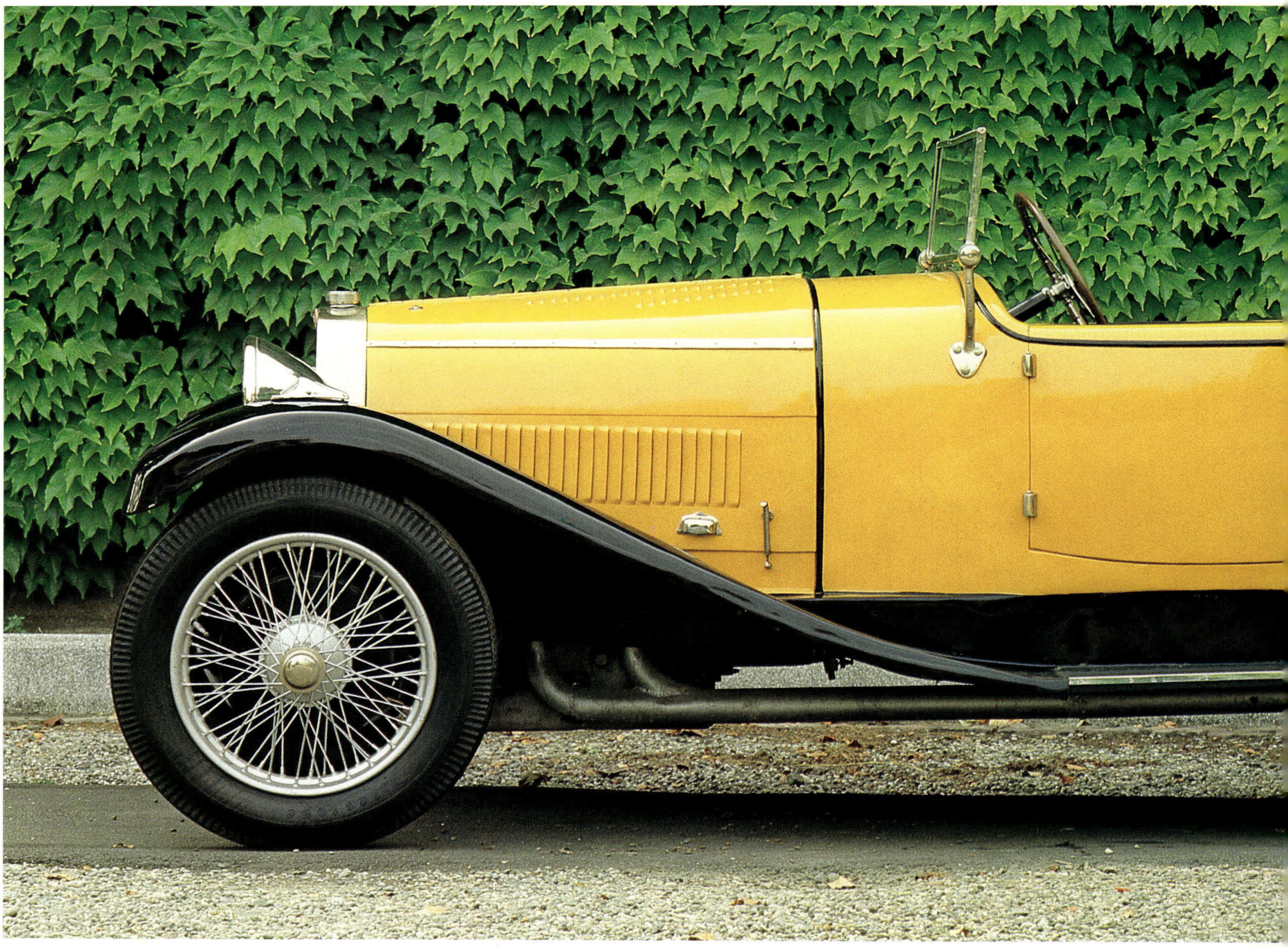

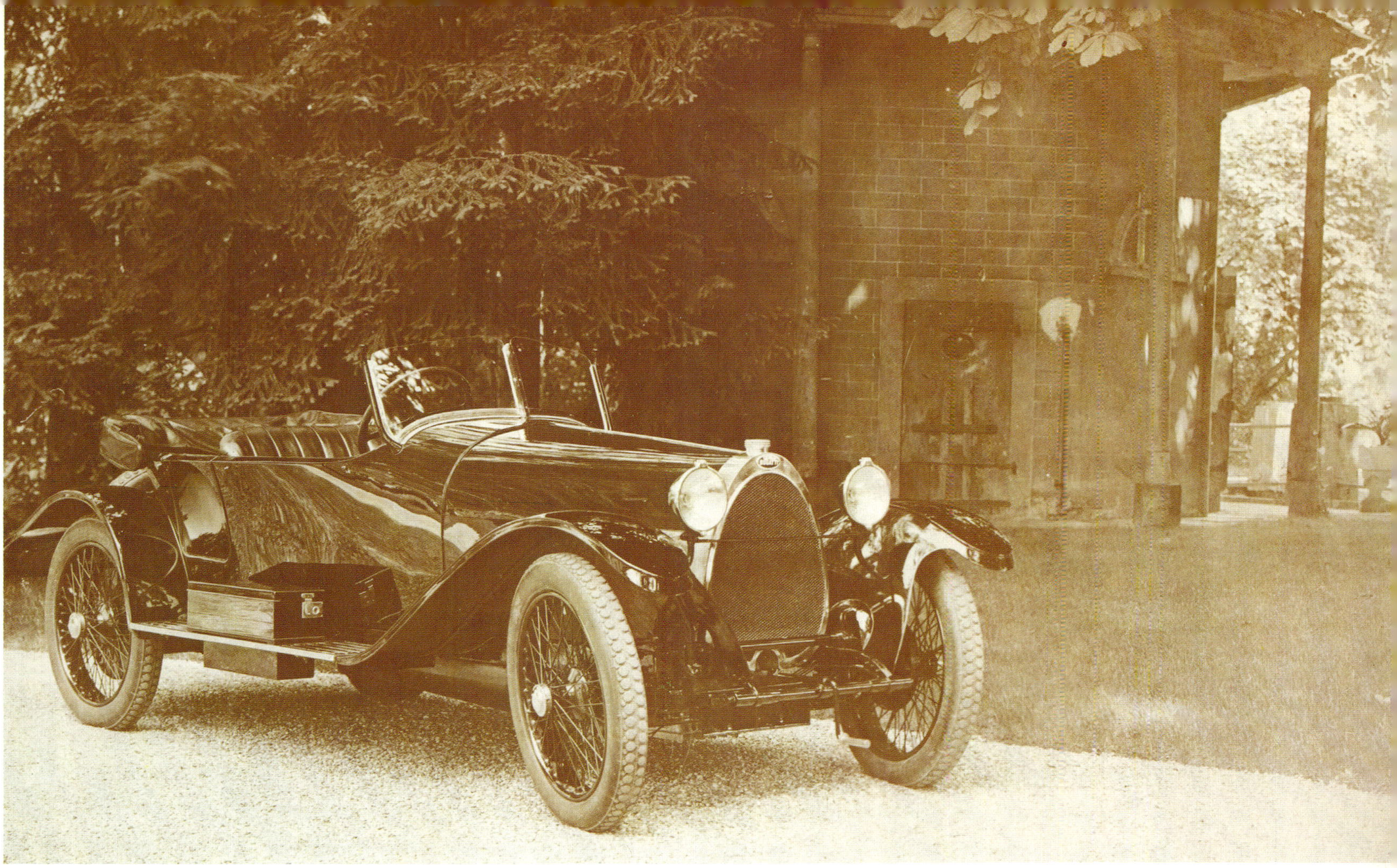

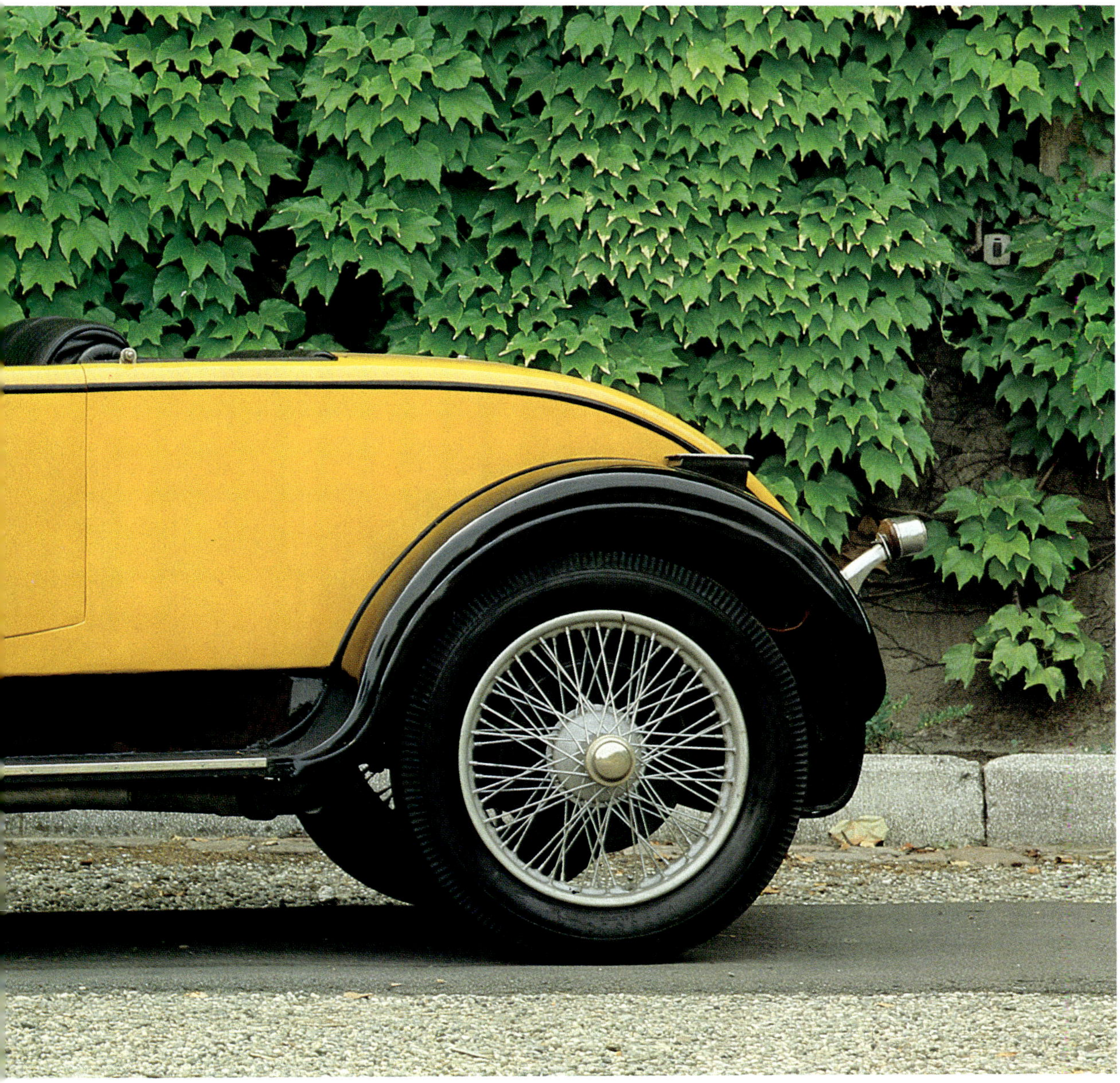

Type 38/38A Tourer
Years made 1926–7
No. made 385

ENGINE

Type	Two 4-cylinder monoblocs, overhead camshaft, roller bearing crankshaft, plain big ends
No. of cylinders	8
Bore/stroke mm	60 × 88
Displacement cc	1991
Valve operation	2 inlet, 1 exhaust per cylinder
Sparkplugs/cyl.	1
Supercharged	38A only
Carburettor(s)	T38: 2 Zenith or Solex T38A: 1 Zenith or Solex
BHP approx.	T38: 75/T38A: 95

DRIVE TRAIN

Clutch	Multi-plate, wet
Transmission	4-speed and reverse, gate change

CHASSIS

Wheelbase	3.12 m (10 ft 2¾ in)
Track	1.25 m (4 ft 1¼ in)
Suspension – front	½ elliptic
Suspension – rear	Reversed ¼ elliptic
Brakes	Cable
Tyre size	(modern) 500 × 19
Wheels	Rudge wire

PERFORMANCE

Maximum speed	140 km/h (87 mph)

LEFT The Type 38 was one of the less successful Bugatti models – especially when fitted with heavier coachwork, which its 2-litre engine could not handle adequately. Its engineering detail in the chassis, gearbox, axles and brakes was good and later, when more power was available from larger engines, most of the Type 38 assemblies were put to good use in other models. Provided by the Musée National de l'Automobile, Mulhouse.

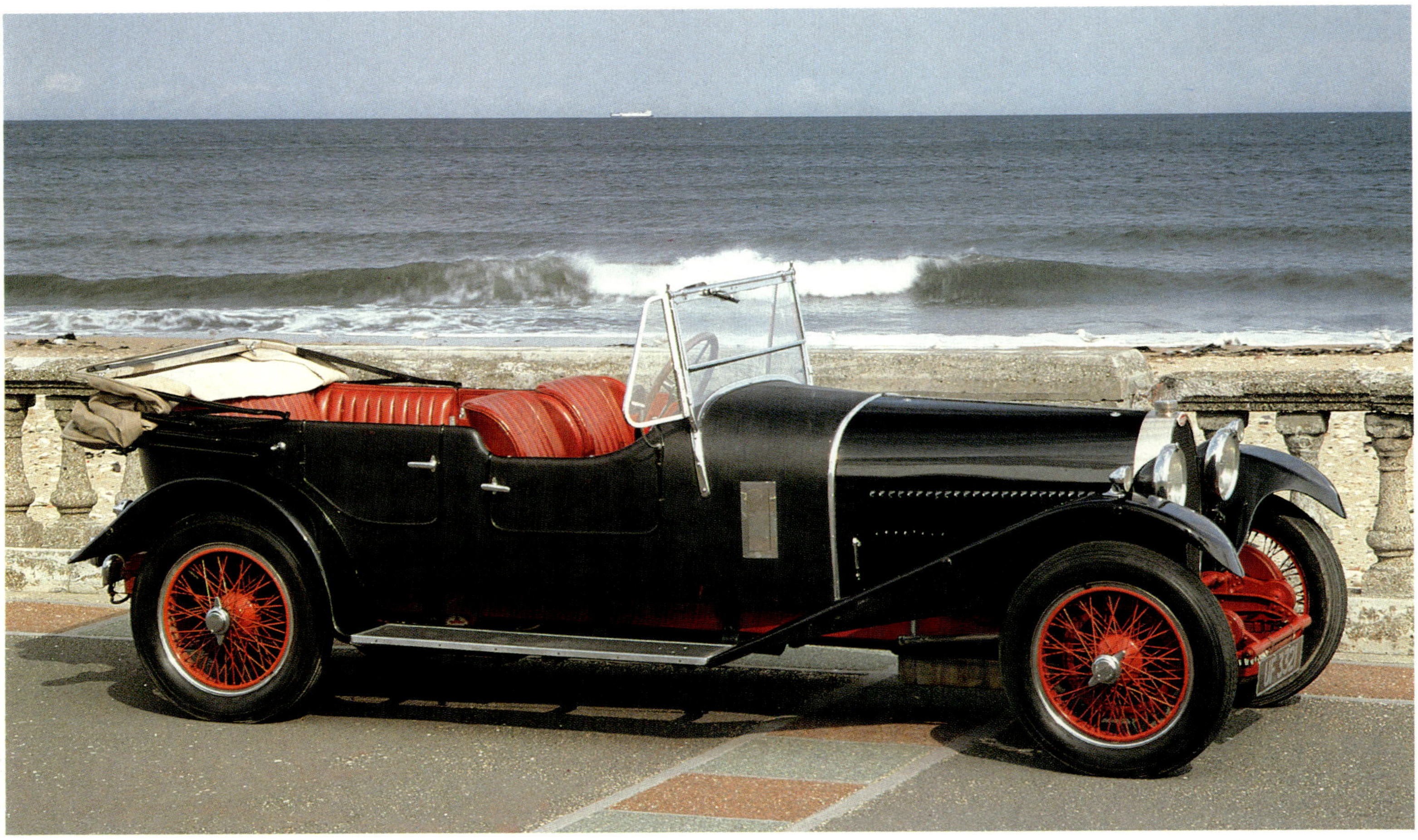

Type 44 Tourer	
Years made	1927–30
No. made	1095
ENGINE	
Type	Two 4-cylinder monoblocs, overhead camshaft, plain bearing crankshaft
No. of cylinders	8
Bore/stroke mm	69 × 100
Displacement cc	2991
Valve operation	2 inlet, 1 exhaust per cylinder
Sparkplugs/cyl.	1
Supercharged	No
Carburettor	1 Schebler
BHP approx.	100
DRIVE TRAIN	
Clutch	Multi-plate, wet
Transmission	4-speed and reverse, central change
CHASSIS	
Wheelbase	3.12 m (10 ft 2¾ in)
Track	1.25 m (4 ft 1¼ in)
Suspension – front	½ elliptic
Suspension – rear	Reversed ¼ elliptic
Brakes	Cable
Tyre size	5.00 × 19
Wheels	Rudge wire
PERFORMANCE	
Maximum speed	145–150 km/h (90+ mph)

ABOVE This typical Type 44 3-litre touring car of 1928 was fitted with a body by Harrington of Brighton for Henry Dupont (of the American Dupont chemicals family). The Type 44 is one of the better touring Bugattis, with all the marque's traditional performance and handling. Provided by Mr G. Little.

RIGHT 1932 Type 49 with Bugatti - built body. Provided by Coys of Kensington.

later replaced by an angle-drive gearbox, allowing the pump to be mounted low down on the sump below the oil level. At the same time (late 1928) a full pressure oiling system was introduced, and the crank layout was changed to the properly balanced 2 – 4 – 2 arrangements where the throws of each half of the crank are at 90° and the rear half is a mirror image of the front half.

The cambox was a single unit and straddled the two blocks as on the earlier 2-litre eight-cylinder car, and the Delco distributor was at the rear as before. The new crankcase was larger to suit the bigger engine, but was again bolted across the frame. A novelty for Bugatti was a vibration (torsional) damper at the front of the crank, the action of which seems to have been spoiled somewhat by being coupled to the crank through rubber bushes, albeit with the use of a friction disc for damping. It was impossible to 'tune' and may well have been ineffective: the several cars tested today have a marked torsional period at mid-range revolutions.

Bugatti had relied so far on French Solex and Zenith carburettors, but now switched to a single American Schebler unit which he had no doubt noticed on the various eight-cylinder Auburns and Studebakers seen in France at the time. This he fitted to a massive water-heated and polished single-piece manifold which enhanced the appearance of the right side of the engine just as the 'bunches of bananas' did on the left. An interesting feature of the engine was a decent float to indicate oil level with a built-in tap which could be opened from above to drain the oil (oil in those days was cheap and you were encouraged to change the heavy untreated '100% pure Pennsylvanian' regularly).

The clutch, gearbox and rear axle were all unchanged from the earlier Type 38 car, although the crown wheel and pinion were now helical for quietness. The brake drums carried cooling fin-rings pressed over the steel drums; other details of springs, brakes and hubs were unchanged.

The chassis came with its own dashboard and bonnet (hood) panels, and the radiator was an enlarged version of the classic Bugatti shape. The dashboard was a walnut panel with two cast aluminium side arms, and had a good display of Jaeger instruments and Marchal switches.

Although many chassis were supplied bare for the customer to arrange his own coachwork, Bugatti was by now starting to make his own bodies at Molsheim, as well as supplying many cars fitted with bodies constructed by his friends at Gangloff, the coachbuilders at nearby Colmar (who indeed had built a coach on his little eight-valve Type 15 in 1910).

The car was universally acclaimed for its smoothness and refinement, and typical Bugatti handling and good performance. Today we must judge a 1928 car by the standards of its competition; if you drive a well-kept Type 44 now you will be surprised perhaps by its easy starting, acceleration, turbine-like smoothness at low speed, marred a little by a torsional period, and a little engine roughness at high speed, but with excellent brakes when pushed hard, and good ride and steering.

Even allowing for the simplicity of the road tests of the motoring journals, the style of Edgar Duffield in *The Auto* may make us smile!

> Colonel Sorel who represents the factory in the British Isles sent the car to my house expecting me, apparently, to spend a week-end on it. I very seldom do that. People who cannot size-up a car in an hour should give up car-testing. And this Bugatti trial was one of the briefest I have made, because I knew, in advance, so much of what I was to discover. I knew that power would be ample, that the action of clutch and gear-box would be perfect, and that the steering and suspension would be unimprovable. All I had to ascertain was the degree to which this straight-eight would behave as a straight-eight should (if it is going to justify its design, of course).

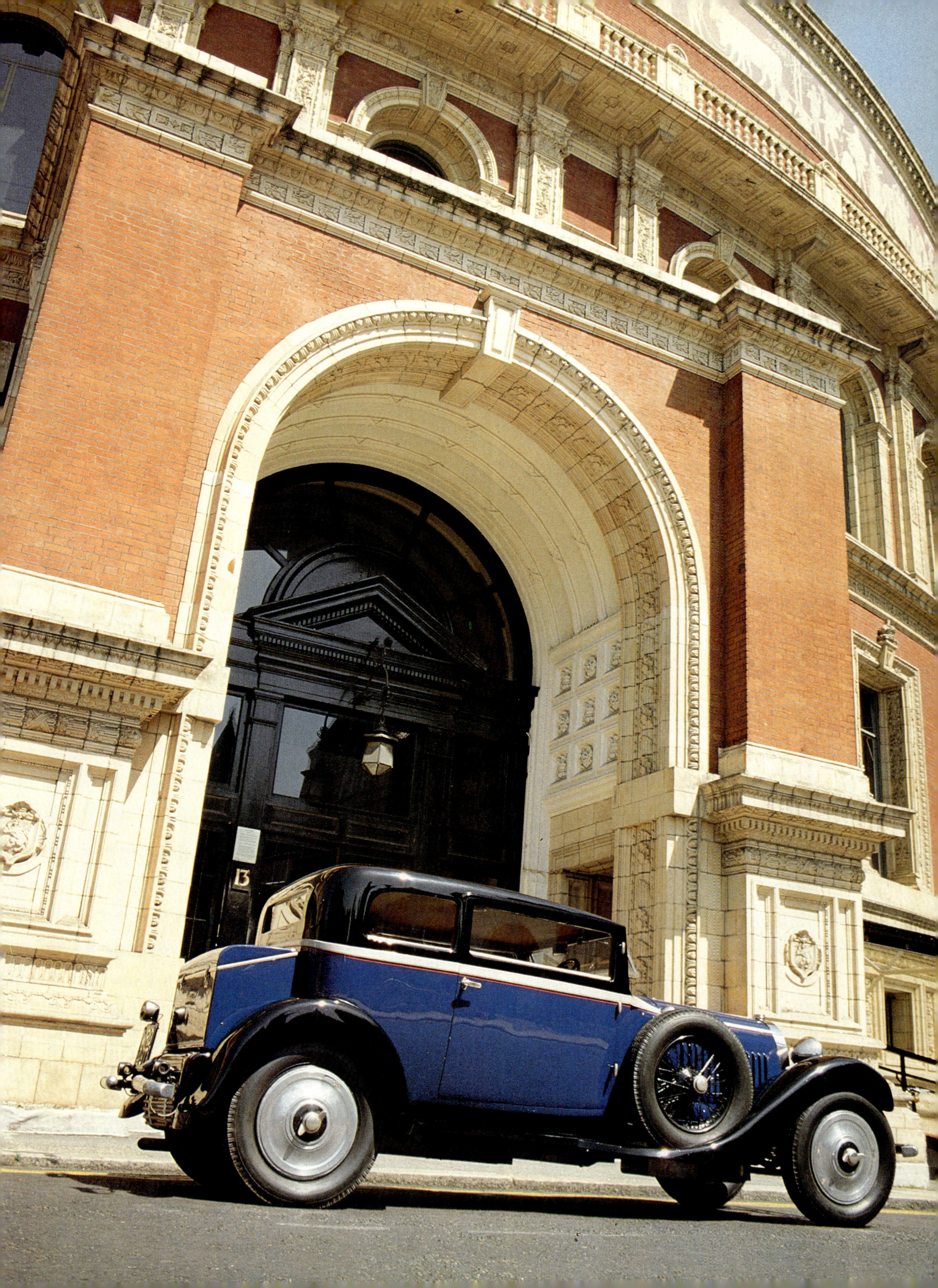
13

Well, the 23.6 h.p. eight-cylindered three-litre Bugatti is decidedly 'sporting' – a much abused word, but I know no single alternative to it – yet it is just as emphatically smooth and sweet and the flexibility on fourth speed is admirable . . .

I really do not know when I have compressed so much motoring enjoyment into so little time. The car had all the old life, every bit as much bite as its engine-dimensions and crankshaft layout promised, but smooth . . . ? The engine was very quiet indeed. The gear-box is incredible to Bugatti fans of five years ago, but is none the less true.

. . . for what my judgment is worth the 23.6 h.p. Bugatti straight-eight is one of the five best, most interesting, most friendly, companionable and altogether delightful motor cars that can be bought in London today.

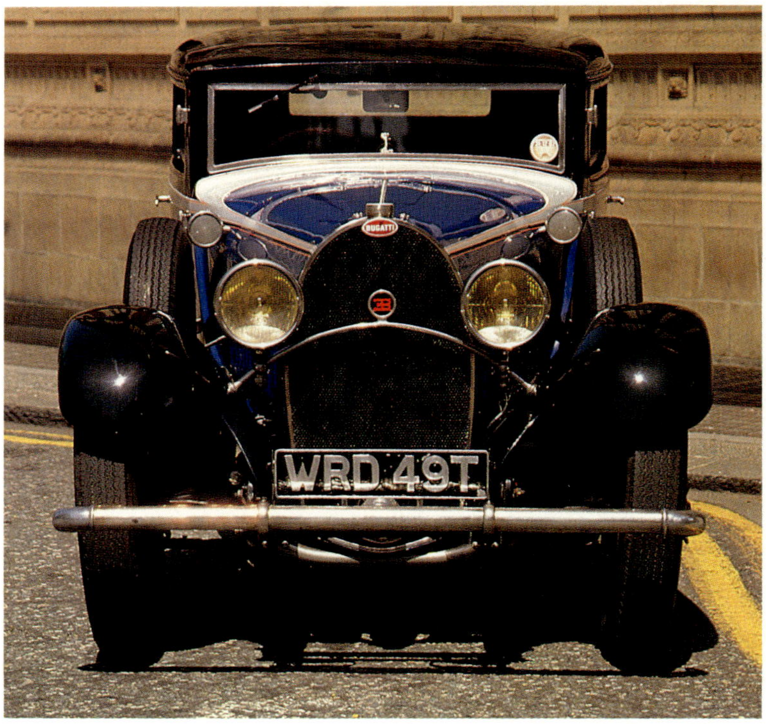

A later test at Easter 1929 at Montlhéry showed clearly that the car was not only fast but reliable. A normal saloon by Van Vooren using the patented Weymann flexible fabric-covered construction, driven by the racing driver Albert Divo and two co-drivers from Molsheim, covered 3009.5 km (1870 miles) in a continuous 24-hour period, the hourly average lying between 124.7 and 126.7 km/h (77.5 and 78.7 mph), with a mean of 125.4 km/h (78 mph).

The production of the Type 44 was exceeded only by the earlier 16-valve Brescia model and totalled some 1100 cars. The first is listed by the factory as October 1927, the last November 1930. In 1929–30 the world was in financial crisis and car sales were universally restricted. The listed chassis price of the model was modest and compared well with cars of similar

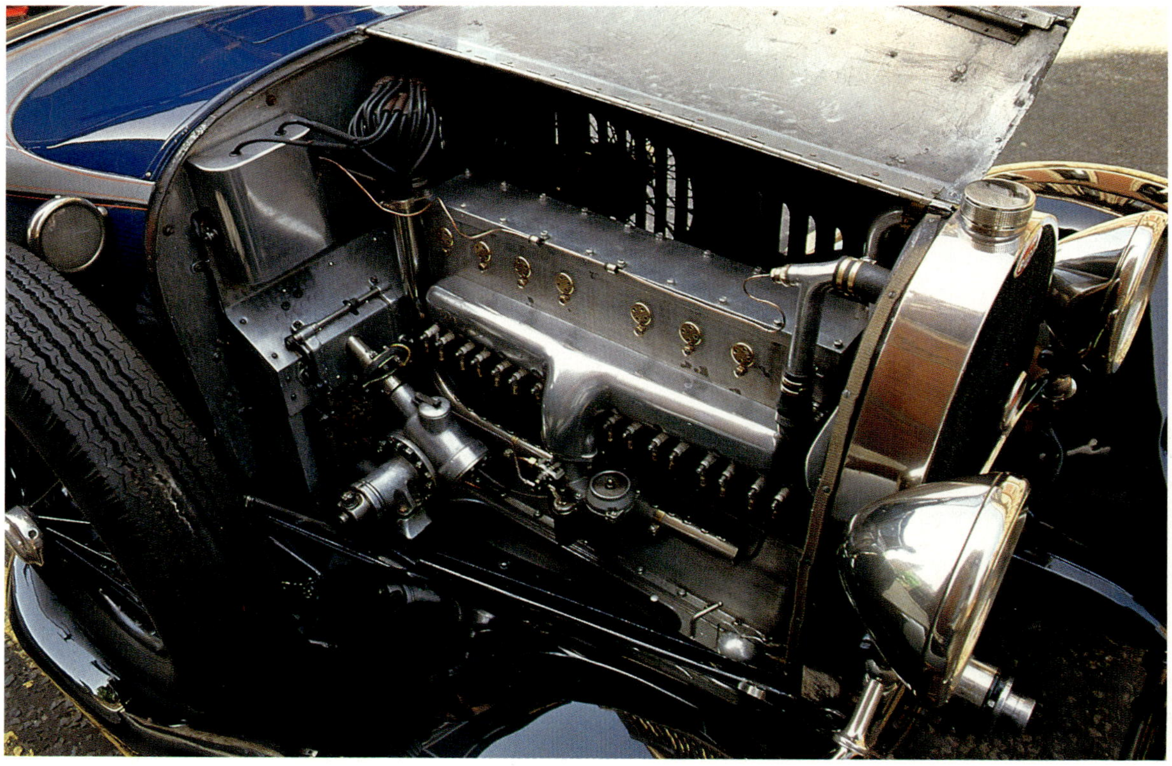

The 3.3-litre Type 49 was similar to the 3-litre Type 44, but had a cooling fan, and twin plugs per cylinder fed from a 16-plug distributor. The dash showed an American influence in its oval instrument panel, but the walnut-covered steering wheel continued the Bugatti tradition. The accelerator pedal was still in the centre between brake and clutch, but the gear lever with a wooden knob on its end was now ball-mounted like its North American sisters. To many the Type 49 was the best of all Bugatti touring models, with the handling, braking and general comfort of the better Bugattis, but without the heaviness and slow gear change of the later and more powerful Type 57. Sales, however, suffered from the financial crisis of 1929-30.

Type 49 Tourer	
Years made	1930–4
No. made	470
ENGINE	
Type	Two 4-cylinder monoblocs, overhead camshafts, plain bearing
No. of cylinders	8
Bore/stroke mm	72 × 100
Displacement cc	3257
Valve operation	2 inlet, 1 exhaust per cylinder
Sparkplugs/cyl.	2
Supercharged	No
Carburettor	1 Schebler
BHP approx.	110
DRIVE TRAIN	
Clutch	Multi-plate, dry
Transmission	4-speed and reverse, central ball change
CHASSIS	
Wheelbase	3.12 m (10 ft 2¾ in), 3.22 m (10 ft 6¾ in)
Track	1.25 m (4 ft 1¼ in)
Suspension – front	½ elliptic
Suspension – rear	Reversed ¼ elliptic
Brakes	Cable
Tyre size	5.50 × 18
Wheels	Rudge wire, or cast aluminium alloy
PERFORMANCE	
Maximum speed	145 km/h (90 mph)

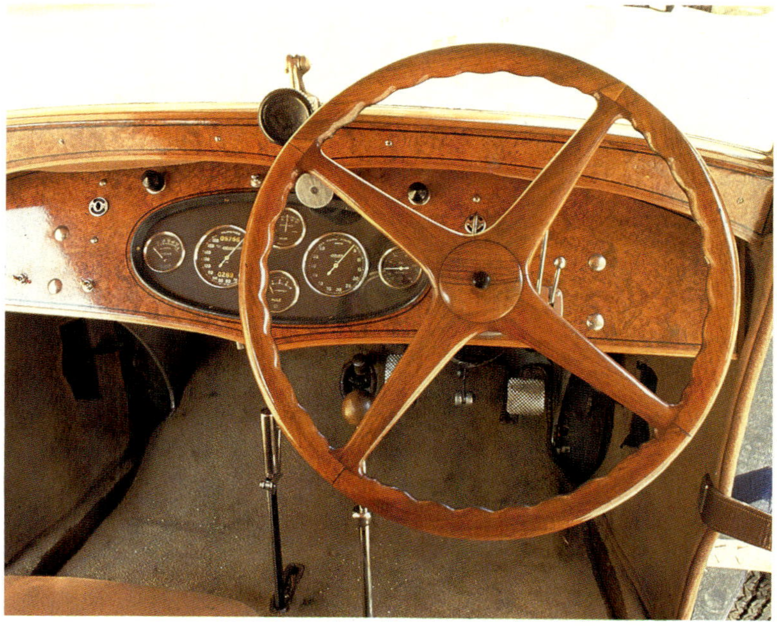

RIGHT A typical 1½-litre Type 40 Grand Sport touring car new in November 1927. The first few cars had a short wheelbase, which was soon lengthened to carry a splendid 'Grand Sport 2 + 2' touring body built at the factory and similar in its lines to the larger Type 43: a variety of other bodies was made by various coachbuilders. Although the output of the four-cylinder engine was modest, the steering, braking, cornering and cruising performance of the car were well up to Bugatti standards – and the model was not expensive in its day! Provided by Mr J. Webb.

quality; in 1928–30 it sold for £550, more or less the same as a 20 hp Sunbeam or Humber, or the comparable Delage. Indeed the listed price of a 20 hp Rolls-Royce of the period was exactly twice the cost of the Bugatti, plus £85 extra for front-wheel brakes!

The Type 49: a superb touring car

For 1931, Bugatti showed an improved model at the Paris and London shows. The new Type 49 differed little from the Type 44, but had an enlarged cylinder bore (72 mm) to give 3.3 litres capacity, and now had a larger radiator and for the first time a fan, demanded by the increasing city traffic in Paris and elsewhere – or the Côte d'Azur in high summer. Other alterations were a ball-change to the gearbox (apeing American cars), and Swiss Scintilla electrics throughout, with a 16-plug distributor feeding two plugs per cylinder. Although the Bugatti had used twin-plug blocks on some of the early racing Brescia cars, his reasons for changing in 1930 are not very clear, and it may well have been more a sales feature to appeal to his clientele than a way of improving combustion or reliability.

Many of the cars were fitted with fine-looking cast aluminium wheels similar in general design to those on the Royale (see page 64), but with appropriately sized 5.25 × 18 in tyres (the Type 44 had retained 19 in wire wheels). The standard chassis price with wire wheels went up from £550 to £625, which more than covered the changes!

The motoring press liked the car and gave it good reviews. Henri Petit from *La Vie Automobile* had had the earlier T44 and enjoyed his new T49, noting the improved acceleration (although the top speed was much the same), quieter gearbox (gears were now ground), and better brakes (in fact they were unchanged).

Production was satisfactory bearing in mind world conditions, although there was often a temporary surplus of chassis when sales lagged behind. The total production was 470 between October 1930 and the end of 1933, a few sales trailing into 1934.

The Type 49 was the last of the Ettore Bugatti-designed single-cam touring cars. Soon his son Jean was to take over as the leading personality at Molsheim, while Ettore concentrated on railcar designs, leaving Jean to develop the twin-cam Type 57.

Many of the marque's enthusiasts would argue that the Type 49 was the best of the Bugatti touring cars, with much of the road handling, brakes and steering that mean Bugatti, and which to some extent were lost on the later Type 57. But perhaps nostalgia colours judgement!

The four-cylinder Type 40

This review of Bugatti touring models would not be complete without reference to the splendid little Type 40, a four-cylinder 1½-litre car introduced in 1926 to replace the Brescia. Sometimes disparagingly referred to as Bugatti's 'Morris Cowley', it was indeed an excellent small car with all the roadhandling that characterized the larger touring models, without some of the starkness of the earlier Brescia; and by Bugatti standards it was not expensive (the chassis price in 1927 was £325!).

Bugatti launched the four-cylinder racing or sports Type 37 at the end of 1925, as described on page 48. In mid-1926 he took the engine from this model and, with a new sump casting with different side arms, fitted it to a new touring frame, stronger than the one on the Brescia. He used the new Type 38 gearbox and rear axle, but with reduced track, a new solid circular section front axle, again with narrower track, the excellent brakes from the T37, and a new radiator appropriate to the model.

The result was a splendid small chassis, initially for coachbuilders to equip, but soon to carry a 'Grand Sport' type, Bugatti-built four-seat touring body very similar to the larger Type 43.

Contemporary press testing was favourable: 'a comfortable and extremely lively car from a famous French factory . . . a real pleasure' said *The Light Car* in June 1927. It went on to describe the car further:

Type 40/40A Tourer
Years made T40: 1926–30/T40A: 1930
No. made 830

ENGINE		**DRIVE TRAIN**	
Type	Monobloc, plain bearing crankshaft	**Clutch**	Multi-plate, wet
No. of cylinders	4	**Transmission**	4-speed and reverse, gate change
Bore/stroke mm	T40: 69 × 100 T40A: 72 × 100	**CHASSIS**	
Displacement cc	T40: 1496/T40A: 1627	**Wheelbase**	2.56 m (8 ft 4¾ in), 2.71 m (8 ft 10¾ in)
Valve operation	2 inlet, 1 exhaust per cylinder	**Track**	1.2 m (3 ft 11¼ in)
Sparkplugs/cyl.	T40: 1/T40A: 2	**Suspension – front**	½ elliptic
Supercharged	No	**Suspension – rear**	Reversed ¼ elliptic
Carburettor	1 Zenith or Solex	**Brakes**	Cable
BHP approx.	60	**Tyre size**	(modern) 5.00 × 19
		Wheels	Rudge wire
		PERFORMANCE	
		Maximum speed	125 km/h (80 mph)

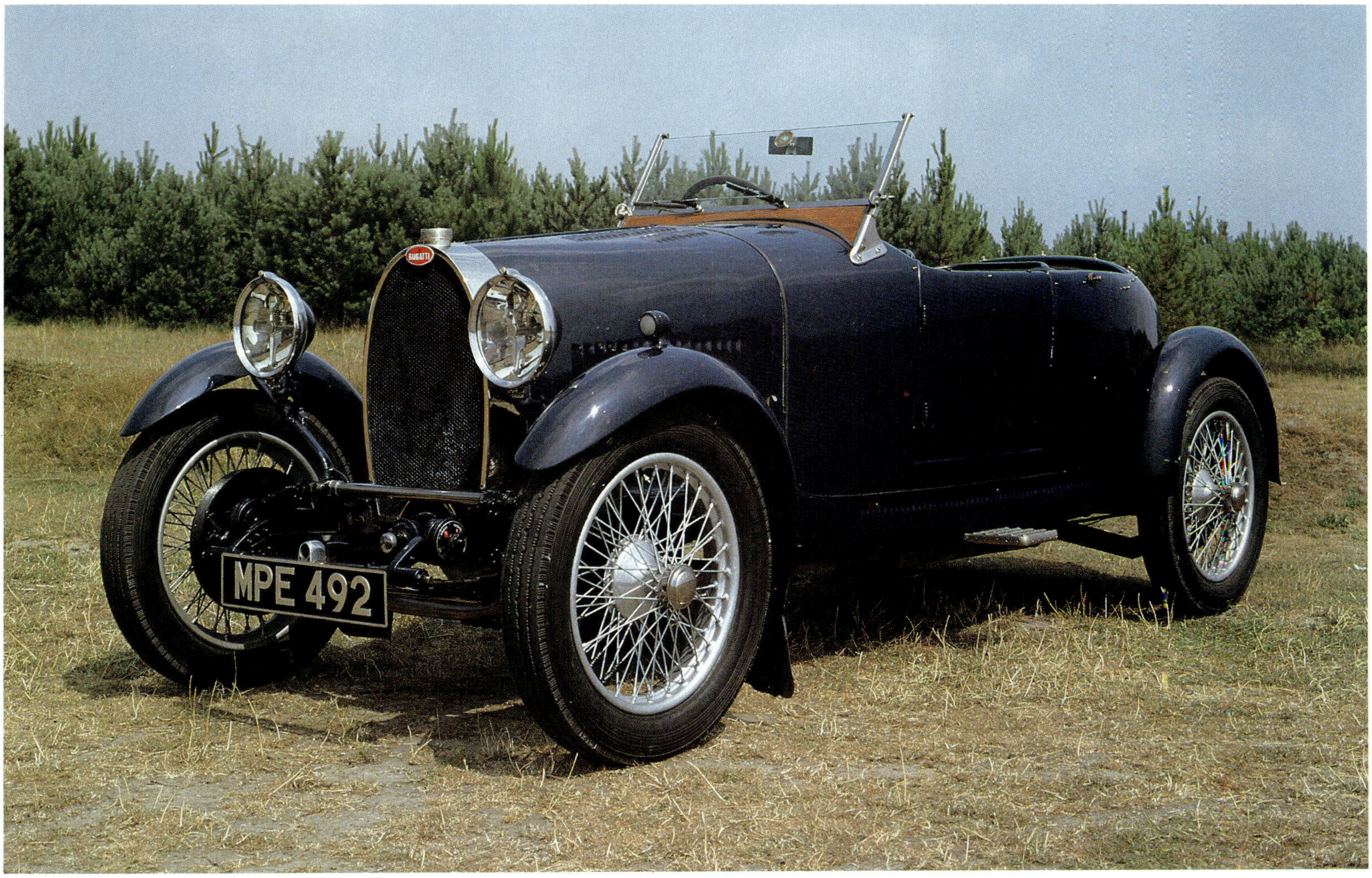

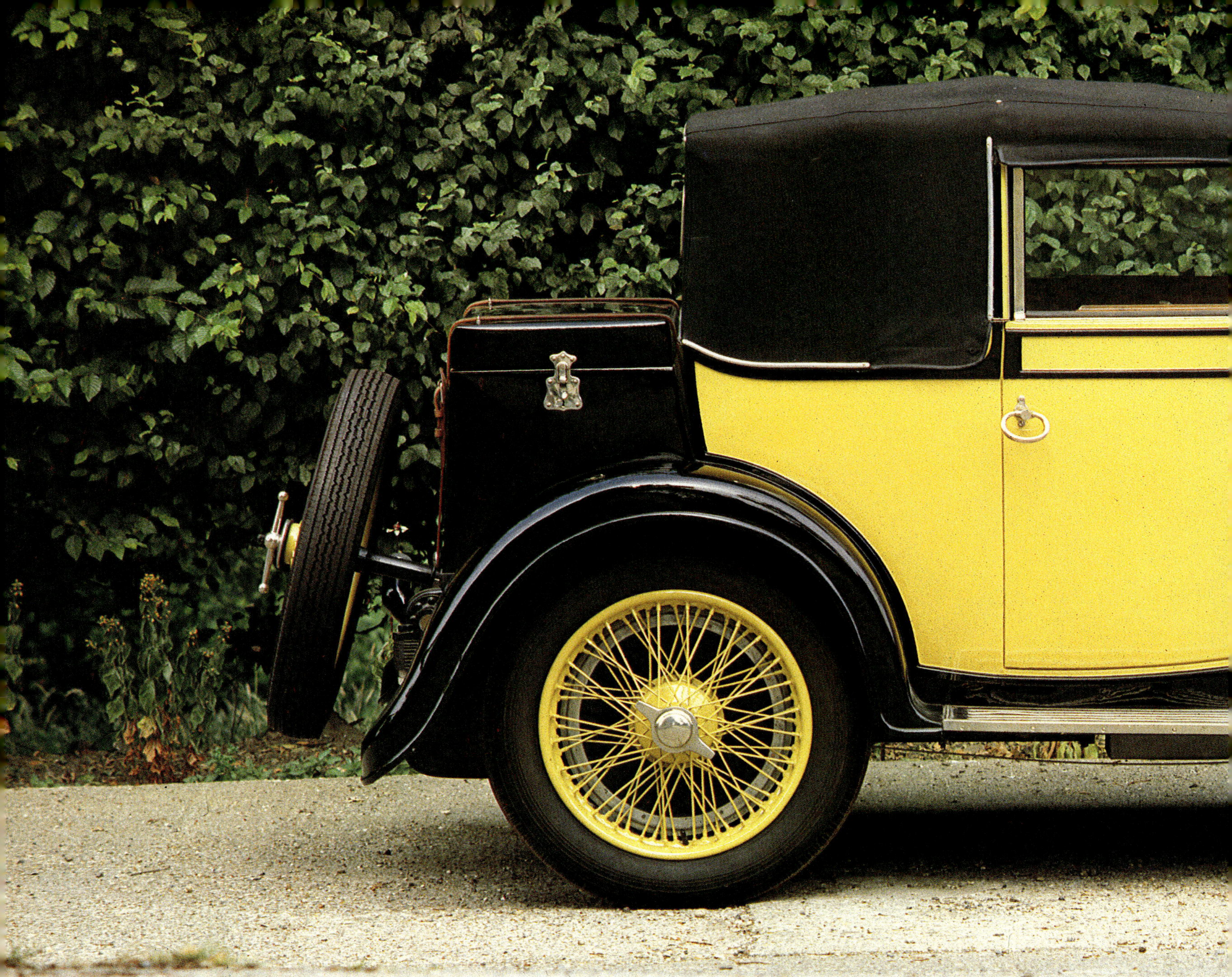

It is difficult to imagine a car of this size more interesting to drive, although in remarking upon the great interest to be found in driving this model we do not wish to be misunderstood and to have the word 'interesting' misconstrued as meaning difficult. The Bugatti is not difficult to drive; it is a car that is well suited to women drivers, but it is very different from the average humdrum, go-as-you-please family hack of about the same size.

In a word, to get any kind of results on the road it has to be driven, and it will not do simply to sit at the wheel and tread on the accelerator as and when required. The explanation of this lies, of course, in the altogether extraordinary capacity of the engine for high revolutions, in the very close gear ratios and in the light construction of both chassis and bodywork.

Upon first starting up the engine we thought that it was too noisy, particularly whilst idling, when it was more or less cold, and we still held this impression at the conclusion of our test. But the striking feature about the Bugatti engine is that, however fast it is revved – and the indicator will register some 4000 rpm if required – it is impossible to produce a period of any kind. Vibration, or in fact, any evidence of high revolutions is entirely absent.

It will be realized, then, that a driver accustomed to conventional touring cars on which, so long as the engine is actually turning over, treading on the gas sooner or later gives acceleration, has certain things to unlearn and learn on taking over a Bugatti. But after a few minutes at the wheel he will get more sheer joy from speed and acceleration than he probably ever achieved in the course of years at the wheel of a more commonplace car with only ordinary powers of acceleration.

Particularly impressive was the functioning of the reversed rear quarter-elliptic springs. We deliberately drove the car at speed over some of the worst roads in the south-west of London, having two passengers on board . . . The brakes we found to be particularly sweet in their action and very powerful; on no occasion in the course of ordinary running did we have to bring them into action to anything like their full extent.

We were also impressed with the comfort and easy controllability of the car. It is a car that can be driven for hour after hour and mile after mile without trace of fatigue to driver or passengers. Steering is finger-light, brakes require little effort for their operation, whilst the comfort of the rear-seat passengers is carefully studied.

The result of this test has been to convince us that Ettore Bugatti . . . has succeeded in turning out a well-designed and thought-out light touring car, capable of speeds and performance generally associated only with racing models.

Production of the Type 40 started in mid-1926 and totalled 780 chassis by May 1931. A small batch of about 35 of a modified model (T40A) was then produced over the next 12 months, a few tailing off into 1933.

The Type 40A was listed with a pretty little American-style roadster body, attributed to Jean Bugatti – but really out of Ford or Chrysler! It had a cylinder block from the T49, with 72 mm bore and twin plugs per cylinder, and other features from the eight-cylinder car, such as a ball gear change. Most of these roadsters were sold in France; this model was never listed in Britain, where customs duties favoured the importation of bare chassis, and a depressed market preferred the high performance model.

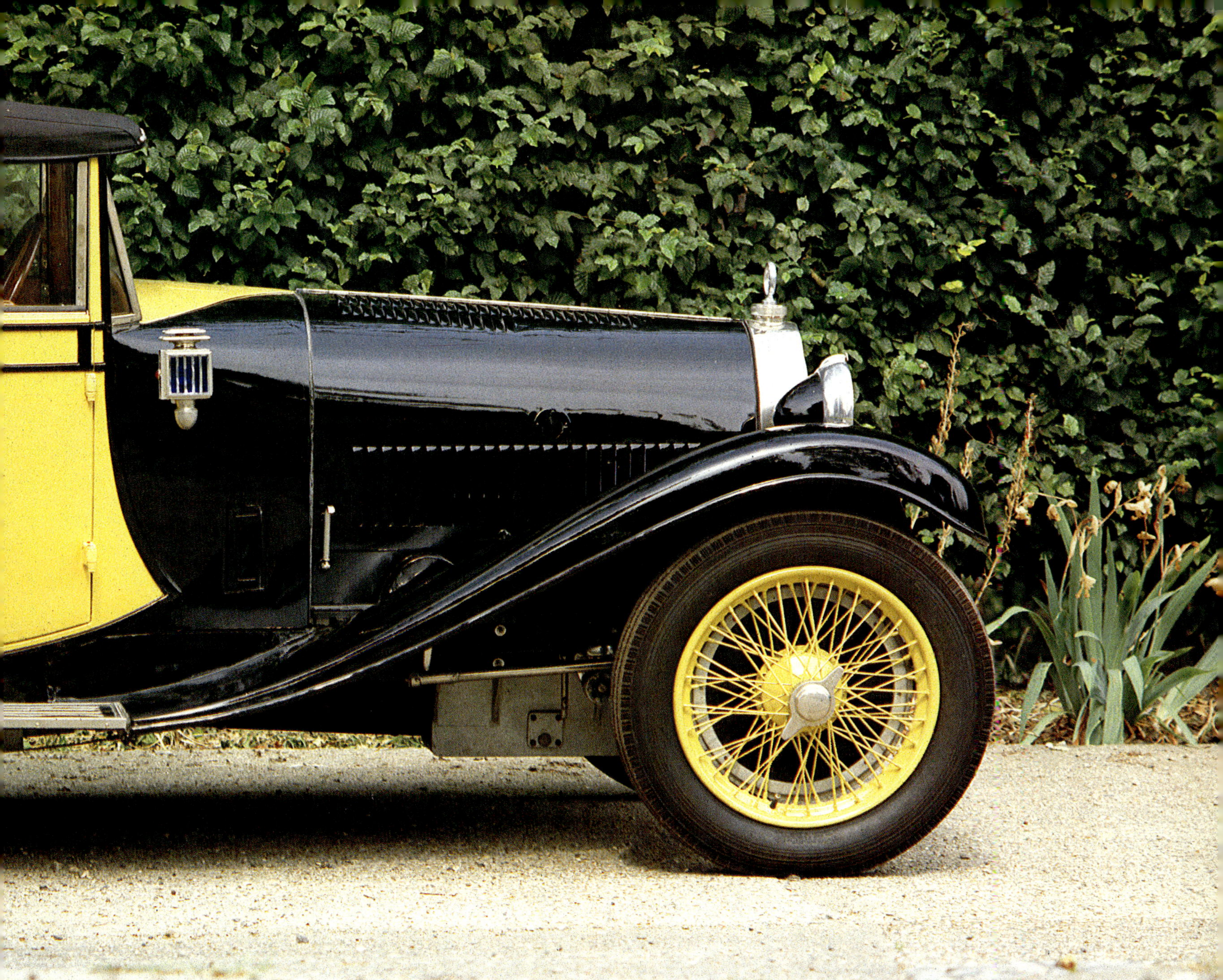

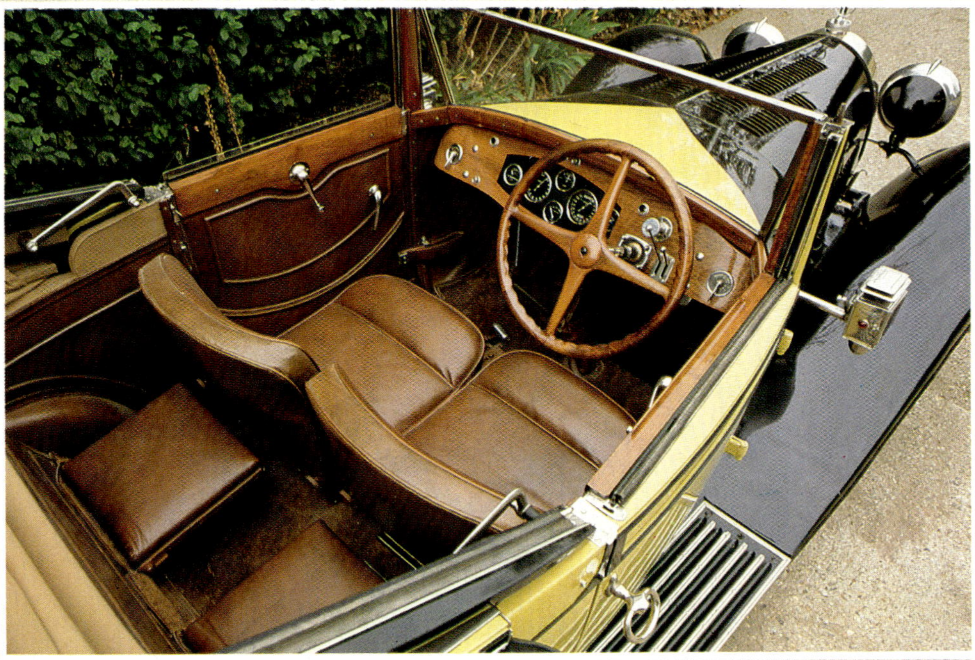

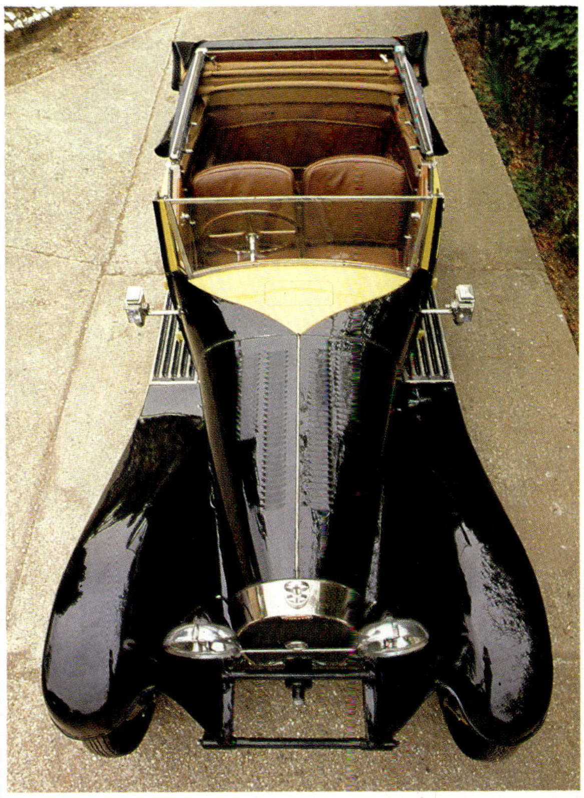

Jean Bugatti designed and had built for his sister Lidia this fine Type 40 coupé, adding a supercharger from the racing Type 37A. The body is based on the classic horse-drawn cab, the fiacre, of a different age. It illustrates the Bugattis' interest in horse-drawn carriage styles. This unique car was acquired from Lidia, Countess of Boigne, in 1972. Provided by Mrs P. Preston.

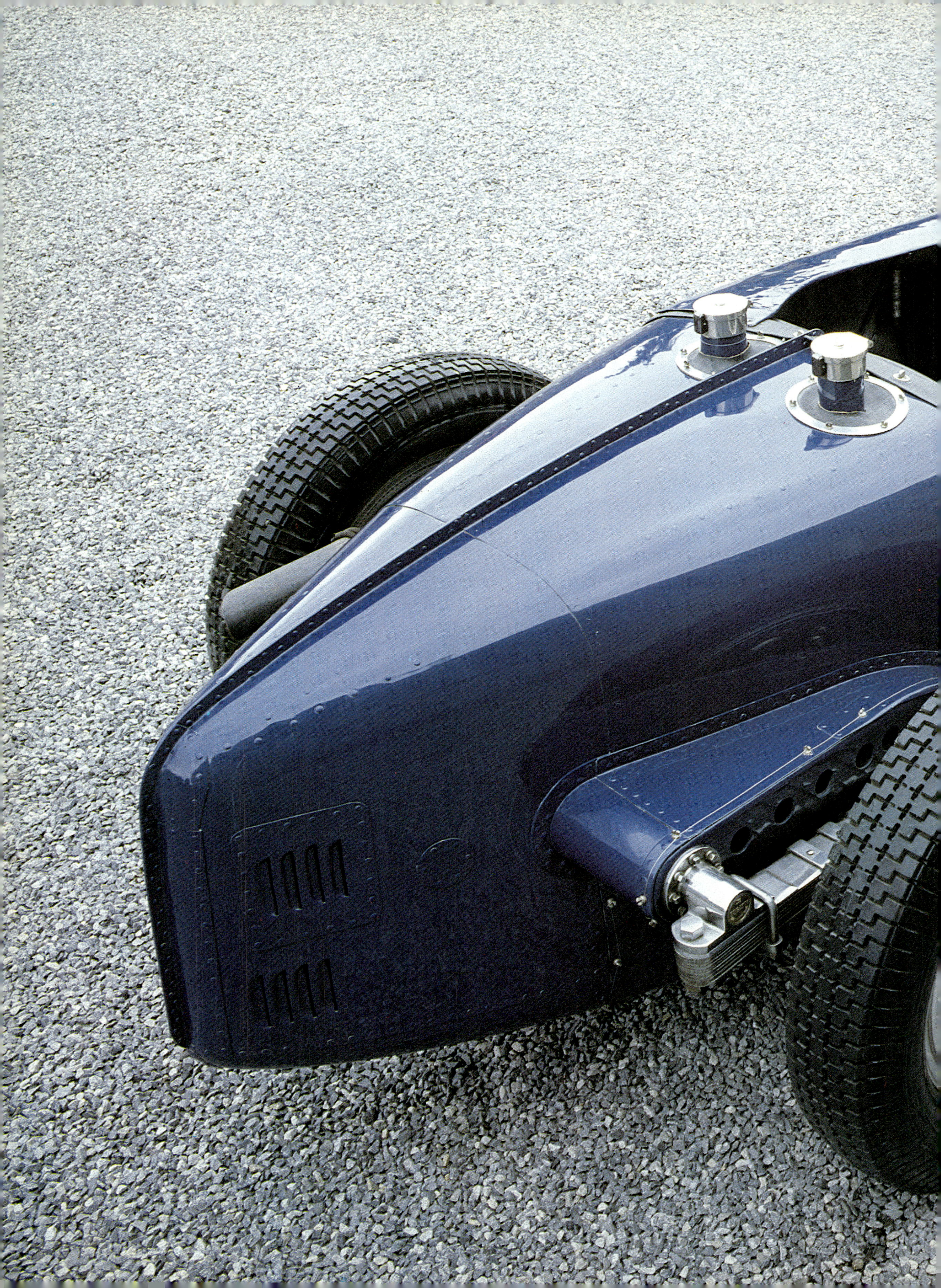

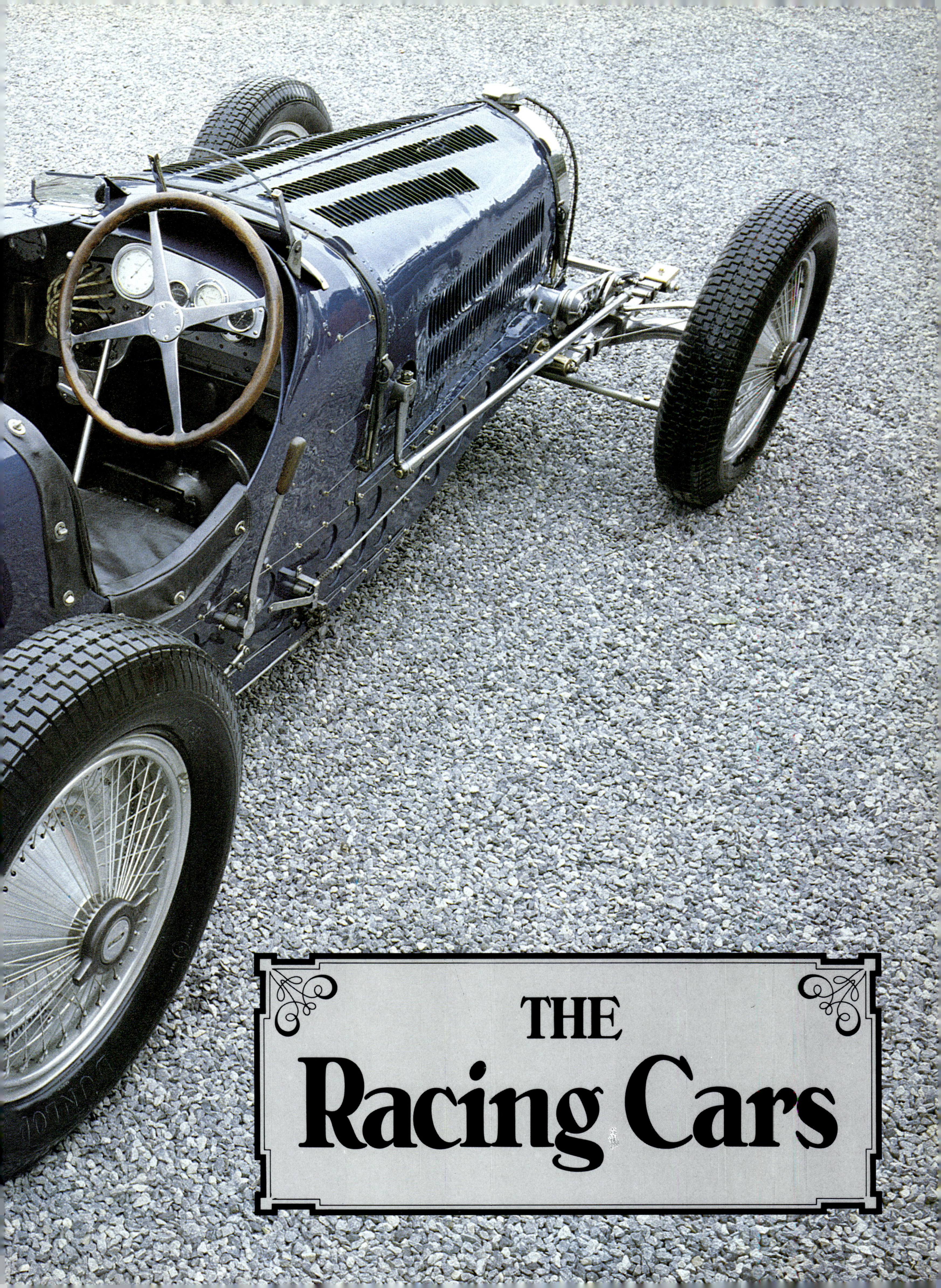

THE Racing Cars

BUGATTI had always been interested in racing and competition cars and understood the publicity and prestige benefits that they could bring. His success with the 1½-litre 16-valve car in 1920 and 1921 had been widely noted and the 2-litre formula adopted in 1923 for international racing gave him the opportunity to widen his ambitions. At that time France was the dominant country in racing, followed by Italy and to a lesser extent Britain which could only offer track events at Brooklands. Germany after the First World War was far from ready to contribute, and Spain was happy to follow behind the others. The United States made its own rules but found it convenient to specify 122 cubic inches (2 litres) as a maximum for engines there.

Strasbourg had been chosen as the district in which to run the 1922 Grand Prix (the 'Grand Prix of the Automobile Club of France'), on a road course near the factory at Molsheim. Bugatti entered four cars using his new eight-cylinder 2-litre engine, with a chassis frame derived from the T22 Brescia model, and intended clearly as the basis of a new eight-cylinder touring car, the Type 30, as described in the previous chapter. He planned originally to run these with 'bolster-tank' bodies, like those on the Type 13 of the year before, but was persuaded by his friend Pierre de Vizcaya (son of his banker), who was to drive one, to have them covered with long-tailed bodies, with cowlings over the radiator and the exhaust coming out of the point of the tail.

The engine was more or less the same as used later on the touring Type 30, although the detail of the early examples differs (oil pump drive, cambox cover and so on). It had eight cylinders, 60 × 88 mm bore and stroke, three ball-bearing main bearings, plain bushed big ends, etc.

The Bugattis had trouble in the race, particularly with the brakes, but three were running at the end, although some way behind the winning Fiat. All the other 18 starters had failed, two Fiats crashing, and the fourth Bugatti had trouble with its magneto driving gears. A few weeks later de Vizcaya in a single entry ran well at Monza in the Italian Grand Prix, coming in third to two Fiats.

The 1923 Type 32 'tank'

So 1922 ended with the new 2-litre Bugatti showing a potential which Ettore could exploit. Unwisely perhaps he allowed de Vizcaya to take two of the 1922 cars, plus three new ones ordered by the wealthy sportsman Martin de Alzaga of Buenos Aires, Argentina, to Indianapolis in 1923 – on a promise, not fulfilled, that the engines would have roller-bearing big ends fitted. The car was an unhappy failure on this high-speed track, only one finishing, the others having bearing and other troubles. Meanwhile Ettore was designing a remarkable 'tank' car, the Type 32. This had a 2 m (6 ft 6¾ in) wheelbase, a rectangular and underslung frame carrying the 2-litre engine, all enveloped by a body that was aerofoil-like in side elevation but rectangular from the front. The crankshaft now did have roller-bearing connecting rods, the big ends being split.

The 'tank' was designed for the 1923 Grand Prix to be held at Tours in central France, where four cars turned up. Bugatti's intuitive approach to automobile design often let him down when he strayed into technical fields: the car's handling was poor, no doubt due to aerodynamic lift, although it was fast on the straight. The race results were a disappointment as Bugatti's faithful Friderich could only manage third place behind the Sunbeams of Henry Segrave and Albert Divo.

It is certain that the results achieved by Bugatti at Tours, the competitive cars he could see around him, and the generally unfavourable press reception of his strange vehicle (even if his friend Gabriel Voisin produced a still odder example) served to deflect him from unorthodox solutions towards a more normal approach. The Italian Fiats were very fine looking, and the Sunbeams looked and worked better than his car.

While it is difficult to imagine Ettore returning to Molsheim in a humble frame of mind, he must have gone back determined to beat the opposition by finding a new approach – after all, he too was an Italian!

The Type 35: beauty and success

The result of the winter of 1923–4 was indeed a new design, the Type 35. Bugatti now remarked that his new car was fitted with a type of body more normal than his aerodynamic solution of 1923 because it made sales easier! This was immediately proved correct when the new Type 35 appeared at Lyon for the Grand Prix at the end of July 1924: on all sides the Bugatti was acclaimed as beautiful, a jewel of a car.

What he had done, brilliantly, was to follow the simple, long-tailed streamlined shape of the Sunbeams and above all Fiats of 1923. The chassis dimensions reverted to those of his successful Type 22 16-valve car, with track 1.2 m (3 ft 11¼ in) and a wheelbase 2.4 m (7 ft 10½ in). He waisted the

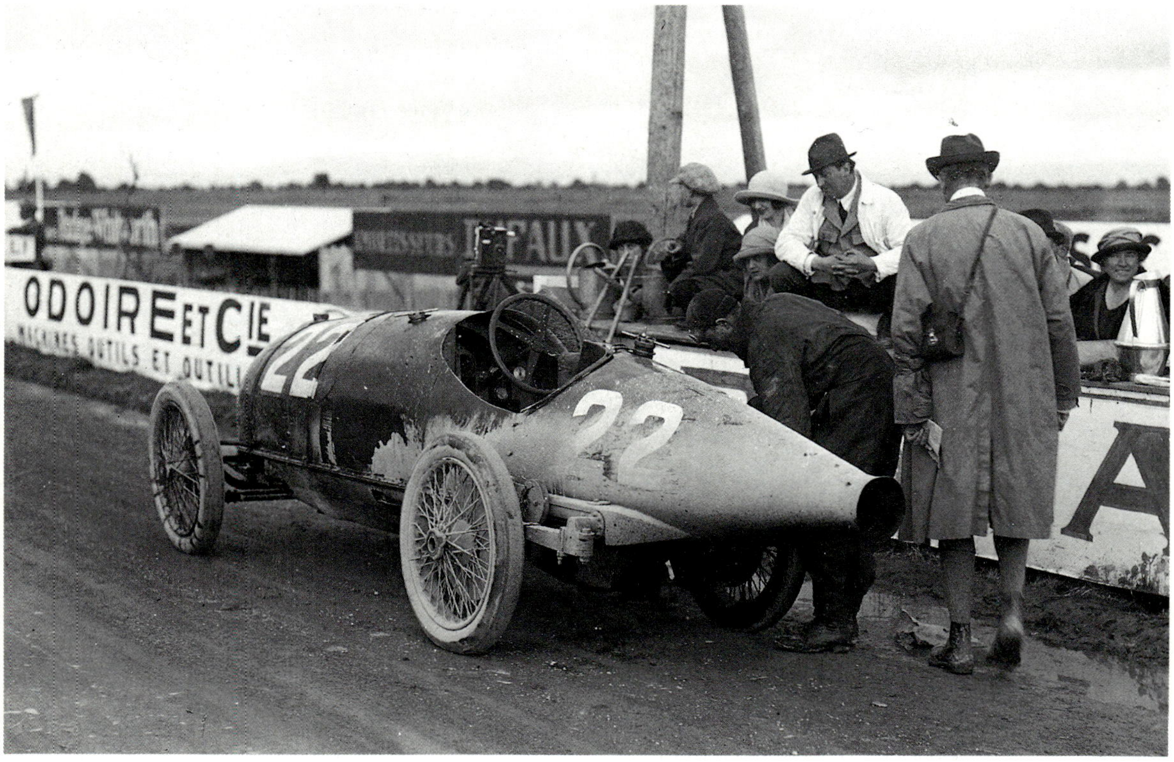

PRECEDING PAGES The ultimate Bugatti two-seat racing car, the 3.3-litre Type 59 of 1933. Despite many novel and effective features, it could not compete with the government-supported German and Italian GP cars. Provided by Mr N. Corner.

LEFT AND BELOW Bugatti's first eight-cylinder racing car was the 2-litre Type 30, four of which entered the 1922 French Grand Prix at Strasbourg. Streamlined bodies with the exhaust coming out of the tail fairing were fitted, but Bugatti's new design of hydraulic brake was not reliable. Felice Nazzaro won in a Fiat, but Bugattis were second and third. Left: Pierre Marco changes a wheel. Below: De Vizcaya comes in for fuel.

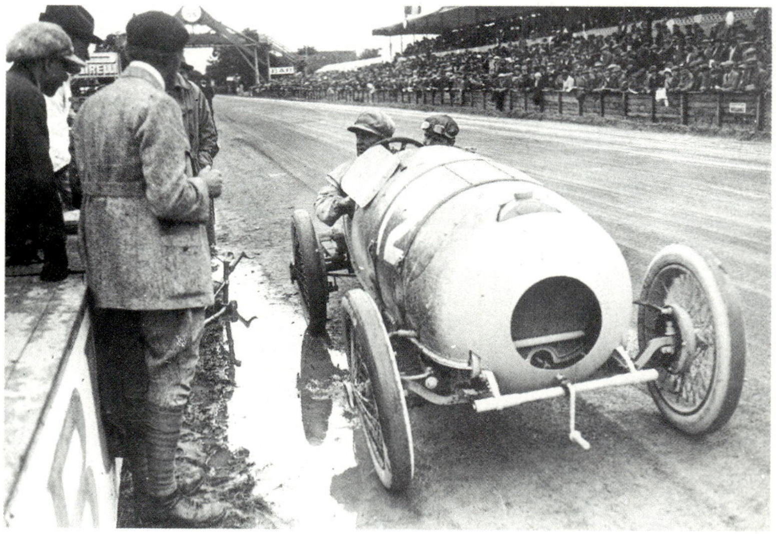

RIGHT Friderich refuelling in the 1923 Grand Prix at Tours in a Type 32 'tank'. His was the only one of the four starters to finish, third and well behind the winning Sunbeams. One car was retained by the factory and is now in the Musée National de l'Automobile at Mulhouse in France.

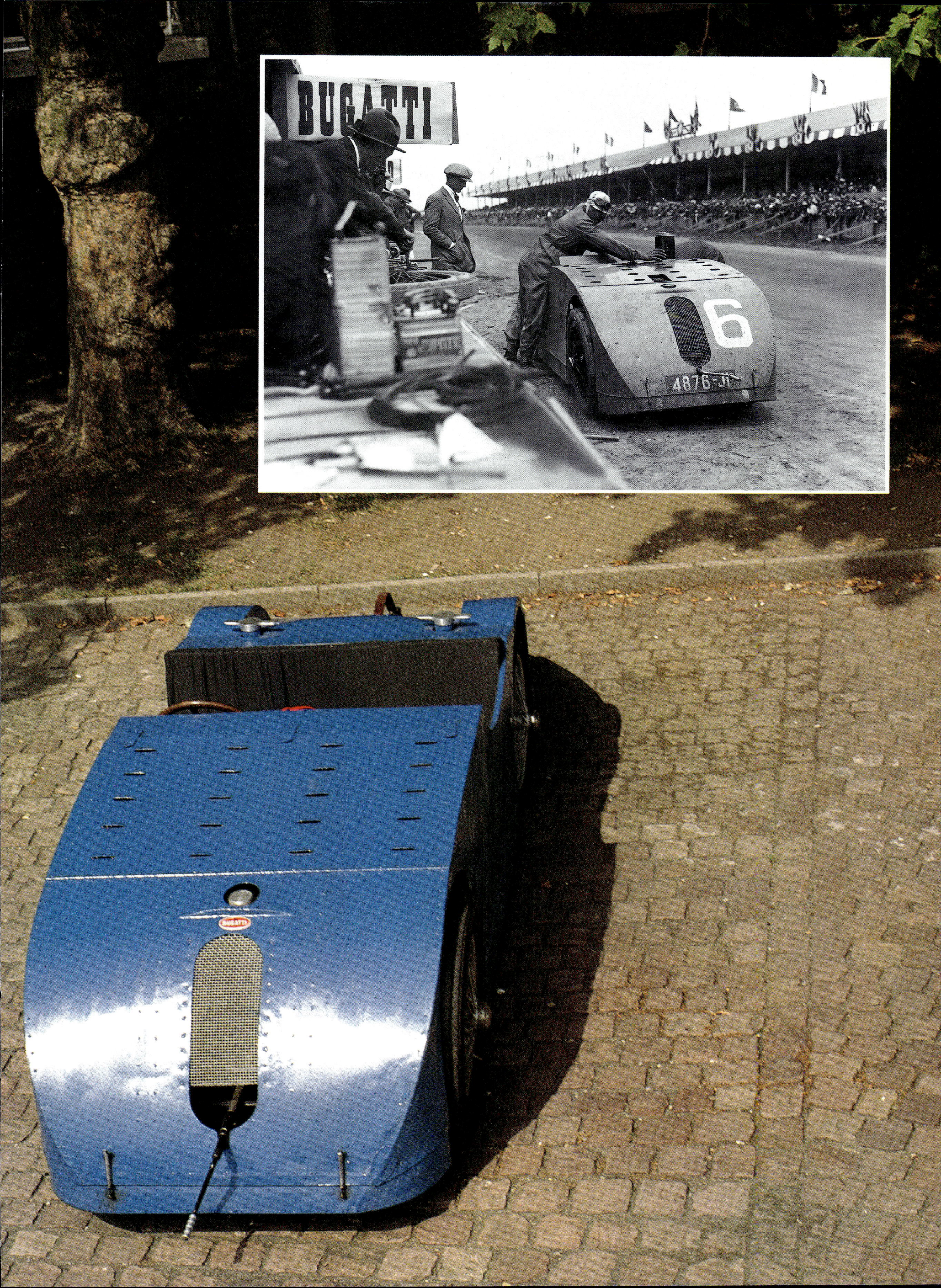
BUGATTI
6

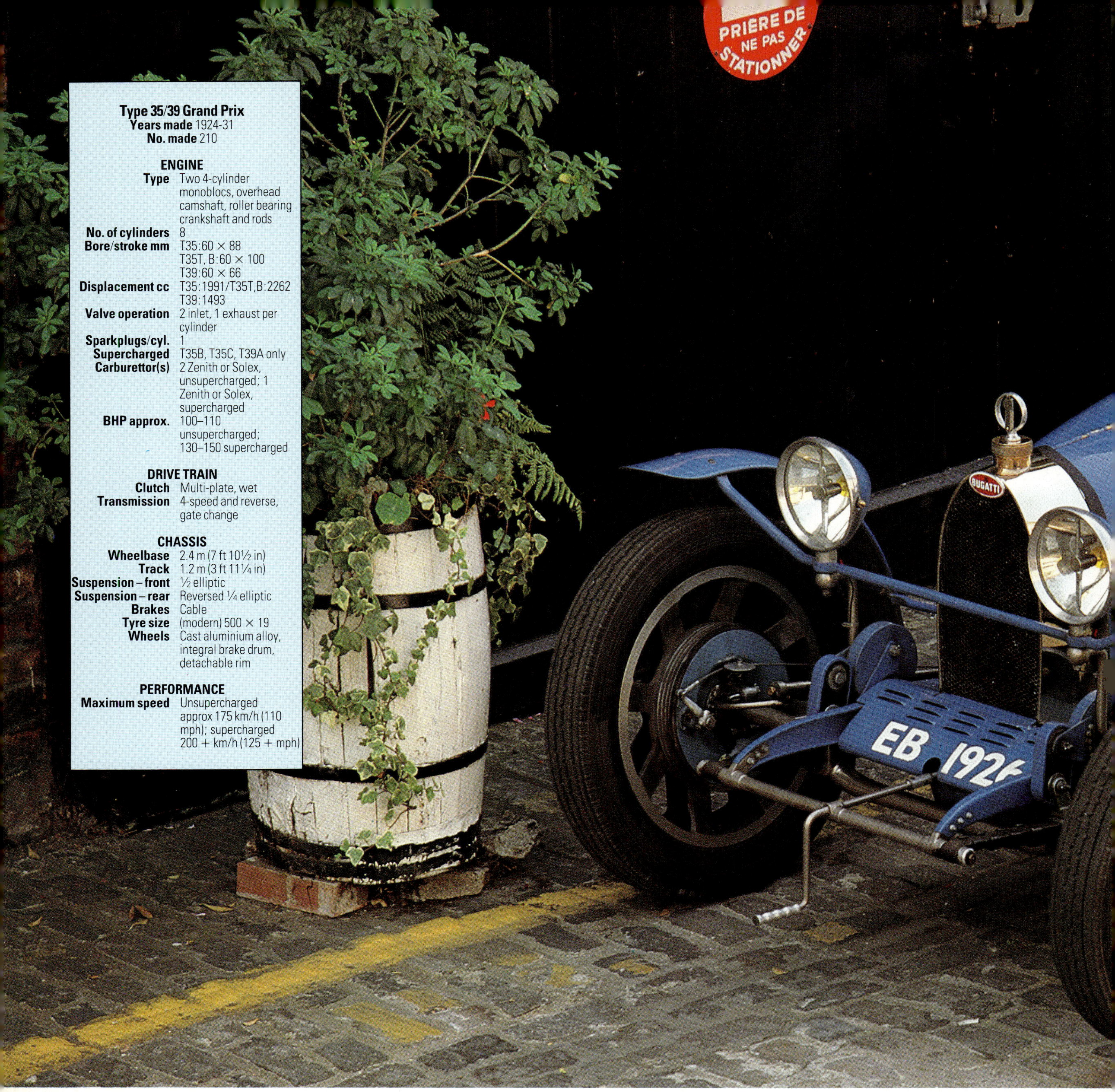

Type 35/39 Grand Prix
Years made 1924-31
No. made 210

ENGINE	
Type	Two 4-cylinder monoblocs, overhead camshaft, roller bearing crankshaft and rods
No. of cylinders	8
Bore/stroke mm	T35: 60 × 88 T35T, B: 60 × 100 T39: 60 × 66
Displacement cc	T35: 1991/T35T,B: 2262 T39: 1493
Valve operation	2 inlet, 1 exhaust per cylinder
Sparkplugs/cyl.	1
Supercharged	T35B, T35C, T39A only
Carburettor(s)	2 Zenith or Solex, unsupercharged; 1 Zenith or Solex, supercharged
BHP approx.	100–110 unsupercharged; 130–150 supercharged
DRIVE TRAIN	
Clutch	Multi-plate, wet
Transmission	4-speed and reverse, gate change
CHASSIS	
Wheelbase	2.4 m (7 ft 10½ in)
Track	1.2 m (3 ft 11¼ in)
Suspension – front	½ elliptic
Suspension – rear	Reversed ¼ elliptic
Brakes	Cable
Tyre size	(modern) 500 × 19
Wheels	Cast aluminium alloy, integral brake drum, detachable rim
PERFORMANCE	
Maximum speed	Unsupercharged approx 175 km/h (110 mph); supercharged 200 + km/h (125 + mph)

frame in at the rear, to follow the lines of a streamlined tail, and splayed the rear springs out towards the wheels. At the front he went one better than Fiat, who had used a circular axle, machined hollow and flange-jointed at the centre, by getting his forge shop to bend up a drilled-out, hollow forging to axle shape, and to close the two ends by forging them back to solid. Then he machined square holes through the axle to form axleboxes to take the springs, as indeed Fiat had done. The result was a forger's *tour de force*, a light one-piece circular but hollow axle.

The gearbox was the same as used on the touring Type 30 with a 'first gear a little stronger' – that is higher geared, but mounted on cross tubes, the arms of the wide casting being cut off. There was an aluminium dash and bulkhead with the traditional Bugatti instruments: an air pump for pressurizing the fuel tank and an indicating air gauge, an oil gauge, a tachometer and the typical clock. There was now one Bosch magneto, mounted once more on the dash, and driven from the camshaft, thus avoiding his lubrication problems with the driving gears of the earlier twin-magneto mounting. The brake layout was now superbly designed, with fully compensated cable work to all four wheels. The wheels themselves were cast and very novel and these are described in detail on page 43. (See also photograph above.)

The new car's engine was basically the same as the Type 30, but the crankcase differed because now a full ball and roller bearing crank was used. Earlier attempts at roller big ends had used split rods and a solid crank. Now Bugatti used one-piece and very light connecting rods and split the crankshaft itself into sections, cottered together in perfect alignment, enabling the rods to be assembled each with their seventeen 8 mm rollers. The detail of the crank was superb by any standards. Made mainly from case-hardened alloy steel of best quality, extensively ground on all important faces, and aligned by varying on assembly the angle of the cross cotter pins, also hardened and ground, the crank could be dismantled and reassembled while preserving the alignment.

This new crank not only got over the big-end lubrication problems of the normal Type 30 engine, which had failed so badly at Indianapolis, but had rods lighter and more rigid than at Tours, so that 6000 rpm could now be reached safely.

The rest of the engine was not much changed. The standard three-valve

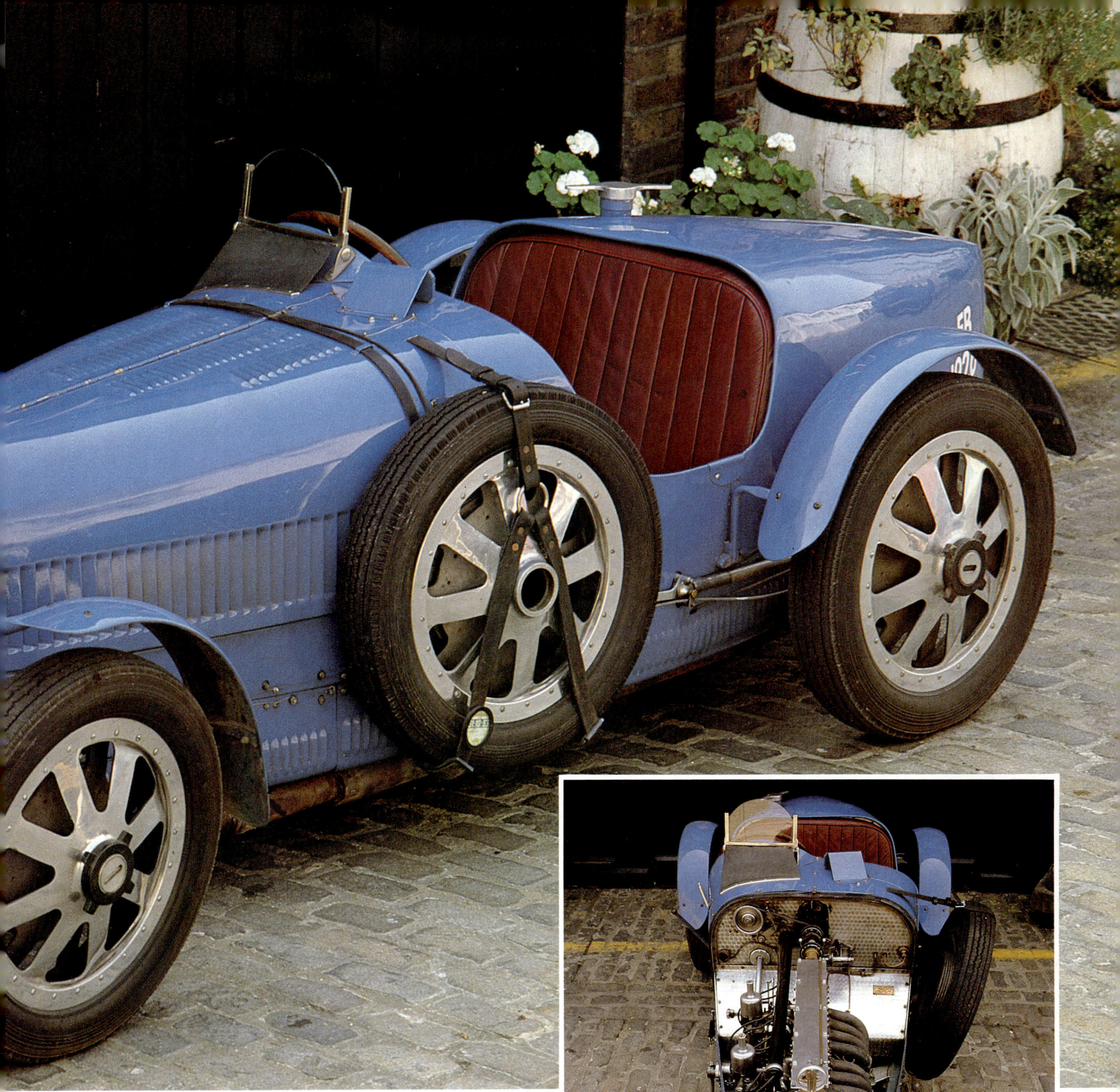

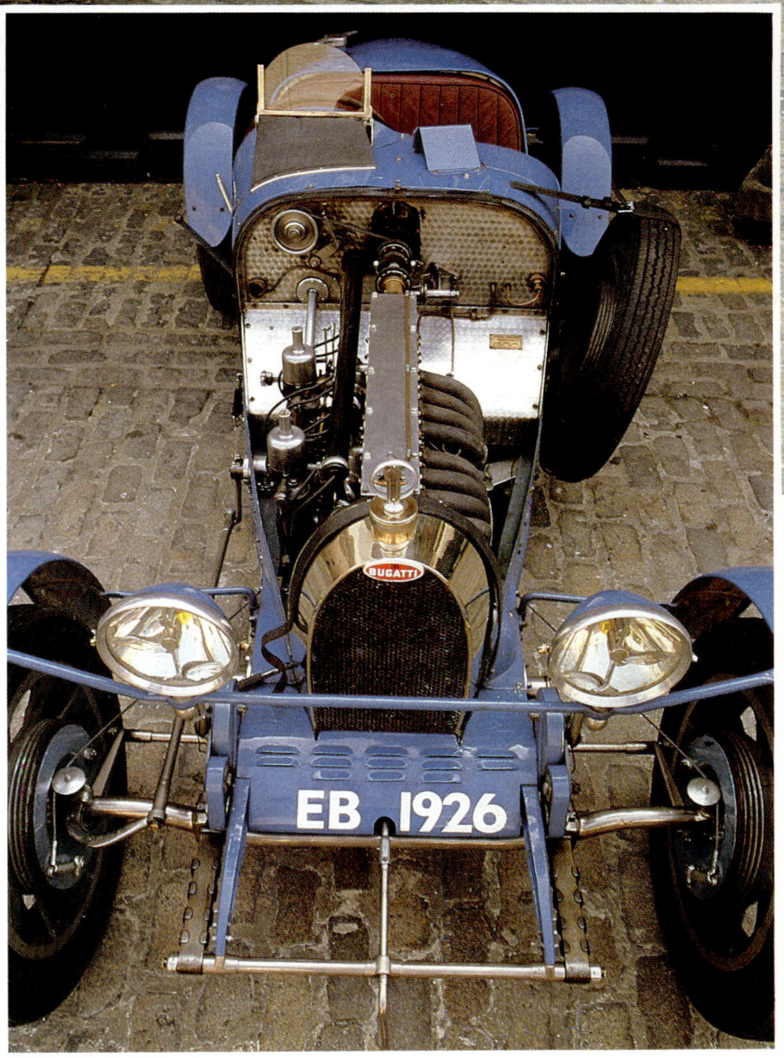

The French Grand Prix at Lyon in 1924 saw for the first time Ettore Bugatti's masterpiece, the Type 35, although tyre trouble prevented any success for the new model at that event. Today a road-equipped Type 35 remains an aesthetic delight, with road manners, handling and performance to match its superb good looks – it will still accelerate with ease up to 160 km/h (100 mph) on the open road. This is a 1926 unsupercharged car.

arrangement was retained, but the valve diameter was enlarged to give better breathing.

Although Fiat had used a supercharger in 1923, Bugatti argued – temporarily! – that supercharging was unethical and stuck to his twin Zeniths. The oil pump was driven from the nose of the crank by a worm gear, and the standard cross drive turned the water pump. Bugatti indeed claimed that his engine was based on the touring engine, and made much of how he used standard parts. The steering box was new and the linkages to the hubs were well designed with polished arms with integral ball ends.

Perhaps the most striking feature from someone who had rejected most bodywork as unnecessarily heavy was the superb line and detail of the Grand Prix body. Never had a car had such a pretty and satisfying body,

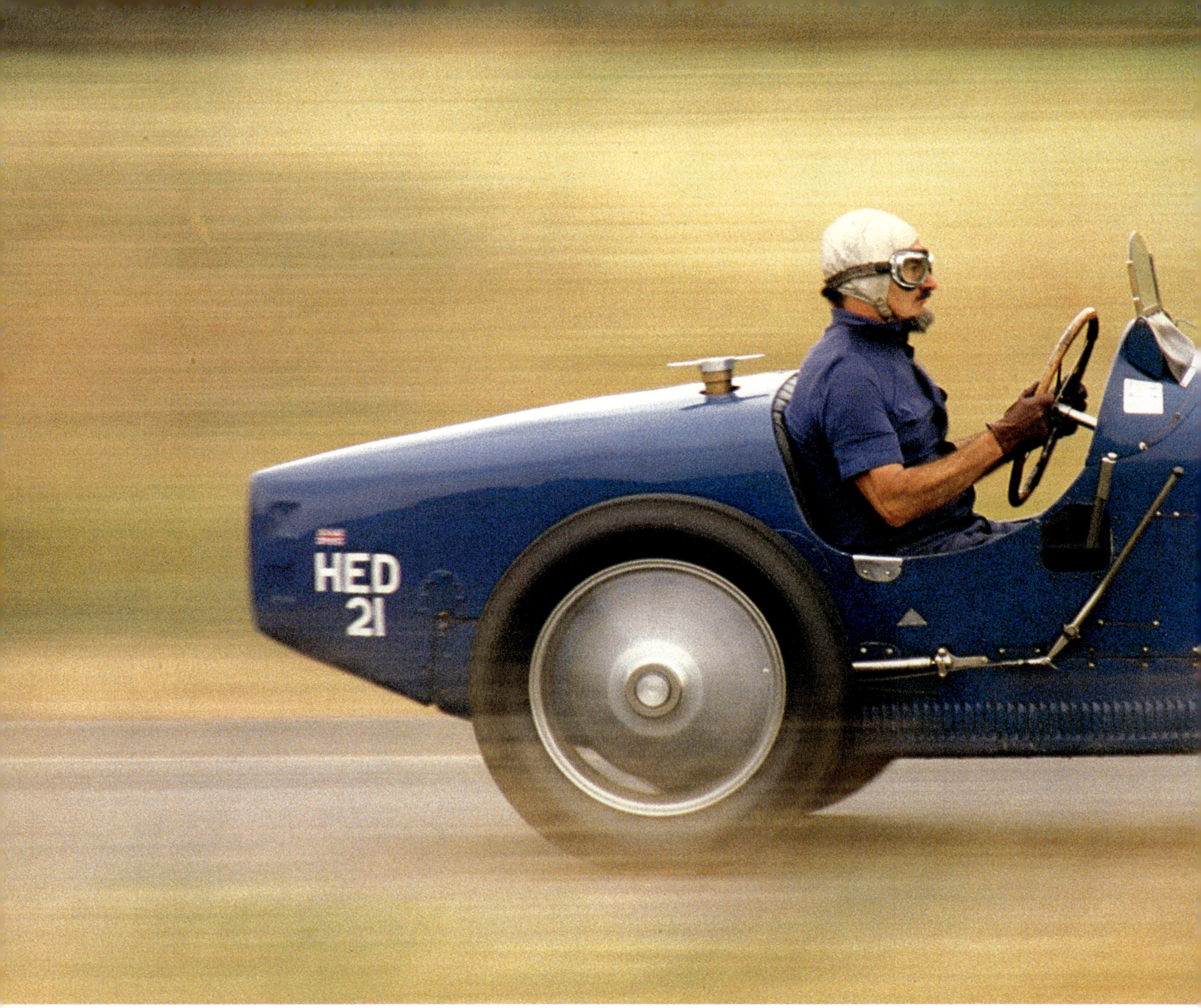
HED
21

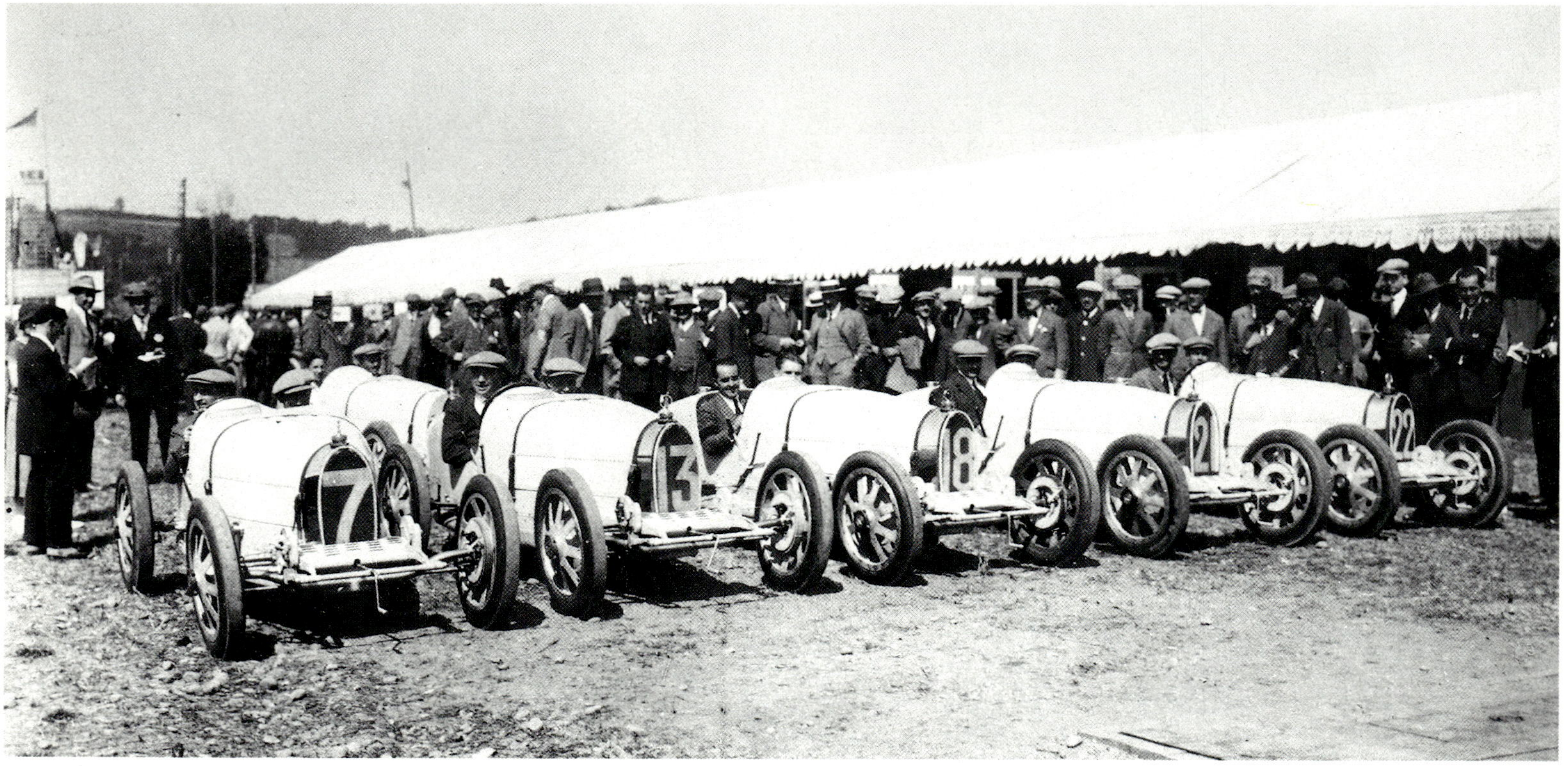
7
13
18
21
22

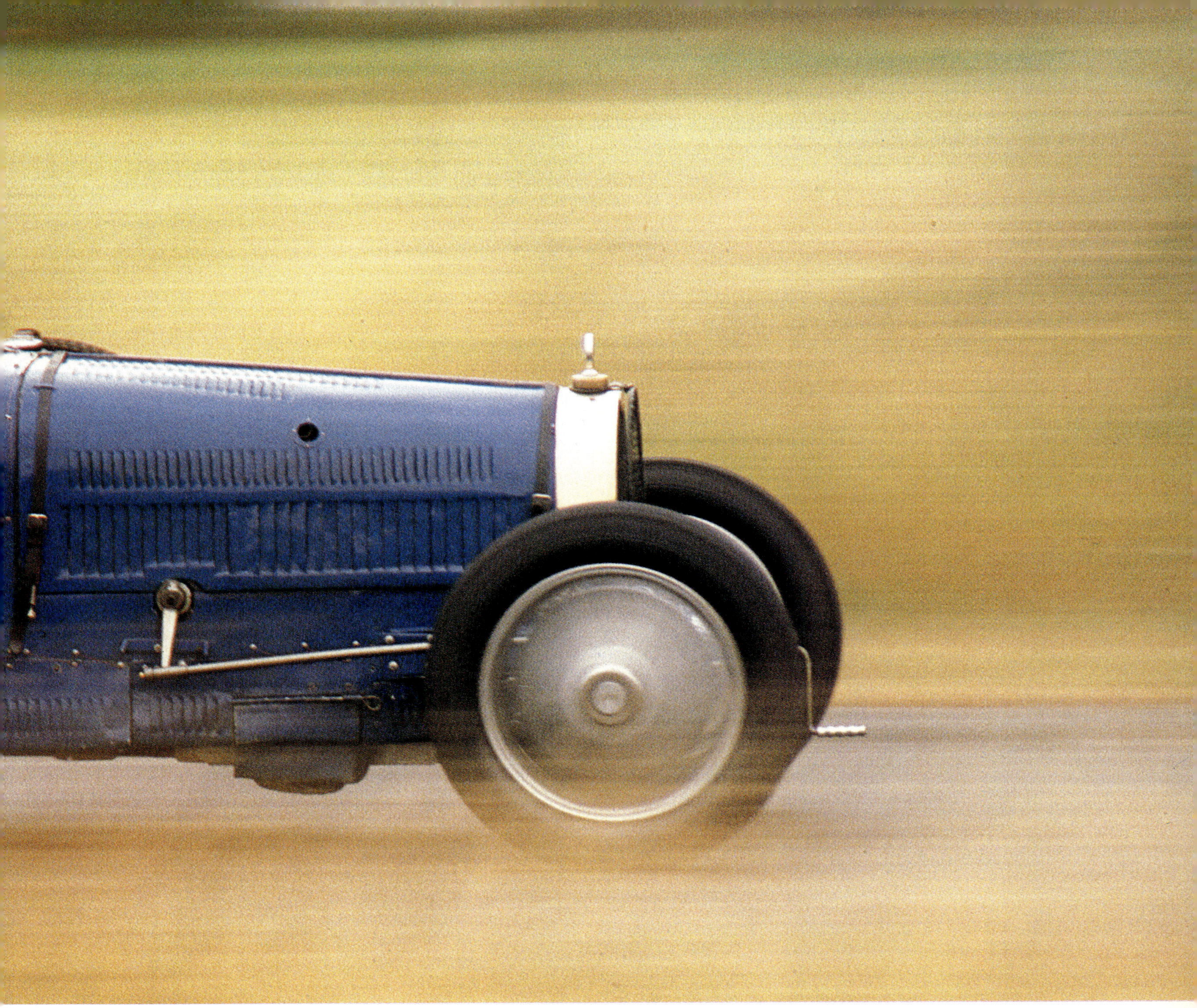

ABOVE The addition of a supercharger and a long-stroke crankshaft produced the Type 35B in 1927. Extremely successful in its day, it has been winning races ever since. This car holds the Vintage record at Prescott hill climb and, running on methanol fuel, has a top speed of over 205 km/h (130 mph), and can achieve a standing start kilometre in less than 27 seconds. Provided by Mr I. Preston.

LEFT Five Bugattis were entered in the Grand Prix at Lyon in 1924, and Ettore himself turned up in the prototype. The handsome appearance of the cars, the superb detail of their aluminium-panelled bodies and their novel cast aluminium wheels, created a sensation. However, the results for the new streamlined racers at this event were disappointing: only two of them completed the race, managing 7th and 8th places.

made up from aluminium panels, extensively louvred and attached to the frame and bulkhead by a multitude of small eared and wired body screws.

But the real novelty of the car was in its cast aluminium wheels, each with eight flat spokes and integral ribbed brake drum with a steel liner, and a detachable rim held on by 32 (later 24) small 6 mm screws. The tyre was of an American size, 20 × 4 in 'Straight Side', which Bugatti ordered specially from Dunlop in England.

The five cars entered in the 1924 Lyon Grand Prix, and the prototype which Ettore drove himself as a demonstrator, were ready in good time and were driven to Lyon from Molsheim. Although they were fast and handled well in tests, disaster struck in the race itself. All the available tyres which had arrived at the last minute were found to be inadequately vulcanized and as soon as the race began started to shed treads. First de Vizcaya ran off the road, hitting a spectator, then Meo Costantini had a tyre wrap round and bend his gear lever. The others began to run out of tyres and only two cars were racing at the end, finishing seventh and eighth to the winning Alfa Romeo of Campari, with Delage second and third.

Bugatti at once reverted to the standard 710 × 90 mm beaded-edge tyres he had used successfully on other cars, and did much better with the Type 35 a month later when Costantini came second to Segrave's Sunbeam at San Sebastián in Spain.

The Type 35, in spite of problems at its début, was an instant success through its obvious performance and superb aesthetic appeal. Orders flooded in from racing drivers and some of Ettore's faithful circle of supporters, wealthy and often titled: the Juneks from Prague, Sir Robert Bird, Glen Kidston and Lord Cholmondeley in Britain, Maurice Bunau-Varilla the owner of *Le Matin*, in France, Count Masetti in Italy. Off the race track the car was astonishingly docile and tractable, as Louis Delage remarked after testing it at the 1924 Paris Salon. Today from a single pull on the handle to start the engine this unsupercharged car can be driven through traffic and accelerate up to 160 km/h (100 mph) on a clear road.

Little change was made in 1925; production was in full swing and races were being won widely. The pressures for more power and speed continued and Bugatti realized he was being left behind without supercharging. So at last he began to work on a Roots-type supercharger, getting help with its design from a French engineer, Edmond Moglia, who had experience to offer.

However, in 1926 Bugatti first enlarged the unblown engine to 2.3 litres by fitting a 100 mm stroke crank to the standard engine (the car now called the 35T – T for Targa) and started a succession of dramatic wins in the famous Sicilian race the Targa Florio. The new supercharged car was tested that year, initially with a small blower in a reduced-stroke 1100 cc version (52 × 66 mm) in the 1926 Alsace Voiturette Grand Prix, and then appeared at Montlhéry for a walk-over in the French Grand Prix in 1½-litre supercharged form (strictly designated Type 39). The same model won at San Sebastián and in the Italian Grand Prix, and came second in the British Grand Prix. Finally the 2-litre supercharged Type 35C achieved a one-two-three victory at the Milan GP at the end of the season. Indeed, 1926 was the peak year of Bugatti's racing success; he was World Champion, winner of all major events and, as he claimed in his advertising, '47 records, 351 first places' in that year!

The car continued with successes in 1927, the first months of which saw the first 'Targa Compresseur', or 35B 2.3-litre, 60 × 100 mm, in the hands of Louis Chiron, and destined to be the ultimate 'single-cam' Grand Prix Bugatti. The World Championship eluded Bugatti that year, going to Delage, while much of the competition found racing too expensive and had withdrawn. In 1928 and 1929 racing suffered from the world recession and, although Bugatti continued to win, Grand Prix racing lost some of its glamour. Then in 1929 the first Monaco Grand Prix around the streets of Monte Carlo was held, the entry dominated by Bugattis with William Grover-Williams (who was of Anglo-French parentage and raced as Williams) winning in his British Racing Green T35B. René Dreyfus won there in 1930, but Bugatti had to be content with Chiron's second in the Targa Florio; but there were other victories that year before the 35 had to give way to a successor.

The twin-cam Type 51

As the decade came to an end and the world economy worsened Ettore became more and more distracted by the problems of his order book, the reduced sales of his touring cars and the lack of customers for his monster Royale, which he had started to develop in 1927 (see the last chapter). Both Ettore and his son knew that more power was needed for the T35B; it was Jean who suggested acquiring a couple of front-wheel-drive Miller racing cars from an American driver Leon Duray, who had come over to Europe to try his luck; a deal was struck – two Millers in exchange for three Type 43 Grand Sport cars which were in stock unsold. The Bugattis now had a pair of engines which they knew were producing much more power than their unit could manage, with a fine twin-camshaft overhead valve design on the same principle as other successful engines that were beating Bugatti.

The Miller engines were dismantled, drawn out, then put on test and they demonstrated over 50 hp more than the best Bugatti had managed! And happily a close copy of the cylinder block and pent-roof two-valve cylinder arrangement could readily be adapted to the crankcase and the rest of a 35B. The result was the ultimate in 2- or 2.3-litre Grand Prix Bugattis, the Type 51.

The car is almost indistinguishable from a 35B, although there are a few give-away details. The wheels are now of the modern well-base type with fixed rims; the blower relief valve hole is lower down on the right-hand bonnet, as the manifolding is different. The magneto is driven from the left-hand camshaft and thus on the left of the dash rather than in the centre – and a Scintilla unit is used rather than a Bosch. Now there are two filler caps for the fuel tank.

The Type 51 was not ready for the 1930 season but was on show in October at the Paris Salon. It made its début in the hands of Achille Varzi who won at Tunis in April 1931; then Louis Chiron won the Monaco Grand Prix with two other 51s third and fourth.

For the next two or three years the Type 51 had many successes for Bugatti, becoming the most attractive and desirable of the smaller Grand Prix cars; some 40 were made in all. But other larger cars were appearing, a 2.6-litre Alfa Romeo, a 2.9-litre Maserati and on the horizon the beginning of the German domination with Auto Union and Mercedes-Benz Grand Prix cars. Significantly the Italians and Germans had state help, which was not available to Bugatti.

Grand Prix oddities

While the T51 was being produced and was racing successfully, Bugatti perpetrated two designs which in retrospect were unwise and wasteful. First he designed, as the Type 45, a 16-cylinder engine in 3- and 4-litre versions, using two banks of eight cylinders with crankshafts geared together – a design he had already used on his aero engine during the First World War, and which had been licensed to the Duesenberg company in the United States. The engine, with a pair of superchargers at the rear, was fitted to a new frame along normal Bugatti lines, but with the rear springs parallel rather than waisted at the rear end. The engine had one-piece blocks with eight cylinders, roller crank bearings, but plain big-end

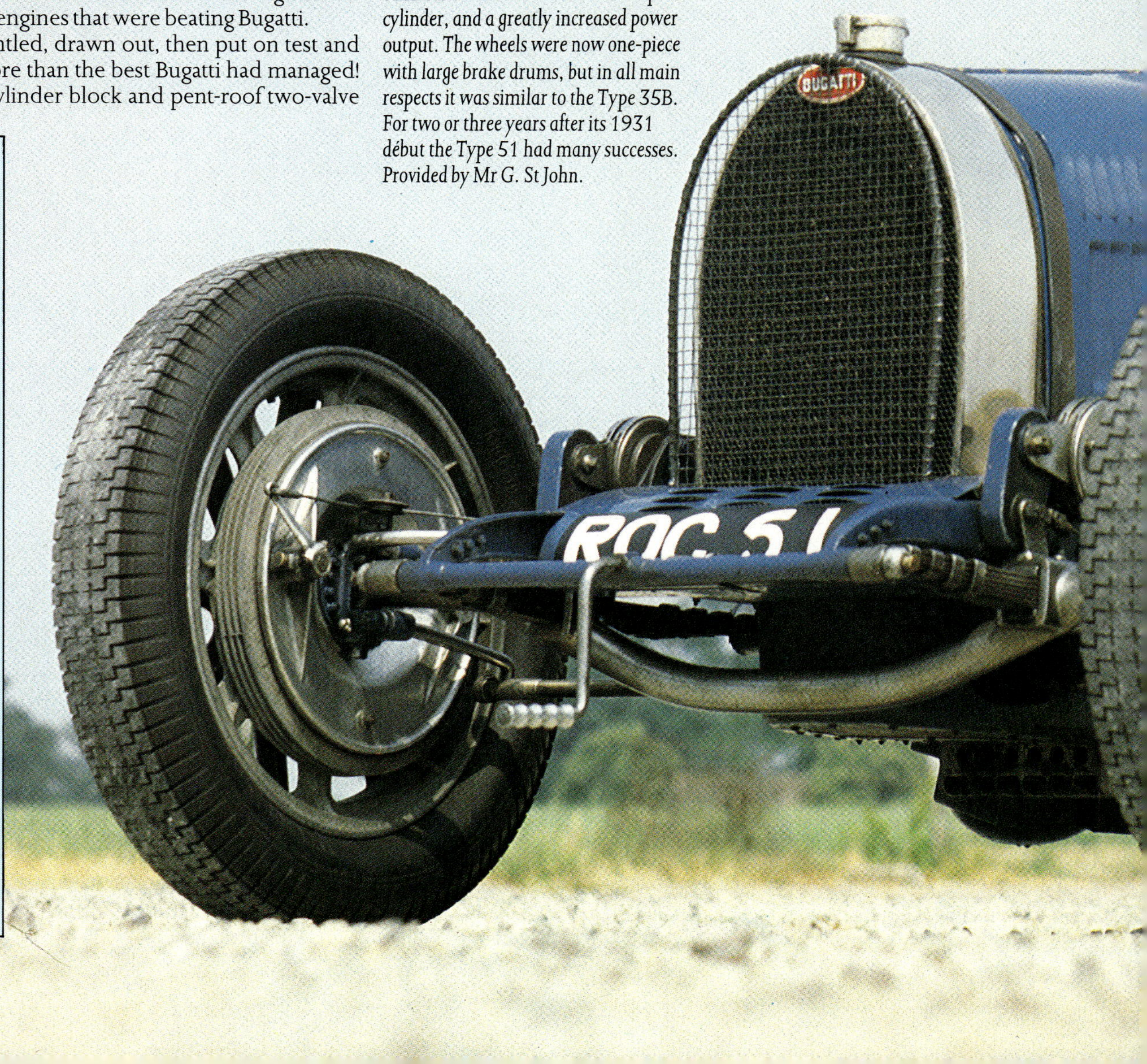

BELOW The ultimate 2.3-litre racing Bugatti was the Type 51, which first appeared in 1931. This had twin overhead camshafts with two inclined valves per cylinder, and a greatly increased power output. The wheels were now one-piece with large brake drums, but in all main respects it was similar to the Type 35B. For two or three years after its 1931 début the Type 51 had many successes. Provided by Mr G. St John.

Type 51/51A Grand Prix	
Years made	1931–5
No. made	40
ENGINE	
Type	Monobloc, twin overhead camshafts, roller bearing crank and rods
No. of cylinders	8
Bore/stroke mm	T51: 60 × 88, 60 × 100 T51A: 60 × 66
Displacement cc	T51: 1991, 2262 T51A: 1493
Valve operation	1 inlet, 1 exhaust per cylinder
Sparkplugs/cyl.	1
Supercharged	Yes
Carburettor	1 Zenith or Solex
BHP approx.	T51: 160–80/T51A: 130
DRIVE TRAIN	
Clutch	Multi-plate, wet
Transmission	4-speed and reverse, gate change
CHASSIS	
Wheelbase	2.4 m (7 ft 10½ in)
Track	1.2 m (3 ft 11¼ in)
Suspension – front	½ elliptic
Suspension – rear	Reversed ¼ elliptic
Brakes	Cable
Tyre size	5.00 × 19
Wheels	Cast aluminium alloy, well base, integral brake drums
PERFORMANCE	
Maximum speed	200+ km/h (125+ mph)

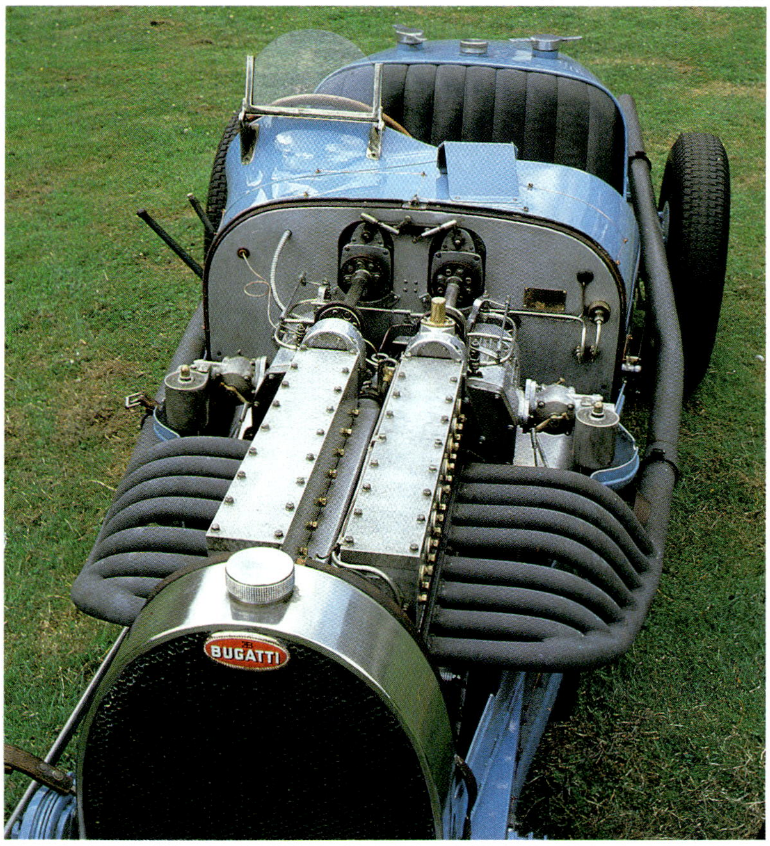

bearings. Its weakness lay in the intermediate gear coupling the two cranks, which was needed to allow them to turn in the same direction. This gear was highly loaded and probably inadequately lubricated; it was the weak point of the design. Two cars only were built and used on a few hill climbs without significant success and were not proceeded with.

The other aberration was a four-wheel-drive racing car, the Type 53. This indeed was the conception of an Italian engineer G. C. Cappa, formerly with Fiat, who persuaded Ettore (or perhaps his son Jean?) to take up and produce the design using a 4.9-litre supercharged engine from the Type 50–54s. Front and back axles were coupled via a transfer gearbox, and for the first time a Bugatti had independent front suspension from a pair of transverse springs. No attempt was made to use constant velocity universal joints, and the steering was not only heavy but also reacted to engine torque. Again a pair of cars was produced, and René Dreyfus and Louis Chiron competed with some success in hill climbs in the south of France. Jean Bugatti brought a Type 53 over to England's Shelsley Walsh hill climb and severely damaged it, although it is said that he broke the hill record unofficially in practice. Again this Bugatti model was not proceeded with.

LEFT The twin bank engine of the Type 45 16-cylinder car, with a pair of crankshafts geared together and a supercharger for each bank. It competed in a few hill climbs in 1929-30 but was never fully developed. One of these cars has now been re-created and contributes splendidly to the Vintage racing scene in Britain.

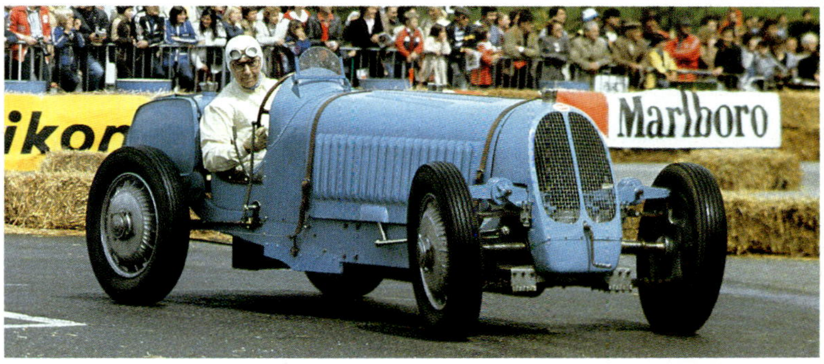

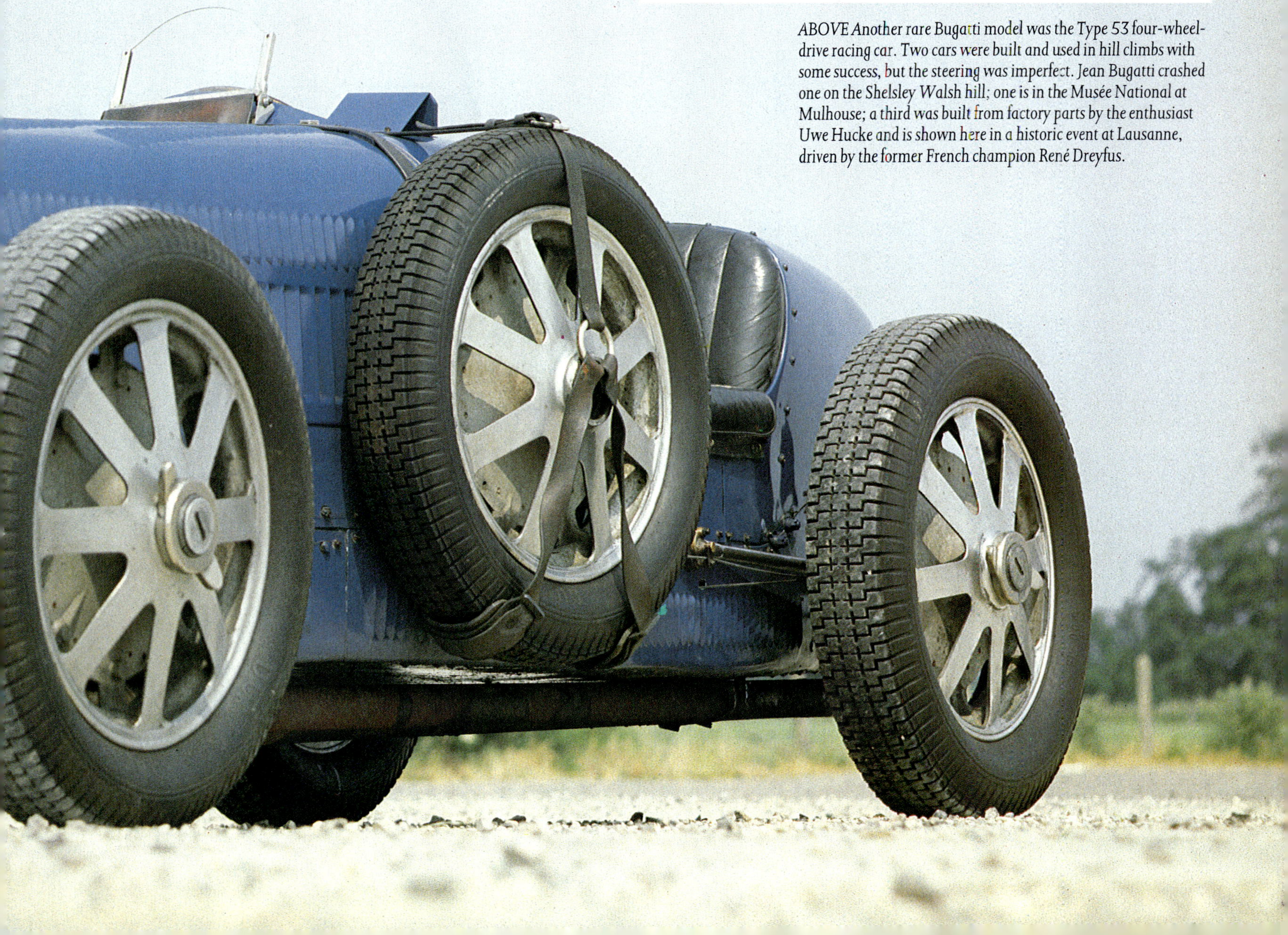

ABOVE Another rare Bugatti model was the Type 53 four-wheel-drive racing car. Two cars were built and used in hill climbs with some success, but the steering was imperfect. Jean Bugatti crashed one on the Shelsley Walsh hill; one is in the Musée National at Mulhouse; a third was built from factory parts by the enthusiast Uwe Hucke and is shown here in a historic event at Lausanne, driven by the former French champion René Dreyfus.

The 4.9-litre Type 54

In his search for more speed Bugatti evolved the Type 54 Grand Prix car using a supercharged 4.9-litre engine from the large sporting Type 50, fitted into a 16-cylinder T45 frame, and with a layout and body similar to the T35/51 cars, but larger and heavier. It was fast, very powerful, but a monster to handle. It appeared first at Monza in September 1931 and had a few successes in 1932–3, the best being first and second (Varzi and Count Stanislas Czaykowski) in the German GP in 1933; in the same year Czaykowski gained the World's Hour Record at Berlin's AVUS circuit in his car, but was killed in it at Monza on a tragic day when two others also died.

Bugatti's rigid spring and axle layout was not suitable for such a heavy and powerful car and its track performance was unhappy even if its speed was high. It is said that the sight of two Type 54s thundering round Brooklands was an experience never to be forgotten.

The sportsman's Grand Prix replicas

Bugatti had always claimed that his racing cars, being based on touring models, were available to anyone. By 1925 he knew that his racing Type 13 Brescia was out of date and now he set out to base a replacement on his T35 GP car, to satisfy the market for a cheaper sports-racing car, and to make the most of the aesthetic appeal of the racing model.

The result was a pair of cars, first an eight-cylinder simplified version of the GP car first delivered in mid-1925, and then at the end of 1925 a version with a four-cylinder engine. The earlier car was the Type 35A, catalogued as the 'Course Imitation', but often called at the works the 'Tecla', from the name of the cultured pearls popular at the time. The second was the T37.

Type 35A 'Course Imitation'
Years made 1926–9
No. made 130

ENGINE	
Type	Two 4-cylinder monoblocs, overhead camshaft, roller bearing crankshaft, plain big ends
No. of cylinders	8
Bore/stroke mm	60 × 88
Displacement cc	1991
Valve operation	2 inlet, 1 exhaust per cylinder
Sparkplugs/cyl.	1
Supercharged	No
Carburettors	2 Zenith or Solex
BHP approx.	75
DRIVE TRAIN	
Clutch	Multi-plate, wet
Transmission	4-speed and reverse, gate change
CHASSIS	
Wheelbase	2.4 m (7 ft 10½ in)
Track	1.2 m (3 ft 11¼ in)
Suspension – front	½ elliptic
Suspension – rear	Reversed ¼ elliptic
Brakes	Cable
Tyre size	(modern) 19 × 4.50
Wheels	Rudge wire
PERFORMANCE	
Maximum speed	145 km/h (90 mph)

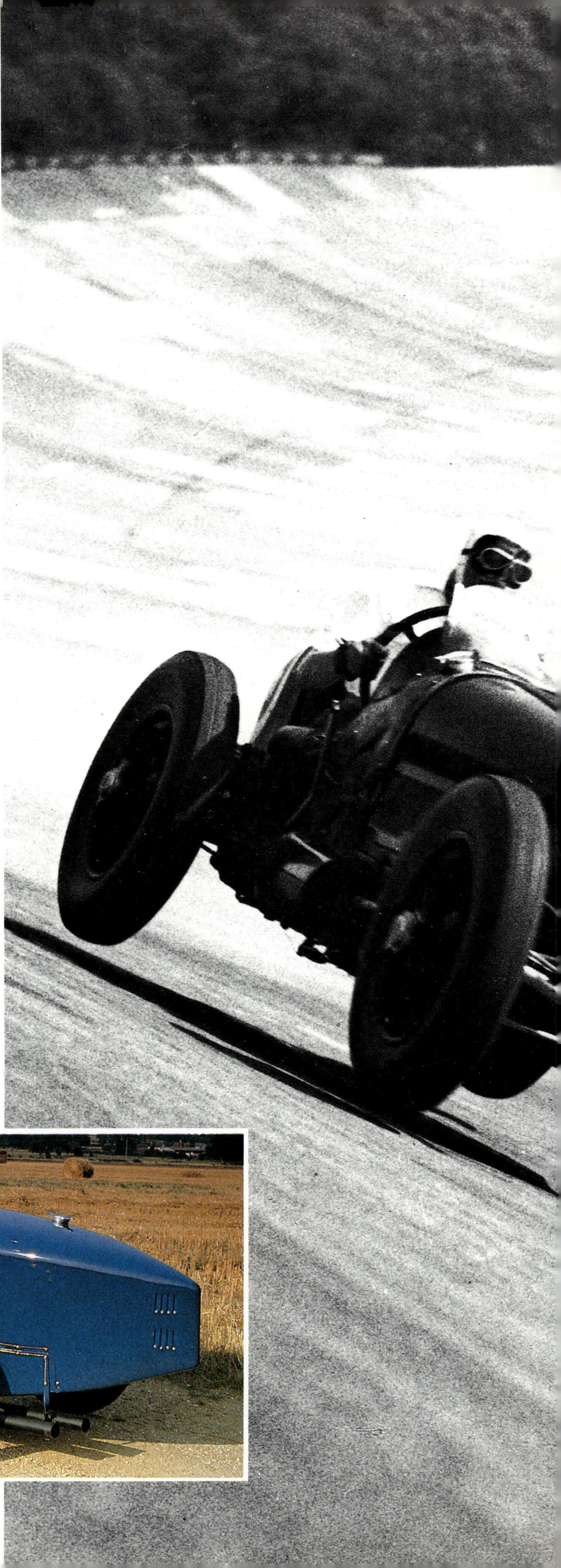

RIGHT Ettore attempted to keep up with his competitors with his Type 54. He used a 4.9-litre supercharged engine from the Type 50 touring car in an enlarged chassis whose general layout followed that of his successful smaller Grand Prix cars. The T54 was a handful, as Kaye Don and a few others found out when thundering around Brooklands at over 200 km/h (125 mph). One car (far right), originally raced by Prince Lobkowitz in Czechoslovakia and now road-equipped, is in the C.W.P. Hampton Collection.

BELOW The success of the Type 35 Grand Prix car created a market for a cheaper, simpler version known as the Type 35A. This sold at less than two-thirds of the price of the T35 and had plain bearing connecting rods and a simplified crankshaft, wire wheels and coil ignition. It had the road manners of its big sister, and a performance quite suitable for road use. This finely restored example uses the original type of narrow, beaded-edge tyres. Provided by Mr T. Cardy.

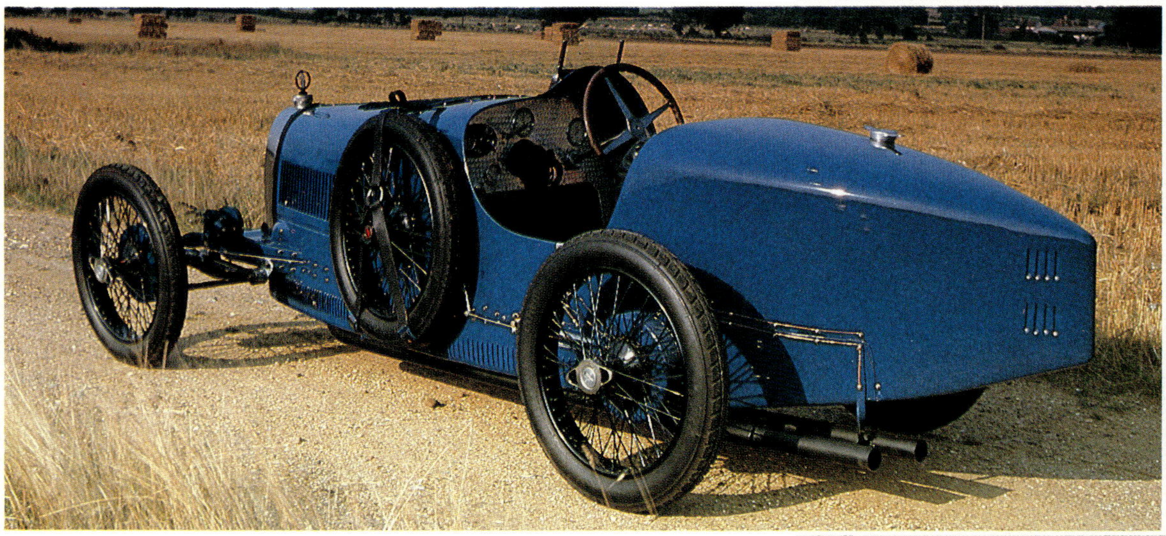

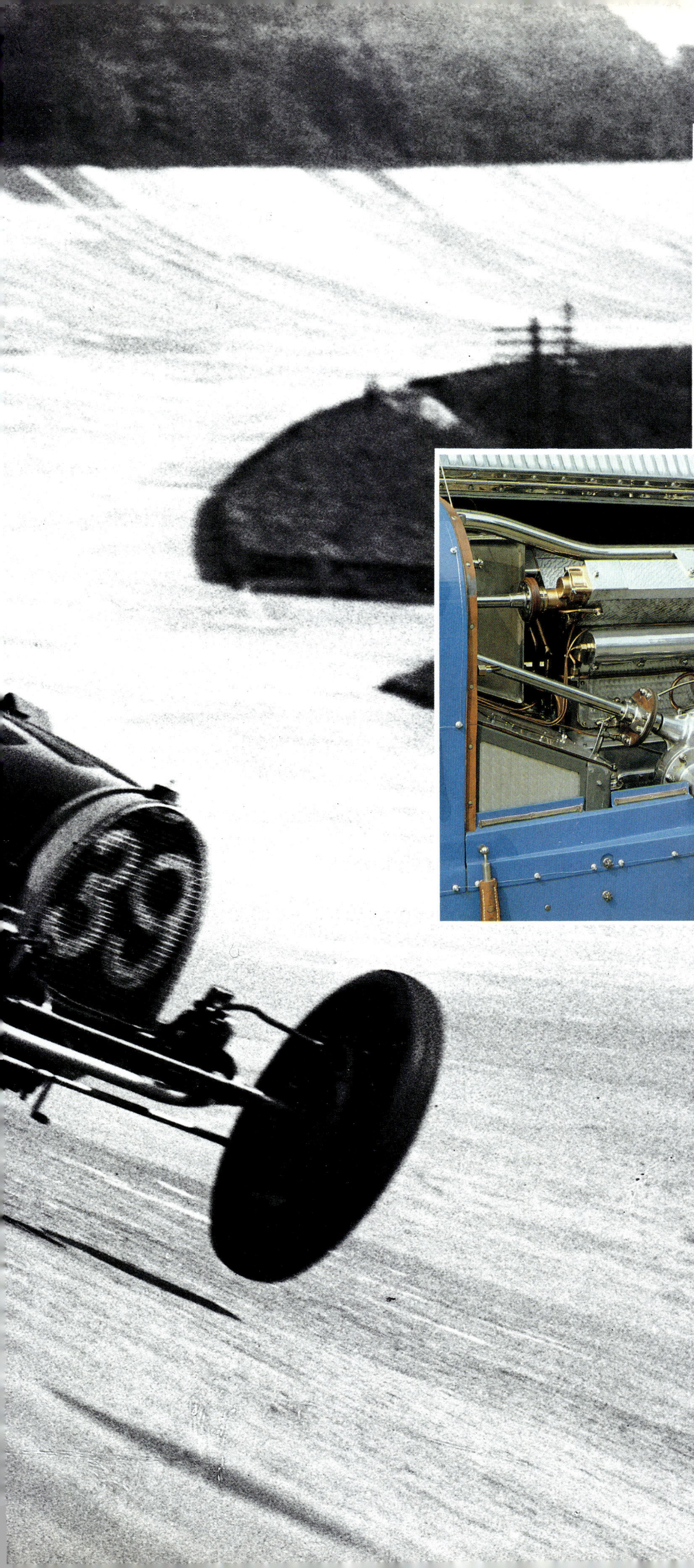

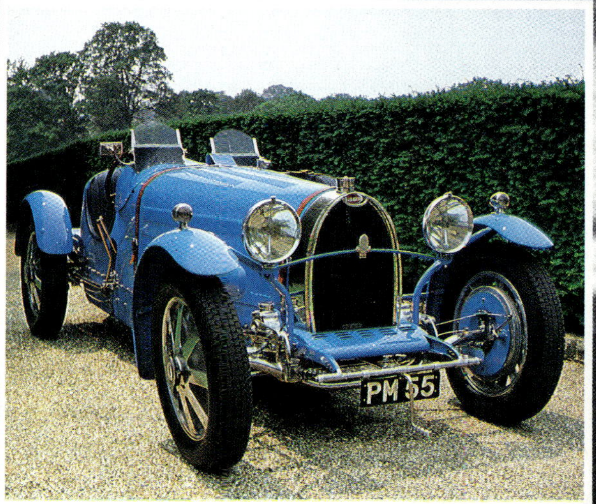

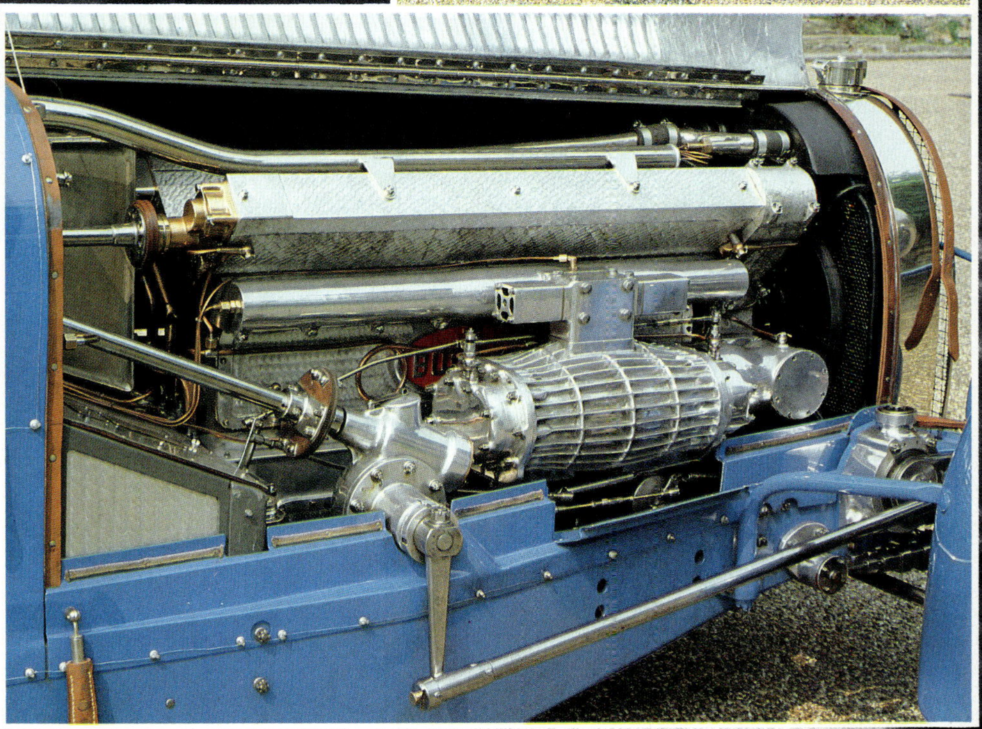

Type 54 Grand Prix
Years made 1932–4
No. made 5

ENGINE

Type	Monobloc, twin overhead camshafts, plain bearings
No. of cylinders	8
Bore/stroke mm	86 × 107
Displacement cc	4972
Valve operation	1 inlet, 1 exhaust per cylinder
Sparkplugs/cyl.	1
Supercharged	Yes
Carburettors	2 Zenith or Solex
BHP approx.	250

DRIVE TRAIN

Clutch	Multi-plate, wet
Transmission	3-speed and reverse, central, gate change

CHASSIS

Wheelbase	2.75 m (9 ft 0¼ in)
Track	1.35 m (4 ft 5 in)
Suspension – front	½ elliptic
Suspension – rear	Reversed ¼ elliptic
Brakes	Cable
Tyre size	6.00 × 19
Wheels	Cast aluminium alloy, well base, integral brake drum

PERFORMANCE

Maximum speed	200+ km/h (125+ mph)

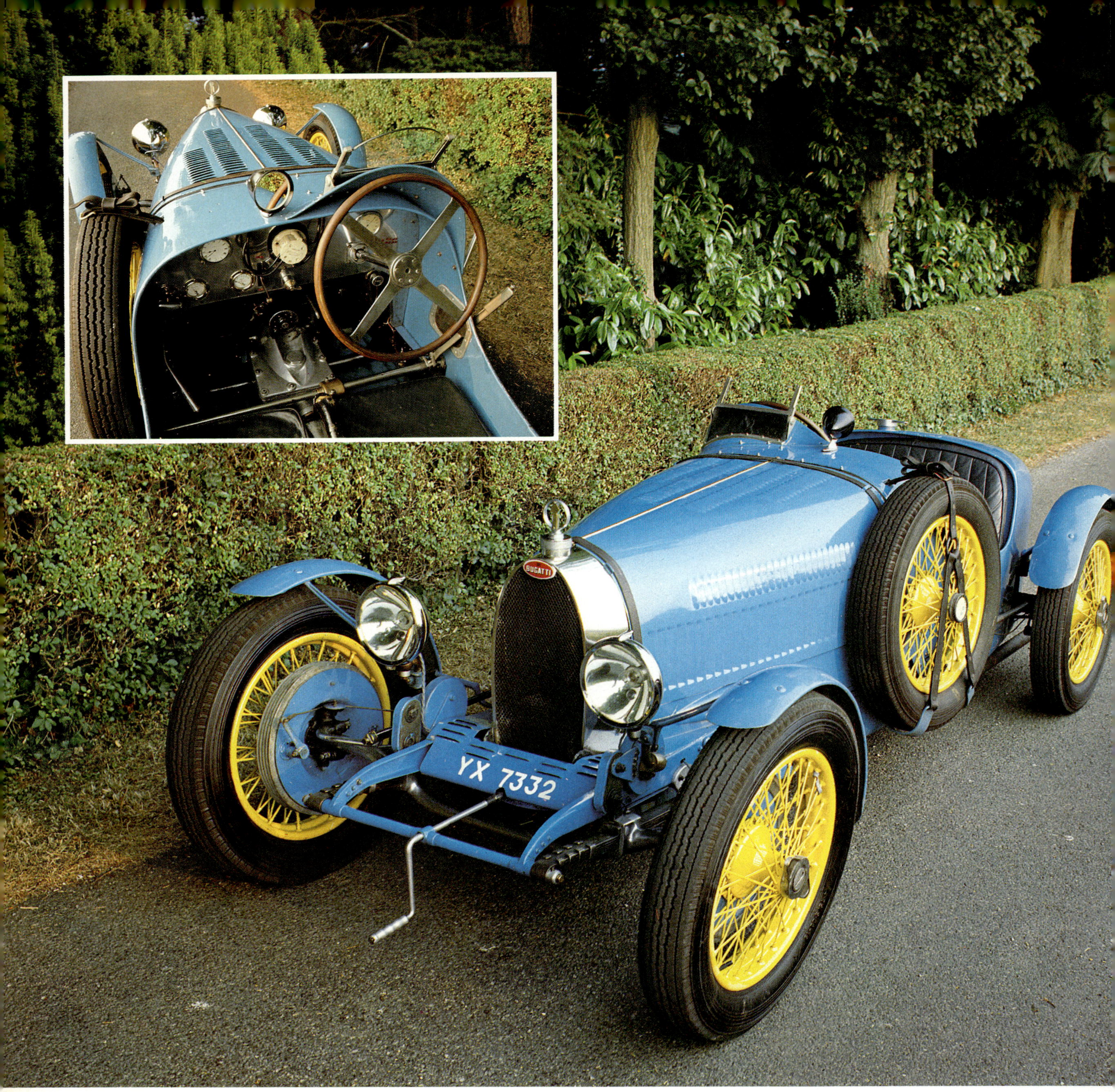

The Type 35A used the standard Grand Prix chassis, axles, gearbox and body, but had wire wheels and brake drums from the late series Brescia model. Where it differed from the full-blooded Grand Prix racer was in the engine, which reverted to the plain big end, three ball-race main bearings of the Type 38 2-litre described in the previous chapter. This had less power and did not relish sustained revolutions over 4500 rpm, but was much cheaper to build and allowed a selling price of less than two-thirds of the full Grand Prix car. It could even be had with aluminium wheels as an extra! It often had electric lighting, and eventually starting, but was never supplied with any form of hood or windscreen in the standard Molsheim version.

The Type 37 was even simpler and was immediately popular, since a four-cylinder, coil ignition, plain bearing crankshaft engine was simple and easy to maintain. It was the 69 × 100 mm, 1½-litre unit used in the Type 40, which came out six months after the Type 37: as a touring model it was intended perhaps to follow the sports-racing version, just as the Type 43 came shortly after the T35B. Although the sequence of development can be surmised from the type number sequence, it is not known whether Bugatti planned the two together or whether this evolution – at a time when development periods were short – was accidental.

In any event the Type 37 was one of Bugatti's most successful models, selling in Britain in 1927 for £550, compared with £1100 for an unblown Type 35, or £675 for the 35A. It had a top speed just under 160 km/h (100 mph) and a good general performance with all the traditional handling qualities of a GP Bugatti.

Then in the spring of 1928 Bugatti inevitably added a supercharger to it, using the small unit from the Type 38 engine, to produce the 37A, and from mid-1928 almost all of the models were so equipped. Apart from the blower drive from the front of the crankshaft, and the blower itself and its manifolding, the other change was to put the magneto in the dash as in the eight-cylinder car; otherwise the vehicle was unchanged, although towards the end larger brakes and drums were fitted using assemblies from the eight-cylinder touring models. The supercharged version was a success, especially in Voiturette (1500 cc) races, which were now becoming popular, and at Brooklands; production continued steadily until 1930, with a few cars delivered in 1931.

The classic Type 59

In 1933 it was Jean Bugatti who was taking the lead at Molsheim while his father spent much time in Paris working on project layouts for his new Bugatti railcar and lobbying the directors of the various railway companies for orders (this was before they were all nationalized into one state railway, the SNCF). A new touring car and its racing counterpart were being worked on at Molsheim, the touring Type 57 and the racing Type 59, only their engines being similar. The touring model is described in the final chapter, but the racing model was really Bugatti's last serious attempt to produce a batch of competition cars to win races and, it was hoped, to sell profitably – which the 4.9-litre Type 54 certainly had not managed to achieve. Oddly enough the racing 59 came out before the touring model went into production, perhaps because there was a substantial stock of earlier models waiting to be sold.

The Type 59 is probably the most beautiful two-seater racing car ever built, bristling with visual pleasures, and the few that remain must be among the most valuable automobiles in the world, certainly of those produced by normal unaided industry. But the car did not achieve what the Bugattis expected of it.

It first appeared in 1933 at the end of the season at San Sebastián and trailed home sixth and seventh. Here it appeared in 2.8-litre form (72 × 88 mm); these dimensions were retained for Monaco the following year, where Dreyfus managed third place. Then it was altered to 3.3 litres (72 × 100 mm), a change made also to the touring car before it was launched in 1934. The engine had a one-piece eight-cylinder block with integral head and inclined valves, as on the Miller-inspired Type 51, but the cups operating the valves on that engine were replaced by small rockers or fingers pivoting on tubes on the side of the cambox castings carrying the two camshafts.

The crank now had six plain bearings properly lubricated by pressure from a dry sump and dual oil pumps. This gear train also drove a gear on the left operating the water pump, the oil pumps by a vertical take-off and, on the touring engine, a dynamo coupled to the end of the water pump. Another gear train on the right drove the supercharger, which now had downdraught carburettors and a manifold from below the blower up to the cylinder block. The starting handle was at the side and turned the crankshaft through bevels on to the water pump shaft.

The clutch was a normal multi-disc wet Bugatti design and the gearbox was similar to the Type 54; a novelty lay in the use of a double reduction

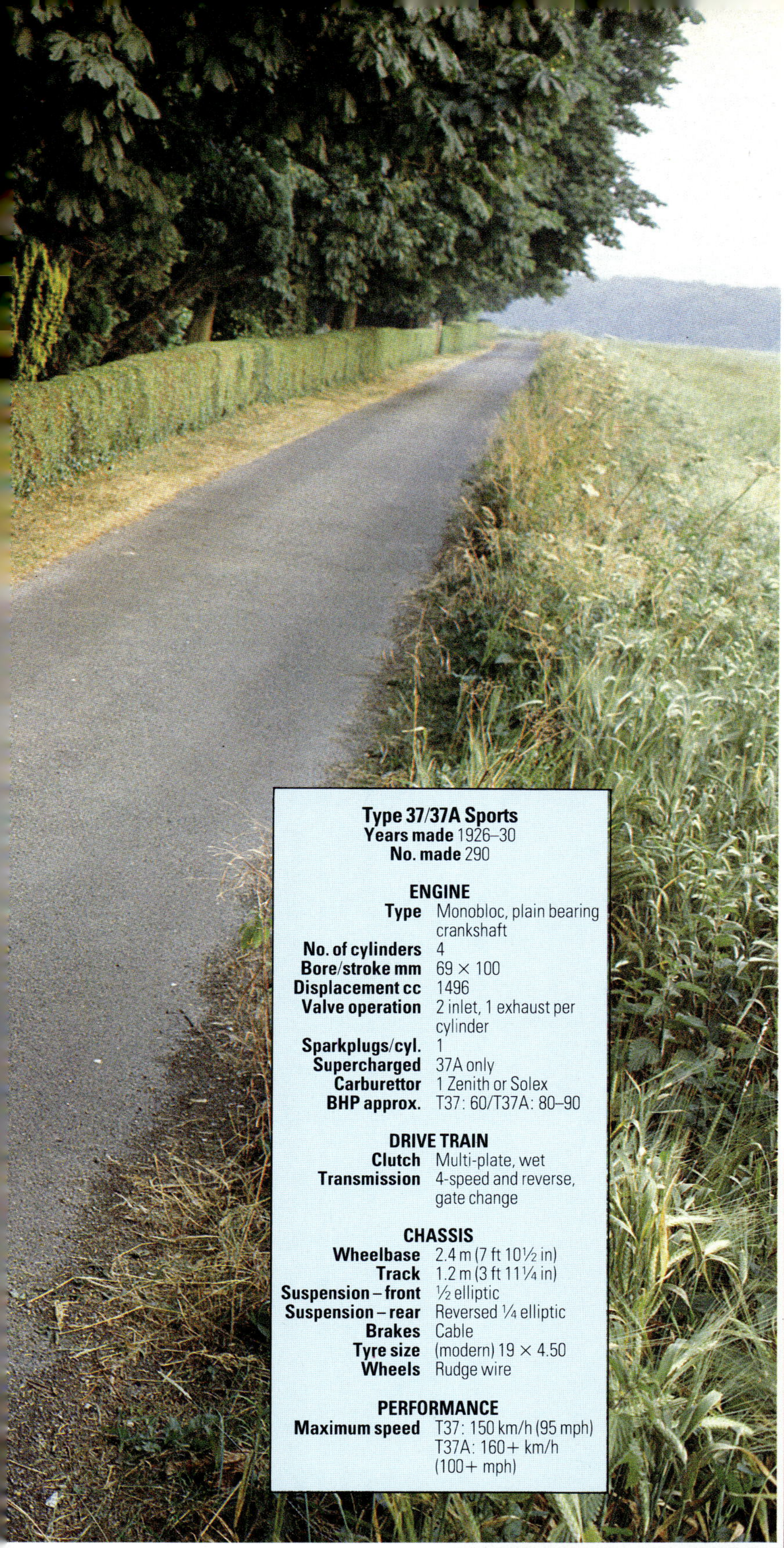

Type 37/37A Sports
Years made 1926–30
No. made 290

ENGINE	
Type	Monobloc, plain bearing crankshaft
No. of cylinders	4
Bore/stroke mm	69 × 100
Displacement cc	1496
Valve operation	2 inlet, 1 exhaust per cylinder
Sparkplugs/cyl.	1
Supercharged	37A only
Carburettor	1 Zenith or Solex
BHP approx.	T37: 60/T37A: 80–90
DRIVE TRAIN	
Clutch	Multi-plate, wet
Transmission	4-speed and reverse, gate change
CHASSIS	
Wheelbase	2.4 m (7 ft 10½ in)
Track	1.2 m (3 ft 11¼ in)
Suspension – front	½ elliptic
Suspension – rear	Reversed ¼ elliptic
Brakes	Cable
Tyre size	(modern) 19 × 4.50
Wheels	Rudge wire
PERFORMANCE	
Maximum speed	T37: 150 km/h (95 mph) T37A: 160+ km/h (100+ mph)

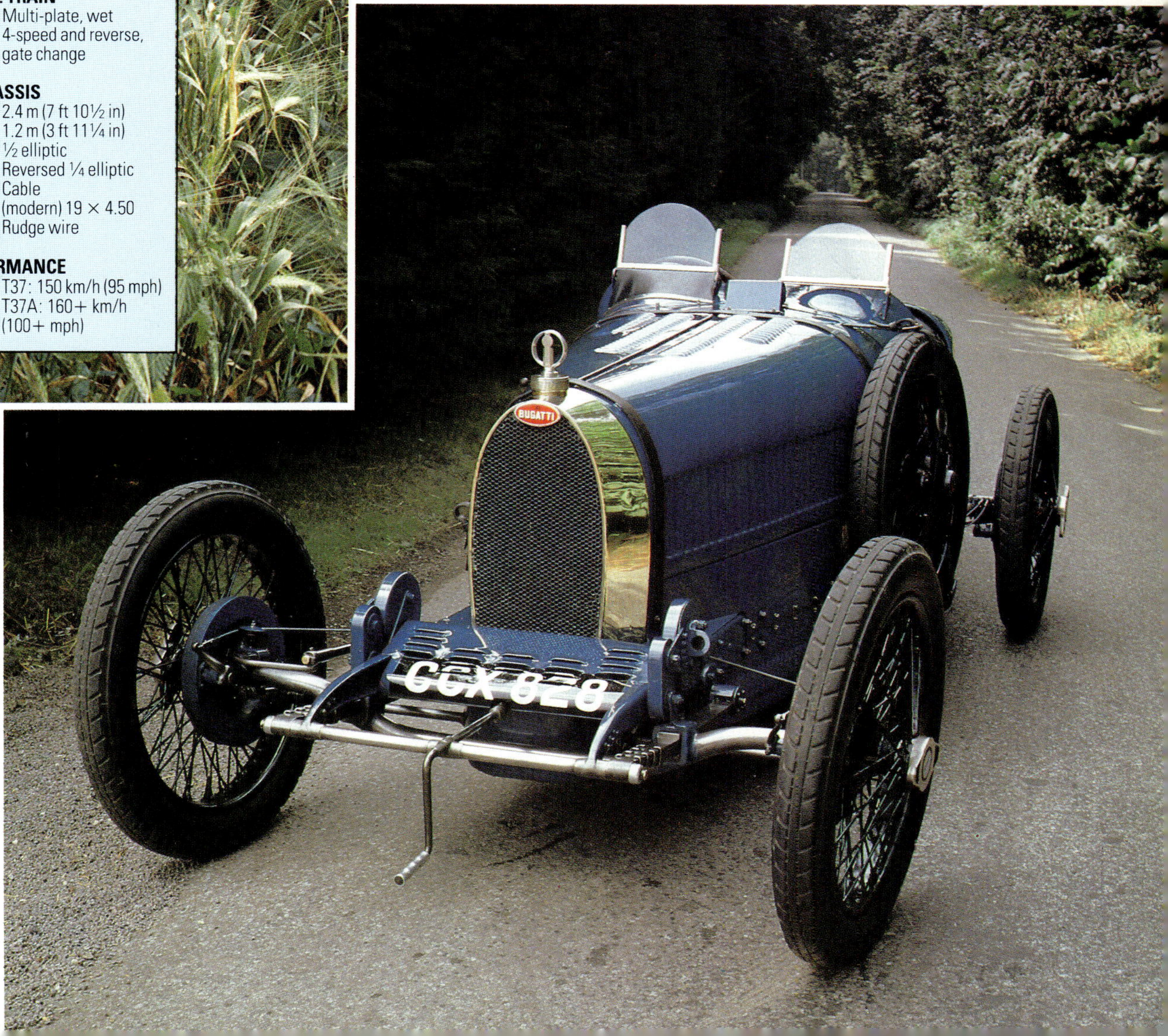

ABOVE The four-cylinder 1½-litre Type 37A was produced as a supercharged version of the Type 37, originally for Voiturette Grand Prix racing, but it proved popular for hill climbs and minor events, due to the simplicity of the engine. Like its eight-cylinder sister, it had a magneto mounted on the dash. Provided by Mr G Perfect.

RIGHT The combination of the simple plain bearing touring Type 40 1½-litre engine with a Grand Prix chassis produced a very popular version of the genuine GP car, designated the Type 37. This had coil ignition and a lighting system and appealed to the enthusiast as a sports car for regular use. Provided by Mr T. Cardy.

rear axle to lower the propeller shaft below the passengers' seats. This had a primary bevel pair followed by a pair of spur gears arranged one above the other which could easily be changed. In practice this seems to have been a source of unreliability as the casing tended to split under gear and axle loads.

The chassis was new, but retained Bugatti's reversed quarter elliptics, with a full-width base at the rear; leaf springs were also used at the front and the axle was hollow with the springs passing through, but now its two halves were threaded together in the centre through a sleeve with right- and left-hand threads. There were radius arms at each side taking front axle torque and acting on de Ram hydraulically loaded friction shock absorbers: complex, very expensive units. The brakes were of large diameter and cable-operated on traditional Bugatti lines. The wire-spoked Bugatti-designed wheels were remarkable: the spokes were radial and dealt only with radial loads, the torque from drive and braking being dealt with by a large number of dogs or teeth between the rim and the brake drum back plate. The rim had one detachable flange for tyre fitting, retained by a split ring. These wheels had a superb appearance, and although the rim and hub proper were light, the drum was of necessity heavy to absorb the energy of a fast and substantial car.

The Type 59 was powerful and fast, but its still traditional suspension and cable-operated brakes imposed limitations on its handling. In 1934 it managed several third places, and won in Belgium (René Dreyfus first, Antonio Brivio second), and at the Algiers GP (Jean-Pierre Wimille). The threat from the government-sponsored German and Italian cars was becoming very real, and Bugatti was forced to decide to abandon racing on the scale he had planned when building the cars. Four of them were sold to Britain, one evidently to Wimille, and one or two were retained at the factory. The British cars were used successfully at Brooklands and Donington by Lord Howe, Brian Lewis, and C.E.C. Martin, and Wimille had several successes over the next three years.

The Type 50B

At least one Type 59 chassis was fitted with a new and larger 4.7-litre engine known as the 50B, based initially on the general layout of the earlier Type 50 but virtually new throughout. The camshaft drive was at the front, as on the T50, and the block was in one piece, with the crank carried directly at the bottom of it (see final chapter).

There were, in fact, several versions of the 50B under development in the 1935–9 period of 3, 4.5 and 4.7 litres, and including versions for racing motor boats and, under French Government contract, for a twin-engined fighter aircraft that was being designed in Paris in 1937–9 by Louis de Monge, an experienced aircraft engineer, to bear the name Bugatti.

Wimille had some success in a Type 59 in various sports car events in 1936–9, sometimes with an unsupercharged 59 engine, sometimes with a 4½-litre 50B unit, including Comminges, Deauville in 1936, Pau, Bône and Marne in 1937 and Luxembourg in 1939, and occasionally in a fine-looking single-seater. There were indeed two single-seaters, a 4.7- and a 3-litre. The former still exists in the Musée National de l'Automobile (Schlumpf collection) at Mulhouse and was a fine car; it took part in the 1936 Vanderbilt Cup in the United States (coming in second) but was not seen much after this. However, it appeared at Prescott Hill Climb in Britain in July 1939, and then in the Bois de Boulogne immediately after the end of the war in Europe in 1945, winning the Coupe des Prisonniers. The 3-litre car turned up at the Cork GP in Ireland in 1938 but was unplaced. These cars 'kept the flag flying', but must have been a severe drain on resources.

The Type 57G 'tank'

Bugatti had built his first tank-like car, the Type 32, for the 1923 Grand Prix at Tours. This was soon abandoned because it looked so odd, and its short wheelbase gave it very poor handling characteristics.

However, in 1936 Ettore, perhaps now as a result of some logical thinking by his son Jean and some able collaborators, evolved a 'tank' version of the Type 57S sports-touring car. This was of relatively long wheelbase and enabled a good-looking and aerodynamically sound body to envelop the chassis. The cars had tuned 57S engines of the standard 3.3

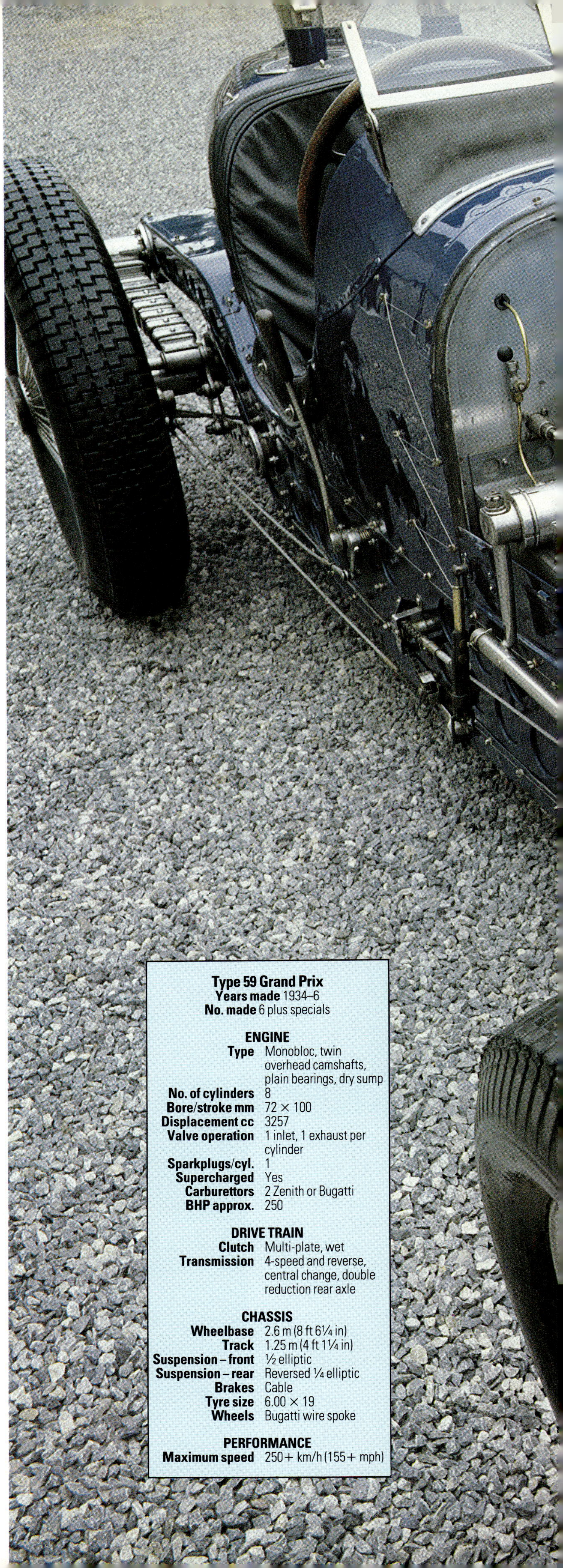

Bugatti's final attempt to lead the Grand Prix scene was with the magnificent Type 59, which had a 3.3-litre supercharged eight-cylinder engine with plain bearings, was full of interesting detail, such as its spoked wheels, and owed much to the influence of Jean Bugatti. The one illustrated here was a works car of 1934, bought in 1935 by Lord Howe, who left it behind after competing in the East London Grand Prix in South Africa in January 1936. It was brought back to Britain after World War 2 and is still raced by its present owner. Provided by Mr N. Corner.

Type 59 Grand Prix

Years made	1934–6
No. made	6 plus specials
ENGINE	
Type	Monobloc, twin overhead camshafts, plain bearings, dry sump
No. of cylinders	8
Bore/stroke mm	72 × 100
Displacement cc	3257
Valve operation	1 inlet, 1 exhaust per cylinder
Sparkplugs/cyl.	1
Supercharged	Yes
Carburettors	2 Zenith or Bugatti
BHP approx.	250
DRIVE TRAIN	
Clutch	Multi-plate, wet
Transmission	4-speed and reverse, central change, double reduction rear axle
CHASSIS	
Wheelbase	2.6 m (8 ft 6¼ in)
Track	1.25 m (4 ft 1¼ in)
Suspension – front	½ elliptic
Suspension – rear	Reversed ¼ elliptic
Brakes	Cable
Tyre size	6.00 × 19
Wheels	Bugatti wire spoke
PERFORMANCE	
Maximum speed	250+ km/h (155+ mph)

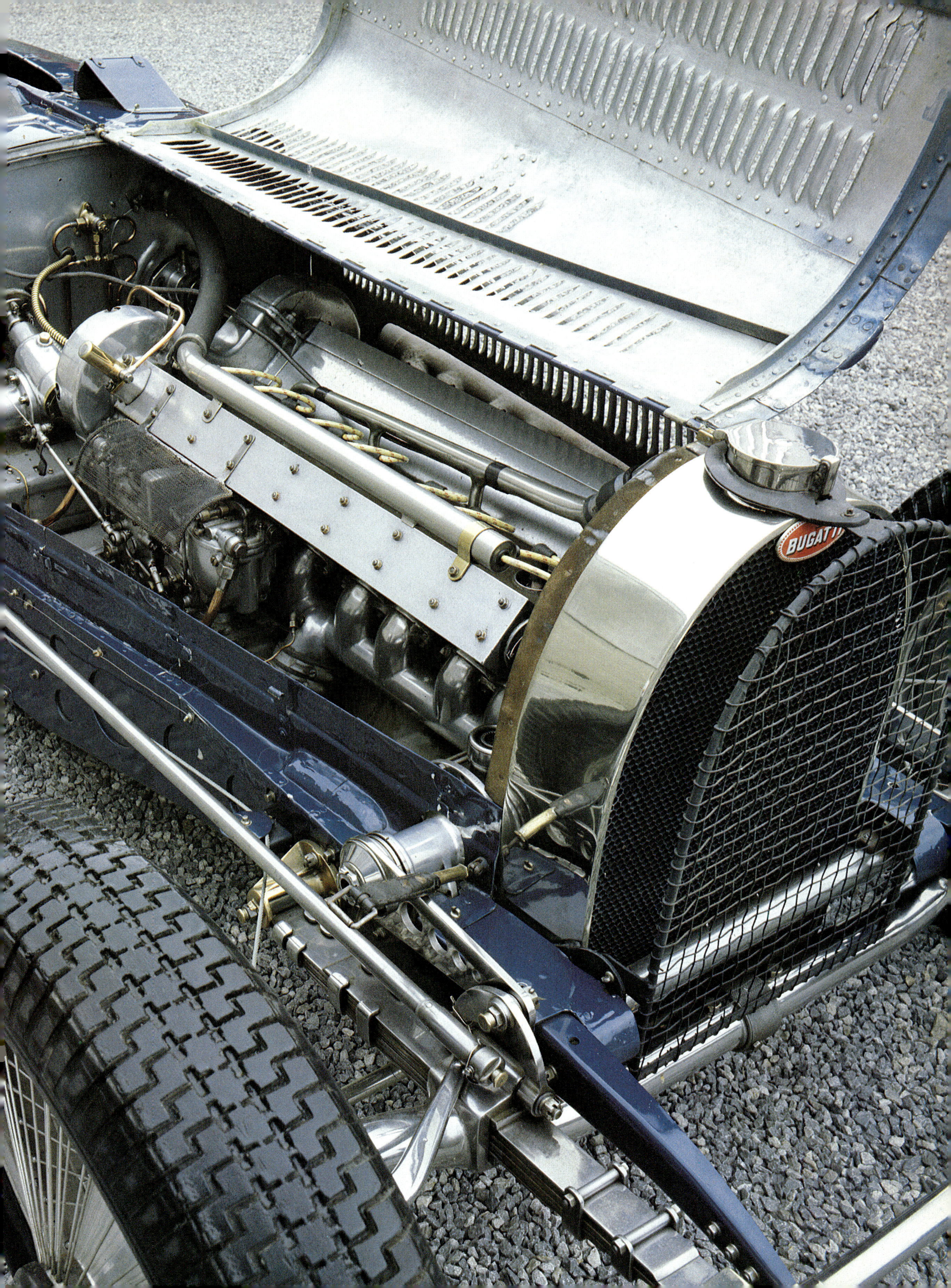
BUGATTI

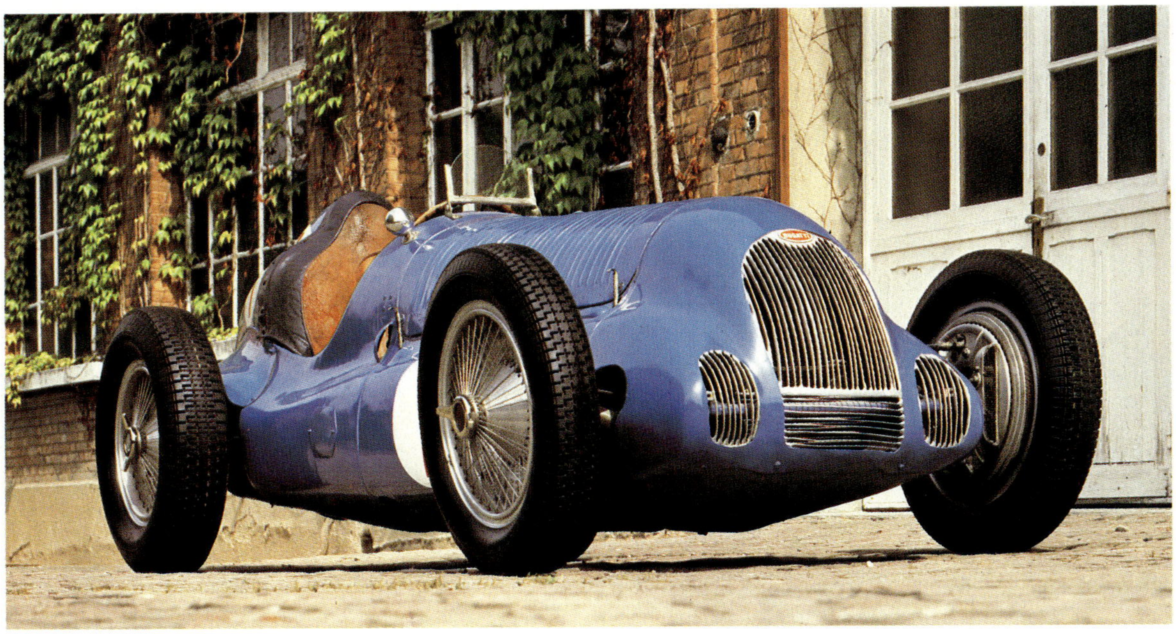

LEFT The single-seat 4.7-litre racing car, known as the Type 50B – which strictly refers only to the engine. The chassis is basically Type 59, with the final supercharged twin-cam engine designed by Jean Bugatti and his small team, led by Antoine Pichetto, at Molsheim. The car had a few pre-war successes. Provided by the Musée National de l'Automobile, Mulhouse.

RIGHT In Paris in 1944 Ettore Bugatti, with his right-hand man Noël Domboy, began to design a four-cylinder 1½-litre racing car, 76 × 82 mm, to be known as the 73C, for post-war use. A batch of 25 was rumoured, and if a driver wanted one he had to help finance the project. The design of the car was good, but development had only just begun at the time of Ettore's death in 1947. Provided by the Donington Collection.

litres capacity, unsupercharged but highly efficient nevertheless.

The Type 57G appeared first in the 1936 French Grand Prix at Montlhéry, three starting, and Wimille and Raymond Sommer winning. Later that year Wimille, Williams, Benoist and Pierre Veyron took a number of Class C world records, including the hour at 217.94 km/h (135.42 mph) and 24 hours at 199.45 km/h (123.93 mph). Success came also in the 24-hour race at Le Mans in 1937 when Wimille and Robert Benoist won at 137 km/h (85.13 mph).

Le Mans was cancelled in 1938 but in 1939 Bugatti entered a single new tank, this time a Type 57C supercharged car, based on a normal touring frame; Wimille and Veyron won at 139.21 km/h (86.50 mph) after a splendid run, Jean Bugatti claiming afterwards that the bonnet or hood was never opened during the race, and that a top speed of over 255 km/h (158 mph) was attainable.

Tragedy came soon after. Jean Bugatti, one evening in August, decided to test the car being prepared for the La Baule Grand Prix; two colleagues closed the main road between Strasbourg and Molsheim by stopping traffic while Jean did a high-speed run. Unfortunately a cyclist appeared in his path from a side road when he was at high speed. Avoiding the man, the car left the road and was wrecked, Jean being killed instantly. So Ettore lost his talented son, war came two weeks later, and for the second time in his lifetime he had to leave Molsheim in front of an invading German army. The factory never recovered from the dual blow.

The Type 73C prototype

Bugatti's final fling in 1944–5 was an attempt to design a 1½-litre racer for sale after the war. However, Bugatti died in 1947 before the car materialized, although the remaining son Roland struggled on with a prototype which was never completed. This and two spare frames and engines were sold by the factory in the 1960s and more or less completed. One lies in private hands and the other two in museums: the Donington Collection in Derbyshire (see photo opposite) and the Musée National de l'Automobile (Schlumpf collection) at Mulhouse.

The Type 251: a Bugatti only in name

In 1953–4 the Molsheim works under the direction of Roland Bugatti engaged the Italian designer Gioacchino Colombo to design an eight-cylinder Grand Prix car for the company, but it was a Bugatti only in name. The transversely mounted engine was of 2½ litres, 75 × 68.8 mm (2432 cc) with overhead camshafts driven from the middle of the crankshaft, as on Ettore's Type 44. The frame was tubular and Roland insisted that Colombo should use a rigid tubular front axle, guided in the centre by a pin moving in a slot! At the rear there was another rigid axle, with de Dion drive. The Type 251 was first tested in October 1955 and then was entered for the French Grand Prix at Reims in 1956; Maurice Trintignant managed some 18 laps before he gave up, stating that the car was a death trap! It went back to the works and was never used again. It is now in dignified obscurity in the Musée National de l'Automobile at Mulhouse, where the badge on the front creates interest and allows it to be labelled a Bugatti.

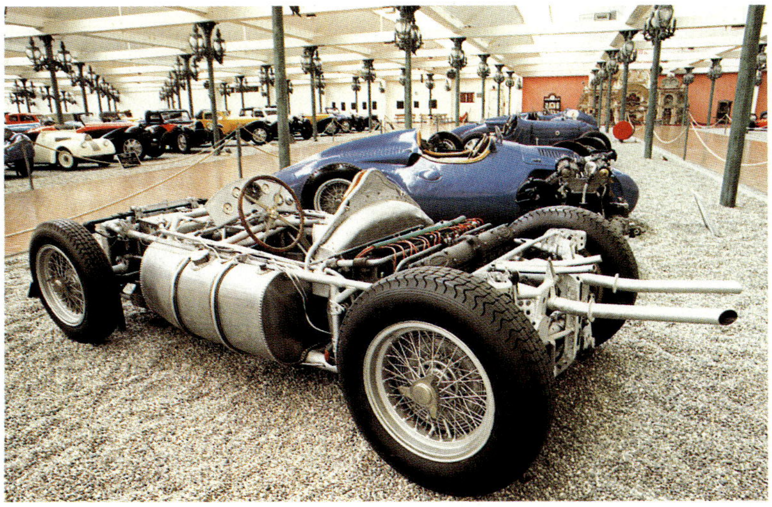

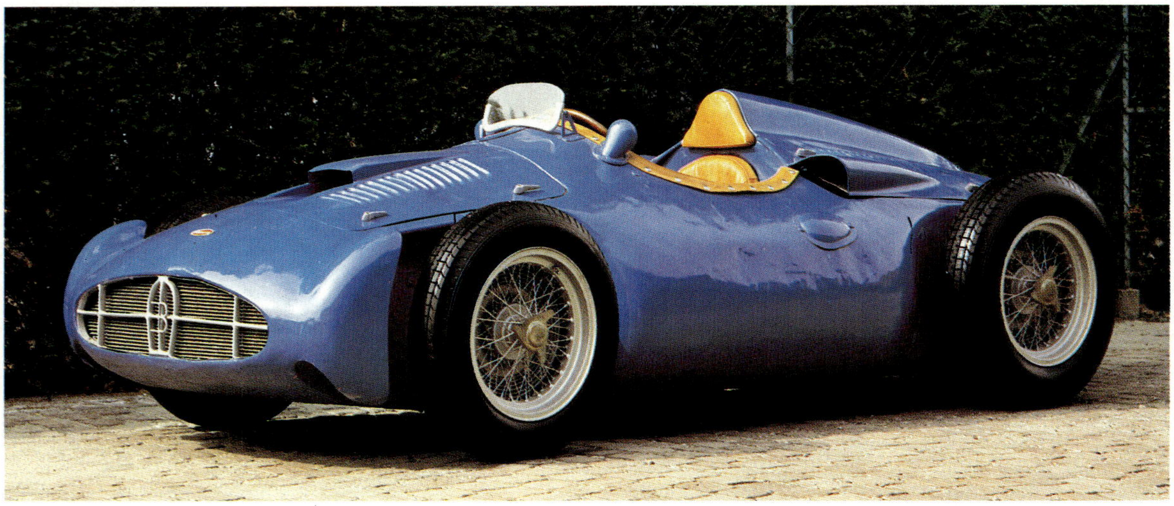

ABOVE AND LEFT Not really a Bugatti, in that no Bugatti with design experience had a hand in it, the 251 was a post-war attempt initiated by Ettore's surviving son Roland in the 1950s to produce a competitive Grand Prix car. Large – but not large enough – sums of money the ailing company could ill afford went into the partial development of this design by the Italian Gioacchino Colombo, and it is clear in retrospect that the end of Bugatti as an automobile manufacturer was being hastened thereby. Fritz Schlumpf acquired the remains of the project. Provided by the Musée National de l'Automobile, Mulhouse.

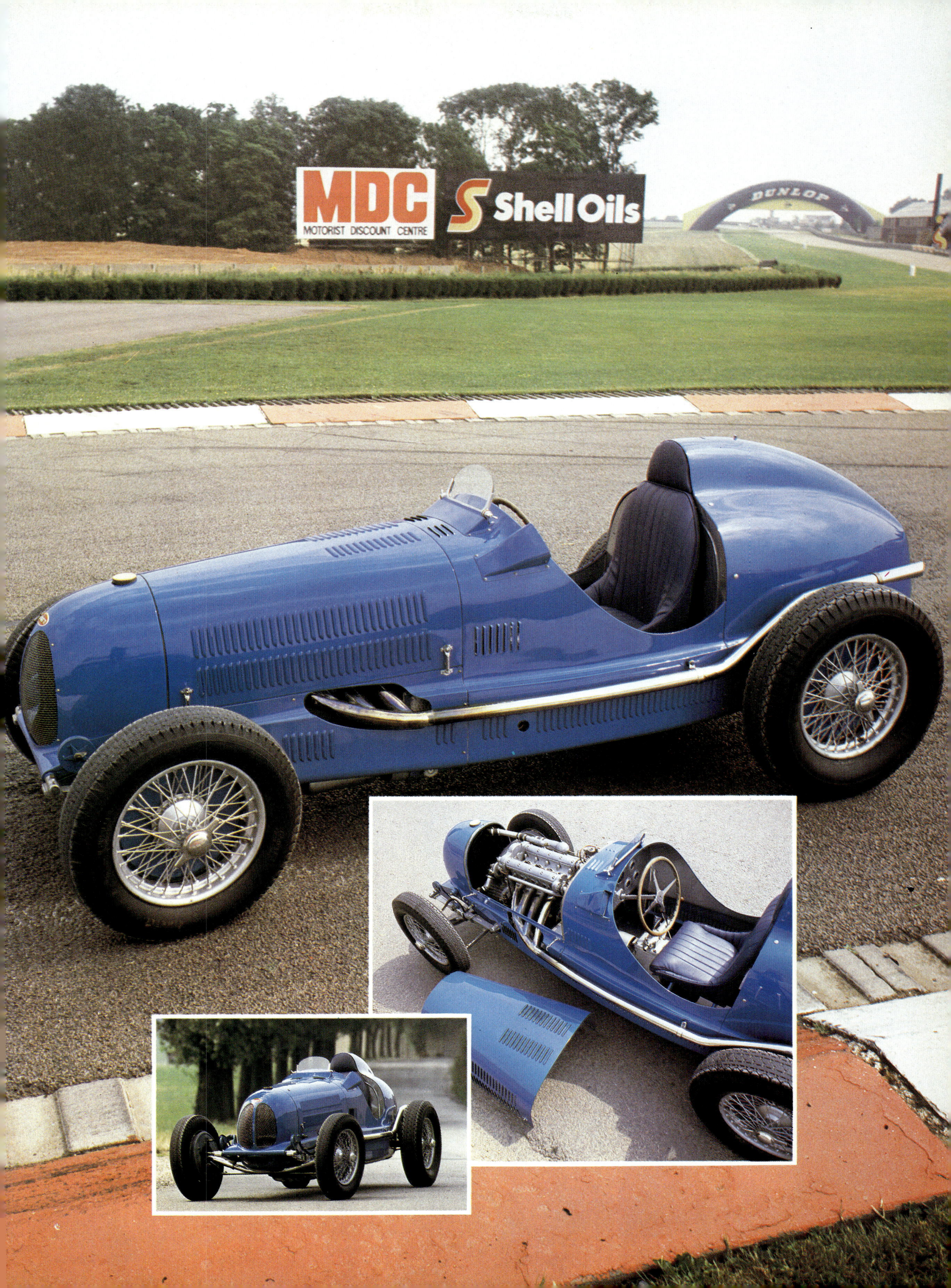
MDC
MOTORIST DISCOUNT CENTRE
Shell Oils
DUNLOP

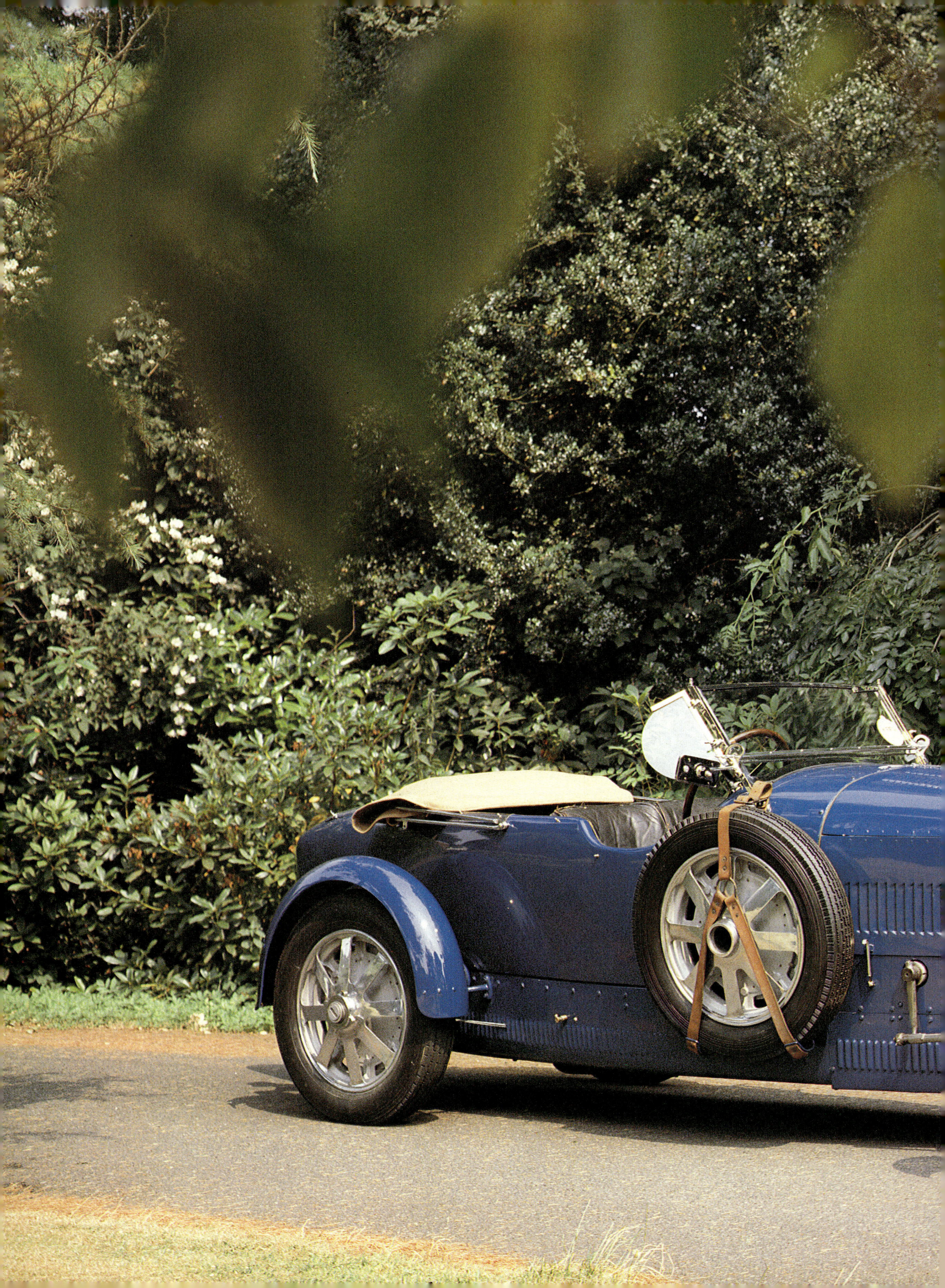

THE Grand Sport Bugattis

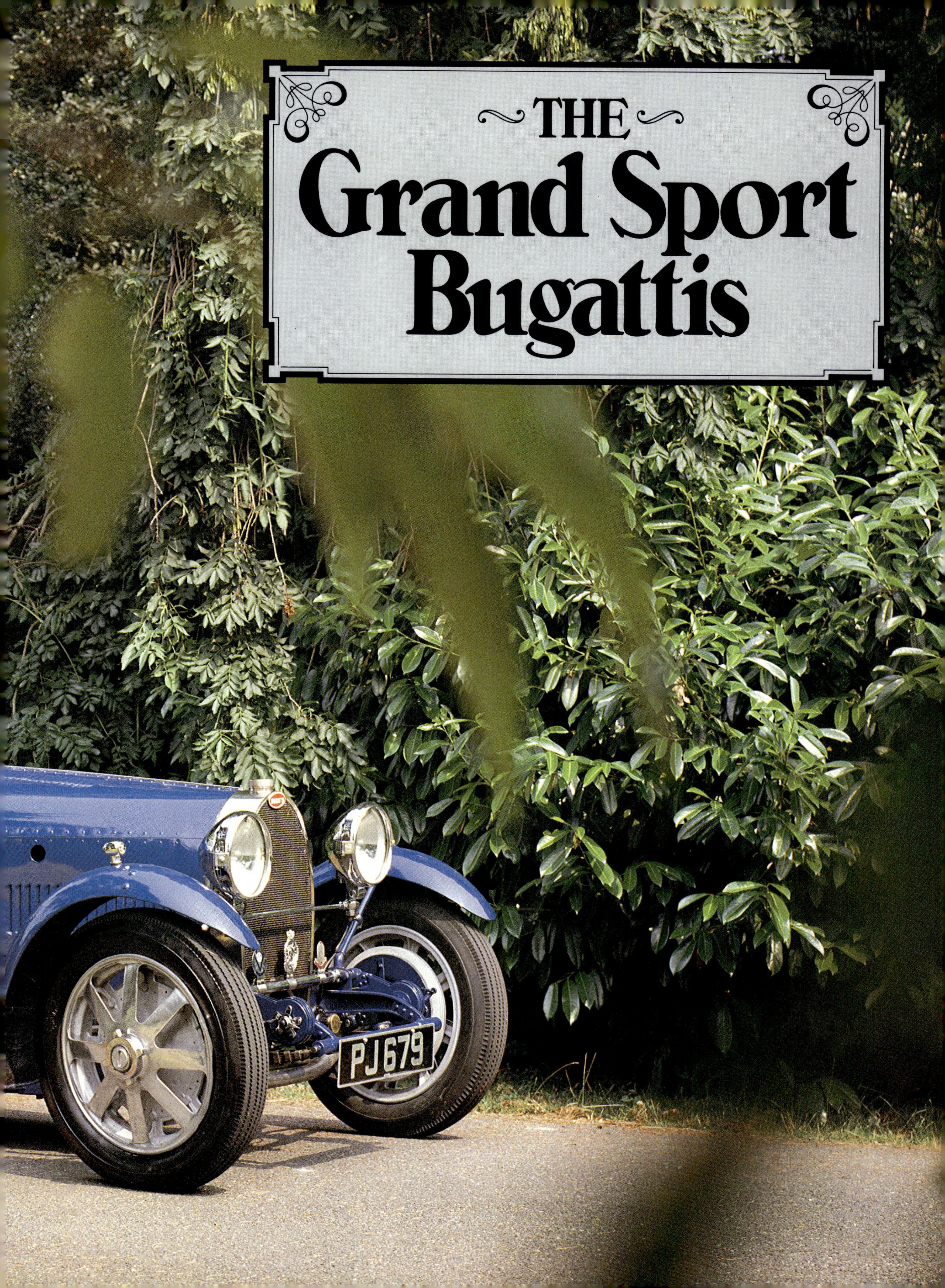

PRECEDING PAGES *The classic Type 43 Grand Sport, the first genuine 160 km/h (100 mph) sports car. Its eight-cylinder supercharged engine is virtually identical to that of the racing Type 35B. This is thought to be the car driven by Sir Malcolm Campbell, rebuilt after its disastrous fire in the 1928 Ulster TT. Provided by Mr G. Perfect.*

SINCE the earliest days of the motor car there has always been a demand for a version that could exploit the main attribute of mechanical road transport, namely speed. Racing was a sport for the track, but it led to a demand for something equivalent that could be used on the road by those who could afford it. A few racing cars were adapted for road use before the First World War, but perhaps it was the 30–98 Vauxhall or the 3-litre Bentley after the war that first offered a 'Grand Sport' car to the public. In Britain it was the Vauxhall by which the others were judged, a four-cylinder 4- or 4½-litre car with 'long legs', good acceleration and a maximum speed of about 140–50 km/h (85–90 mph).

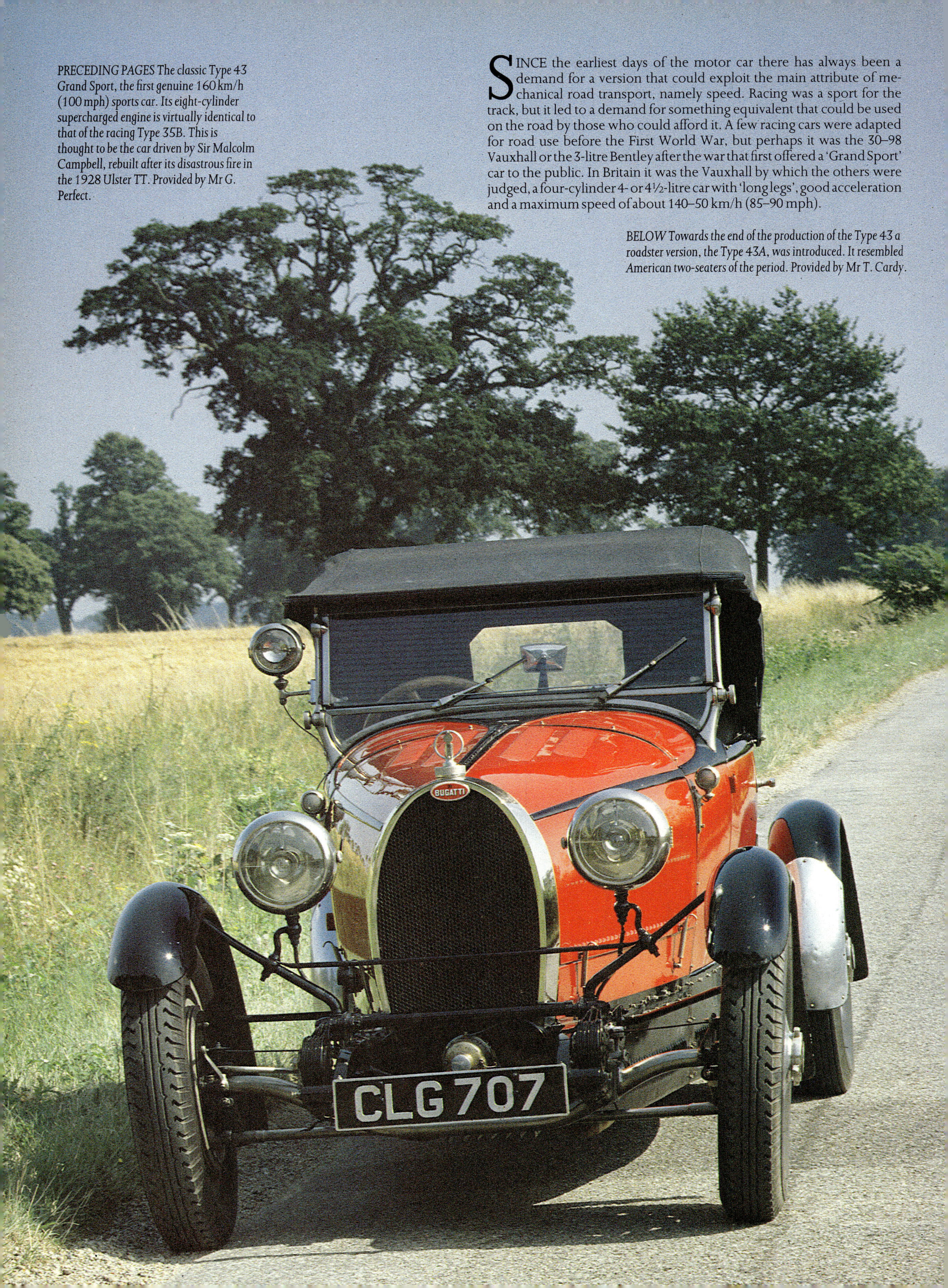

BELOW *Towards the end of the production of the Type 43 a roadster version, the Type 43A, was introduced. It resembled American two-seaters of the period. Provided by Mr T. Cardy.*

But taking a long view of the development of the sports car there are two important landmarks to be noted when Bugatti took a successful racing chassis and adapted it as a production 'Grand Sport' car for road use. He did this for the first time in 1927 when he converted the successful racing Type 35B into the T43, and later in 1931 he repeated it by turning the T51 into the T55. Thus Bugatti can be given credit for evolving the first 100 mph (160 km/h) road car, although the 'blower' Bentleys and 1750 Alfa Romeos were then in the same mould!

The great Type 43

The outstanding feature of the normal unblown Type 35 racing car when driven was its almost startling flexibility. It could 'potter' in top gear, ignition retarded, at 32 km/h (20 mph), and accelerate away cleanly. When the supercharged Type 35C came out at the end of 1926 it had the same characteristics, enhanced indeed by the blower, but with a radiator not really large enough to allow prolonged idling, which was not expected of a racing car, and with bodywork hardly suitable for road use.

The 2.3-litre Type 35B appeared in early 1927 and at the same time came the Type 43 on a new frame with waisted side longerons to allow the body to follow their contours as in the racing car, but with the rear reversed quarter-elliptic springs outrigged to full width. The engine was identical to the Type 35B (eight-cylinder, 60 × 100 mm, 2.3 litres, three valves per cylinder, Roots supercharger running at engine speed), although the lower crankcase had narrower rear mounting arms to fit the normal touring type front end of the frame.

The front and rear axles and gearbox came straight from the Type 38 (see page 28), but now cast aluminium wheels were used as on the racing car. As the car was heavier these wheels had the larger brakes and drum diameter from the Type 38, but the wheels still had detachable rims. Although the first of the 35B Grand Prix cars retained the smaller brakes, they were soon fitted with the large-drum wheels from the Type 43.

The radiator was from the Type 38, and there was no fan. The dash was similar to the racing car, and used the same magneto mounting, but had more instruments and electric lighting and starting. A dynamo was driven from the front of the engine and the starter was clamped to the rear of the crankcase on the right-hand arm.

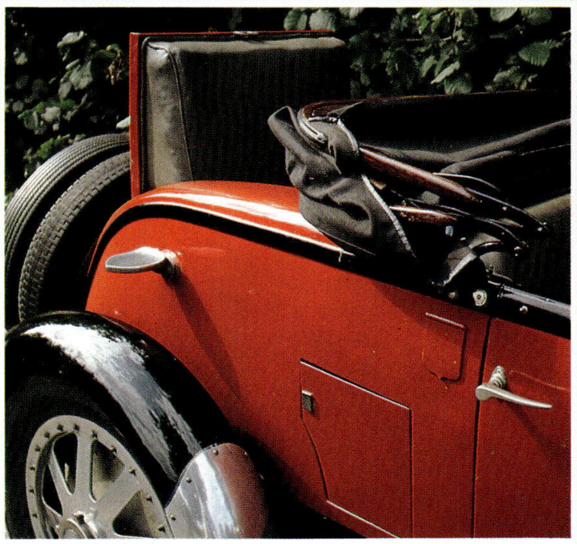

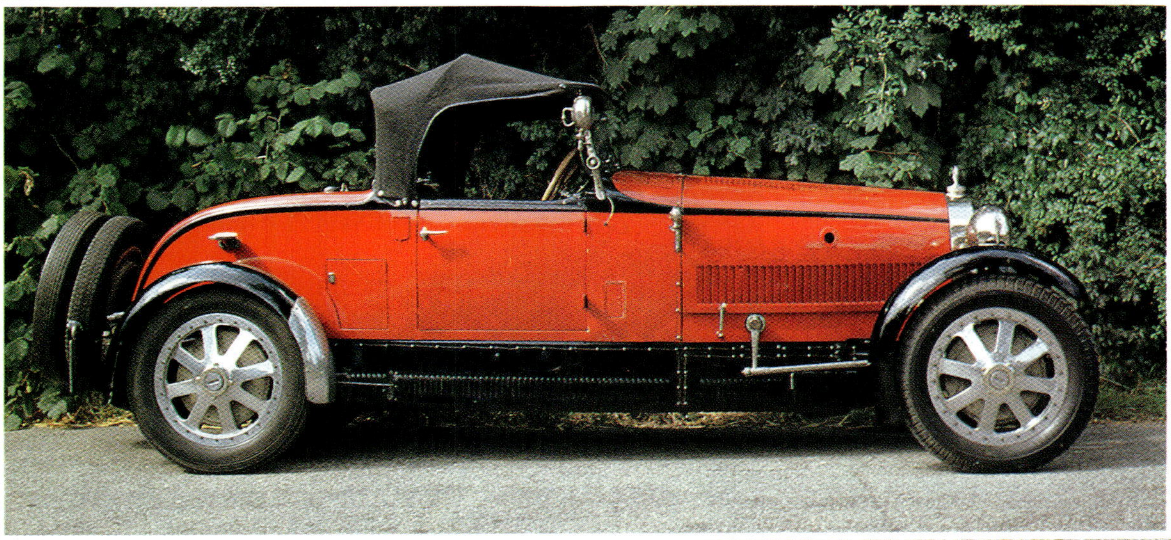

Type 43/43A Grand Sport

Years made	T43: 1927–30/T43A: 1931–2
No. made	160
ENGINE	
Type	Two 4-cylinder monoblocs, overhead camshaft, roller bearing crankshaft and rods
No. of cylinders	8
Bore/stroke mm	60 × 100
Displacement cc	2262
Valve operation	2 inlet, 1 exhaust per cylinder
Sparkplugs/cyl.	1
Supercharged	Yes
Carburettor	1 Zenith or Solex
BHP approx.	120
DRIVE TRAIN	
Clutch	Multi-plate, wet
Transmission	4-speed and reverse, central change
CHASSIS	
Wheelbase	2.97 m (9 ft 0½ in)
Track	1.25 m (4 ft 1¼ in)
Suspension – front	½ elliptic
Suspension – rear	Reversed ¼ elliptic
Brakes	Cable
Tyre size	(modern) 5.00 × 19
Wheels	Cast aluminium alloy, integral brake drum, detachable rim
PERFORMANCE	
Maximum speed	170 km/h (105 mph)

The body drew inspiration from the racing car, with a fine line in plan and elevation, but had only a single door on the left for the sake of body stiffness. The passenger's seat folded and you could climb into a small compartment at the rear, two of you if you were small enough! Indeed the official designation was '3½ places'.

The windscreen was fixed and had no wiper, but many cars converted to a folding screen. A light tubular frame carried the hood, which was very well thought out and gave the car a splendid appearance when erected, and even better when folded away.

The first Type 43 was delivered in March 1927, and the car was an immediate success in spite of its high price – more indeed than the racing model. The total production was some 160 cars, mainly between 1927 and 1930, with a few during the following three years and a couple thereafter.

Ettore himself used to demonstrate its flexibility by putting the car in top gear, starting it on the starter, and accelerating away! Certainly, although not able to corner as quickly as the racing car, its road performance was excellent and obviously suitable for fast long-distance runs, cruising happily and with surprising comfort at about 125 km/h (80 mph).

It was an automobile for the well-to-do sportsman or woman – a car that could compete in Alpine trials or rallies, or be raced in handicap events at Brooklands, and especially hill climbs. The factory sponsored teams in the 1928 and 1929 Tourist Trophy race in Ulster. In 1928 the three cars were driven by Lord Howe, Malcolm Campbell and the works driver Dutilleux, who was the only one to finish. Howe managed the fastest lap in his class before retiring, but Campbell's Type 43 had a spectacular fire at the pits, which extensively damaged it.

In 1929 four works cars were entered in the TT again, three starting (with Divo, Williams and Count Carlo Conelli) but unhappily none finished. Type 43s also appeared at long-distance races at Brooklands, and at Phoenix Park in Dublin, but generally without much success. No doubt the extra weight of the car put a heavier strain on the engine and running gear, which nevertheless did not have much effect on its performance in short events, or in high-speed road use. However, it has always been a much sought-after model since its appearance in 1927, with a great reputation due to its combination of performance and suitability for long-distance touring. The typical performance today is a top speed just over 160 km/h (100 mph) with windscreen up, a standing quarter mile in less than 17½ seconds and very good brakes by vintage standards.

By 1929-30 the single-door Grand Sport body was proving unpopular for normal usage, and the American-style roadster with its rear-folding 'rumble' seat ('dickey' in Britain, *spider* in France) was in vogue. Bugatti now produced a Jean-inspired version, called the 43A with two doors and the hinged *spider* at the back and an elaborated dashboard; there was even a hatch for golf clubs! The body was heavier than the earlier version and the mechanism was less accessible, but it kept sales going.

The real problem with all 43s in the hands of owners who had paid high initial prices lay in the long-term unreliability of the Grand Prix crankshaft. The rollers on its connecting rods had an extremely hard time, especially if the oil was not allowed to warm up gently; the rollers had to accelerate and decelerate during each revolution of the engine – an inherent feature of an engine with a necessarily short connecting rod – and would skid if the engine was not allowed to warm up at constant speed. This skidding then wore flats on the rollers. Carbon deposits from the rich mixture on which the engine ran polluted the oil and eventually blocked the oil ways in the crankshaft.

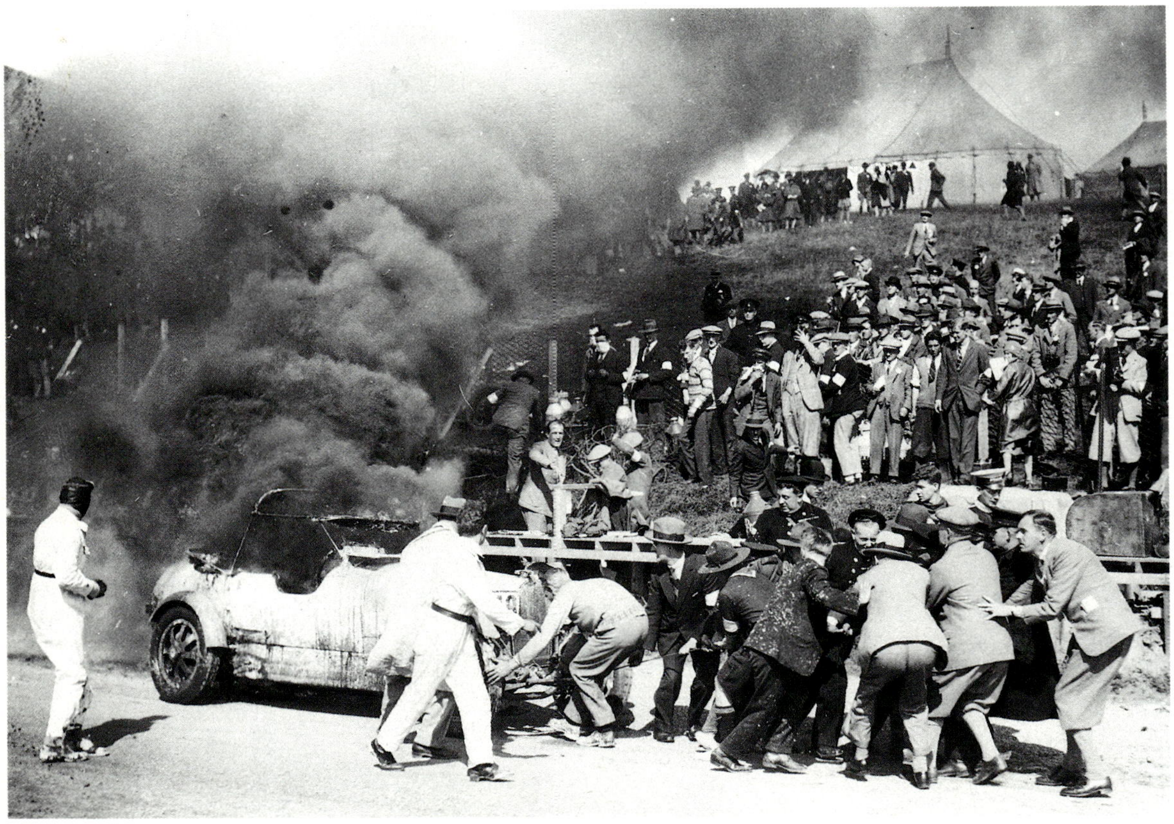

ABOVE Campbell's car on fire at the pits in the 1928 Ulster TT (see below).

Type 55 Super Sport
Years made 1932–5
No. made 38

ENGINE	
Type	Monobloc, twin overhead camshafts, roller bearing crank and rods
No. of cylinders	8
Bore/stroke mm	60 × 100
Displacement cc	2262
Valve operation	1 inlet, 1 exhaust per cylinder
Sparkplugs/cyl.	1
Supercharged	Yes
Carburettor	1 Zenith or Solex
BHP approx.	130
DRIVE TRAIN	
Clutch	Multi-plate, dry
Transmission	4-speed and reverse, central ball change
CHASSIS	
Wheelbase	2.75 m (9 ft 0¼ in)
Track	1.25 m (4 ft 1¼ in)
Suspension – front	½ elliptic
Suspension – rear	Reversed ¼ elliptic
Brakes	Cable
Tyre size	5.00 × 19
Wheels	Cast aluminium alloy, well base, integral brake drum
PERFORMANCE	
Maximum speed	180 km/h (112 mph)

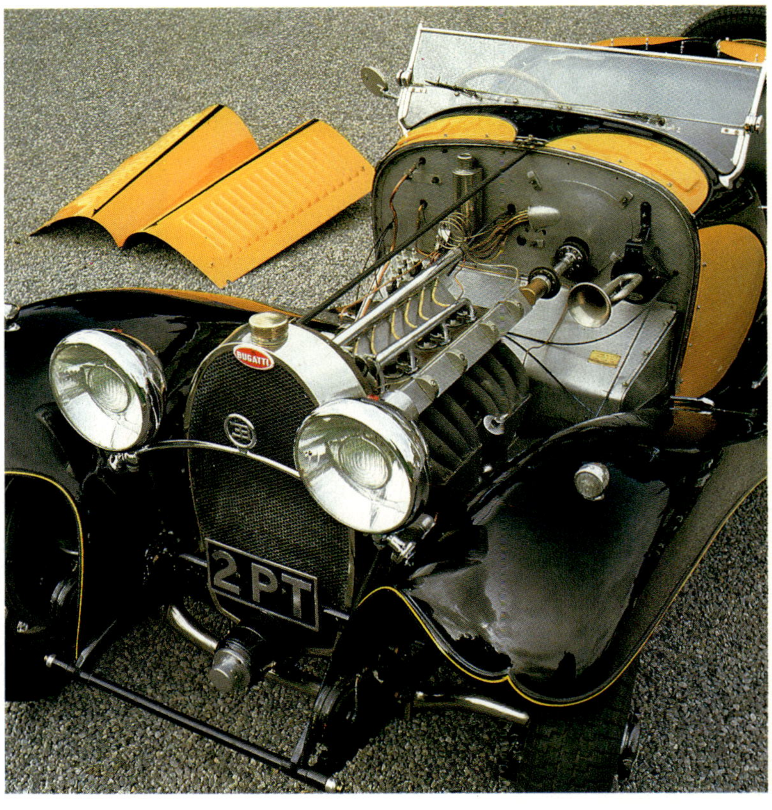

RIGHT AND FACING PAGE To many the Jean Bugatti-designed Type 55 roadster is the most beautiful sports car ever produced. Superb performance and handling combine with the flowing lines. Provided by Mr N. Corner.

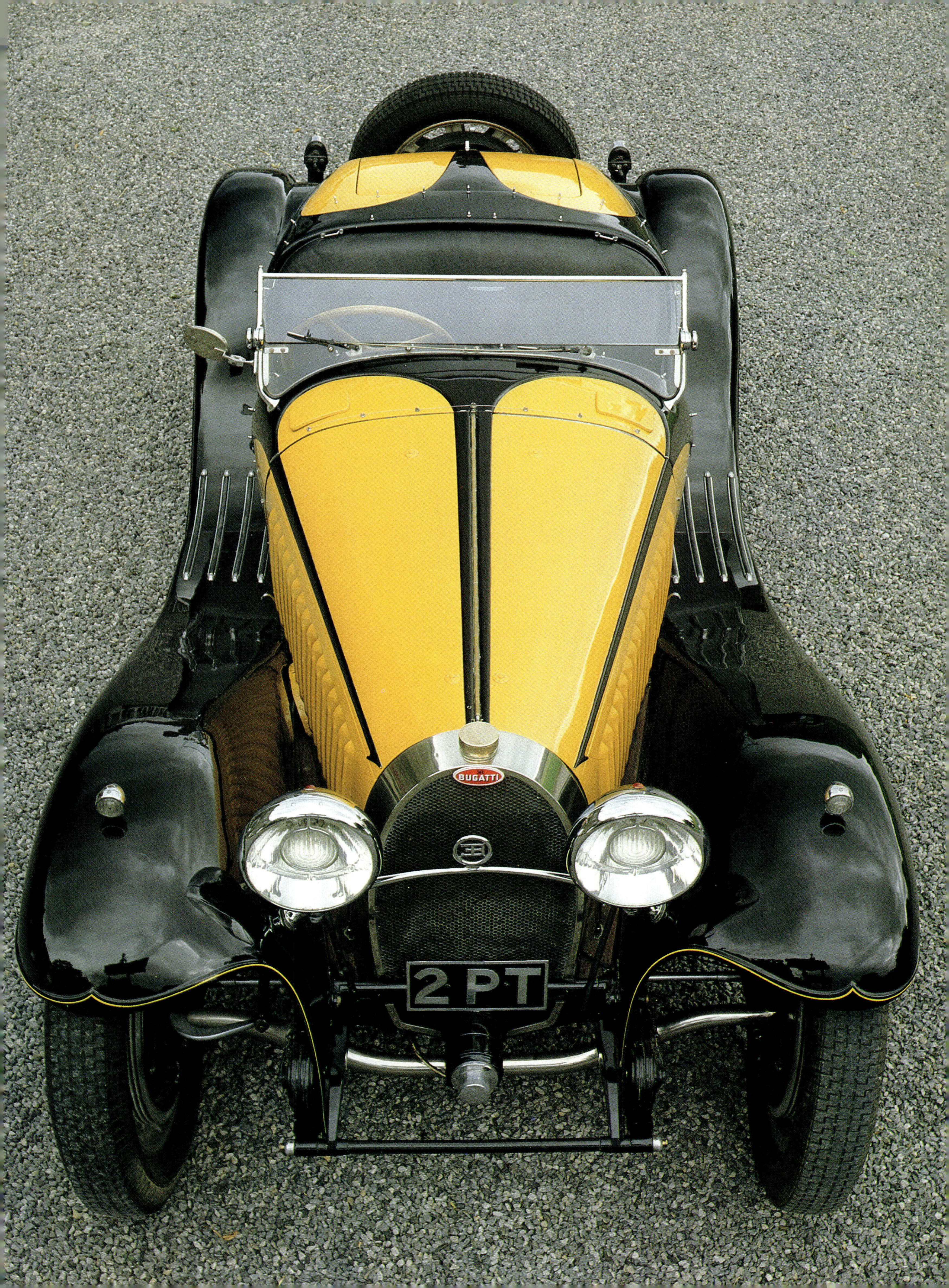
BUGATTI
2 PT

A racing 35B would not do a large mileage annually and would in practice be dismantled regularly. A well-to-do owner of an expensive Type 43 would often drive his car too fast when cold and was unlikely to take his engine to pieces very often (say every 10,000 km) to clean and re-roller the crank. The result was that many a Type 43 suffered connecting rod bearing seizure, usually with the rod coming through the crankcase, to the owner's great displeasure and cost!

The beautiful Type 55

The mystique of a Grand Sport Bugatti, the performance and perhaps the superb noise from the exhaust, the blower and all those gears and ball races continued to draw customers to the best Molsheim could offer. Jean Bugatti, whose eye for line and interest in bodywork were developing, now produced what by any standard is an aesthetic and engineering masterpiece, the Type 55. This was based on the development of the successful Type 51 twin-cam racing car into a Super Sport car in the same way that the 43 had grown out of the 35B.

There were a number of Type 45/47 chassis frames at Molsheim from the abortive 16-cylinder vehicle which had not gone into production, although a few had been used as the 4.9-litre Type 54 racing car. In 1931 at Jean's instigation a 2.3-litre Type 51 engine was fitted to one of these frames, using T43 front and rear axles, and a touring gearbox with ball change in a new cast casing straddling the frame, together with a new radiator, to produce the Type 55 chassis.

For this chassis Jean sketched out a two-seat roadster body without doors, but cut down sides to allow access for a driver and passenger, and a curved rear end cleverly waisted, along the lines of the T43A. Long flowing wings with running boards were used at the side, curved and domed in front elevation, with separate Scintilla headlamps. There was a small *spider* seat at the rear and a pair of spare wheels at the back, the well-base cast aluminium wheels of the racing car being retained. A pretty two-seat coupé with a fixed head body and the same mudguard treatment was designed and produced at the same time, although the open car proved the more popular.

The result was a flamboyant, rather 'Americanized' two-seater, probably the most beautiful sports car of all time. Aesthetic judgement of the car's appearance may be subjective, but no one could question its magnificent performance. The works talked of a top speed of 195 km/h (over 120 mph), which was no doubt a little exaggerated but 175 km/h (nearly 110 mph) was certainly not: remarkable for 1932, and with acceleration to match. Although the T43 liked a rich mixture for power, and suffered sooting of plugs at low speed in traffic, the twin-cam engine's combustion was much cleaner, docile in urban use and trouble free. *Motor Sport* tested a roadster in July 1932 and was enthusiastic:

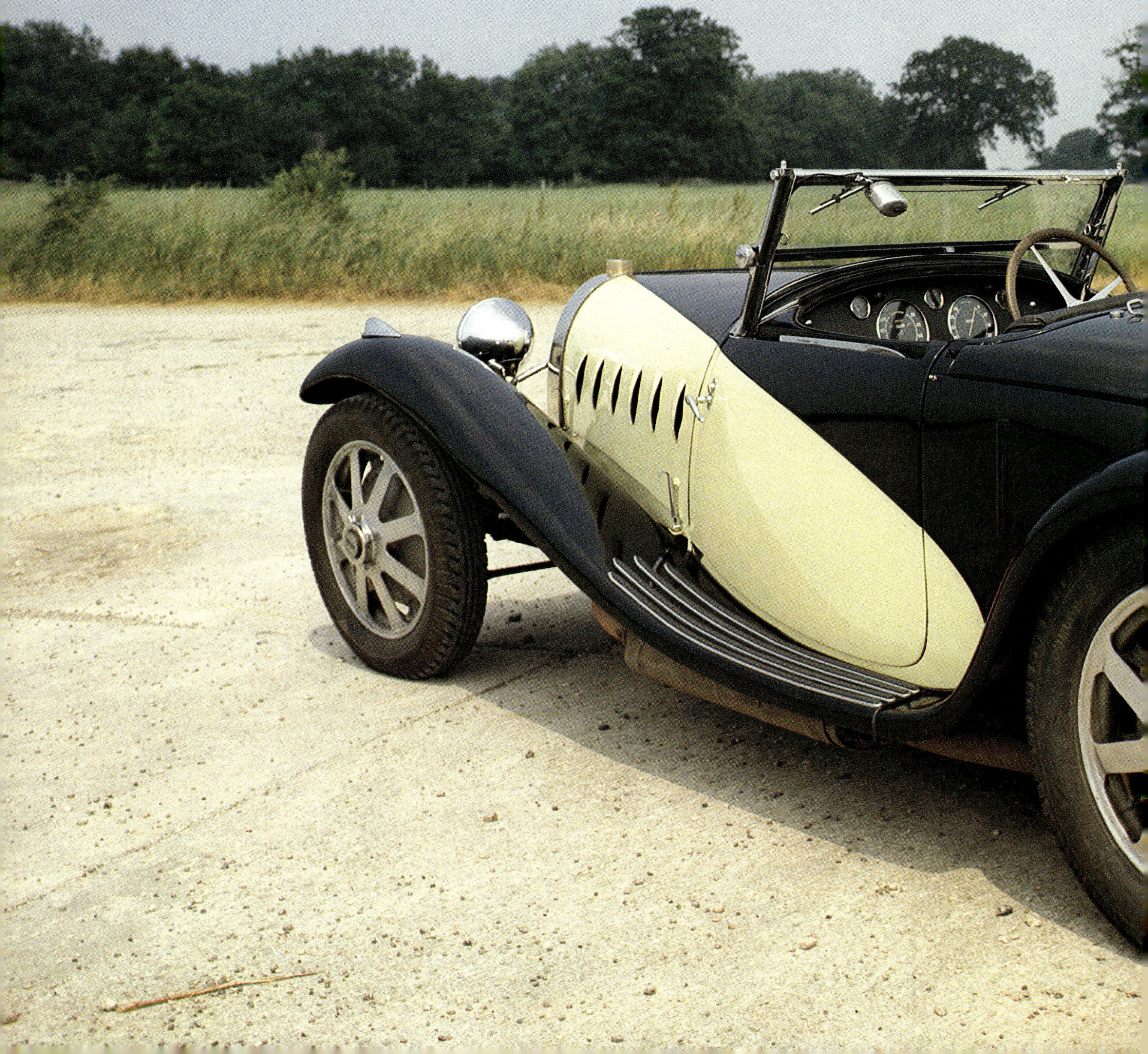

The car we tested was fitted with a smart and comfortable two-seater body finished in black and red, with a large luggage compartment at the rear. Pneumatic upholstery was installed, and the whole car was a great advance on the rather spartan bodies which were traditional on the faster Bugattis.

The streets of South London presented their usual crowded appearance and provided a good test of the '2.3's tractability. The exhaust note is subdued, and in top gear one hears nothing more than a pleasant hum. Changing down to accelerate, one caught a suggestion of the real character of the car, the blower and its gears making a most stimulating sound which can only be rendered as 'hurra-a-a-,' a remark with which we entirely agreed!

In the new 2.3 the driving position is much more upright than in the average sports car, deep wells being provided on each propellor shaft. The steering wheel comes right into one's lap, with the gear lever, brake, and ignition control under the left hand. A sloping windscreen does its work effectively, and altogether the car is perfection to drive. The crowded state of the roads made it inadvisable to exceed 100 m.p.h. although we were told that at 5.30 one morning the speedometer did creep round to 112. At speeds above about 80 the sound of the blower and its gears rises above audibility, and one glides along as in a fast aeroplane, with no sound but the rushing wind. Cornering, of course, is effortless, and if a bend is taken too fast, the car seems to correct the error without help from the driver.

Production of the Type 55 was much less than of the 43, only 38 being made compared with 160 of the latter. The first car was shown at the Automobile Show in Paris in October 1931, going to the Duc de la Trémoille; others soon went to the Bugatti race driver Meo Costantini and King Leopold of Belgium (a faithful *Bugattiste*). Twenty-three cars were delivered in 1932 and the rest followed in the next three years.

Most of the cars had the Jean Bugatti roadster body. A few chassis carried bodies by well-known coachbuilders such as Van Vooren and Figoni. Today the Type 55 is one of the most sought-after models.

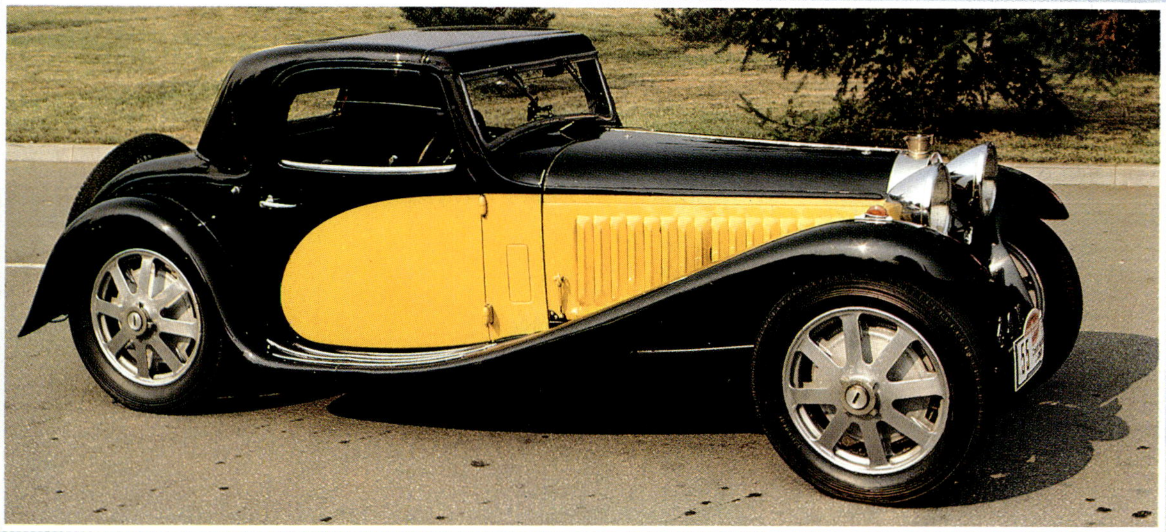

The Type 55 factory-built coupé (left) is as handsome as its roadster sister. Below is a Figoni-bodied car originally entered in the 1932 Le Mans 24-hour race with Weymann coachwork, driven unsuccessfully by Louis Chiron and Guy Bouriat. The car was then fitted with this body and used successfully in pre-war rallies. Provided by Mr G. St John.

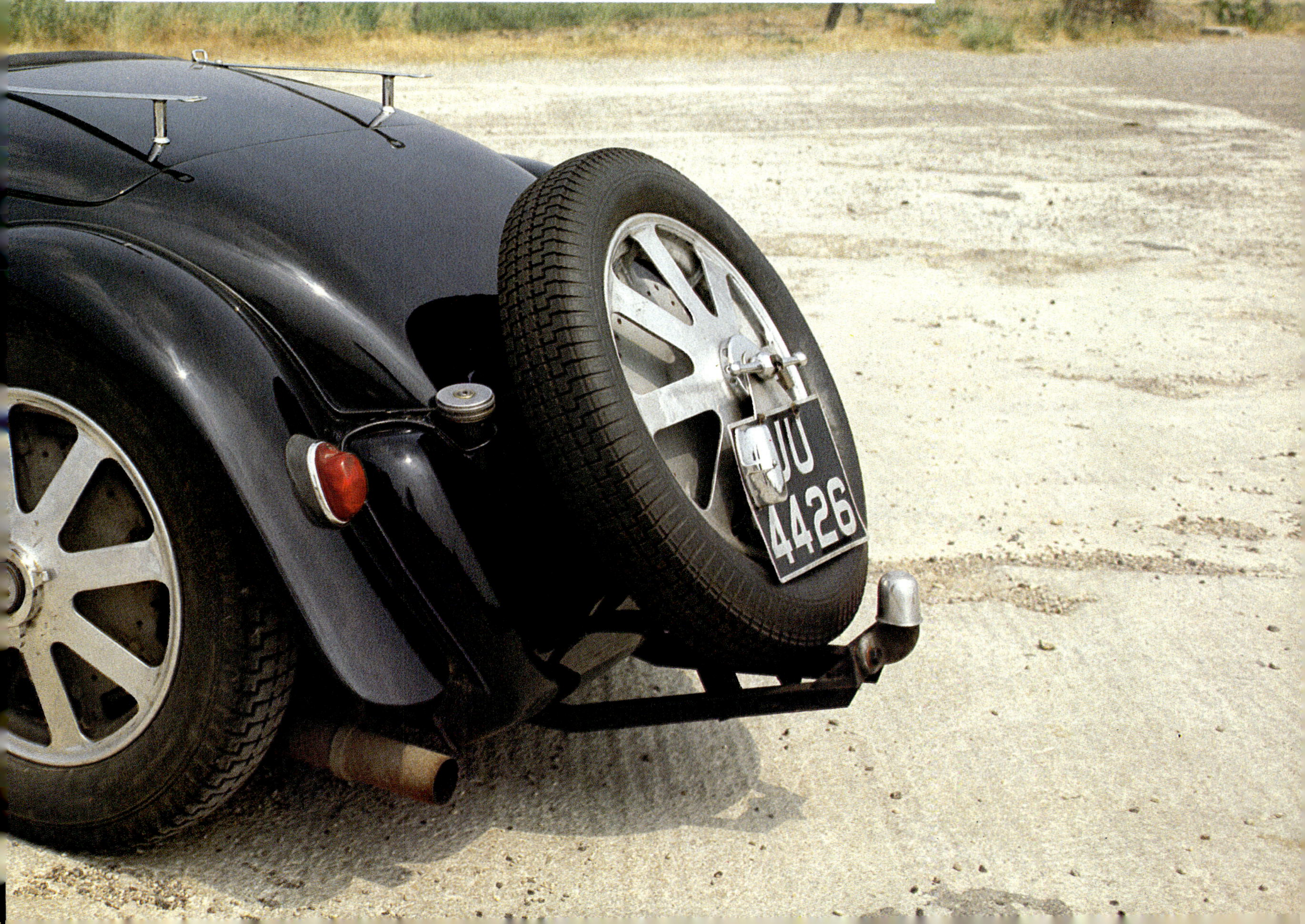

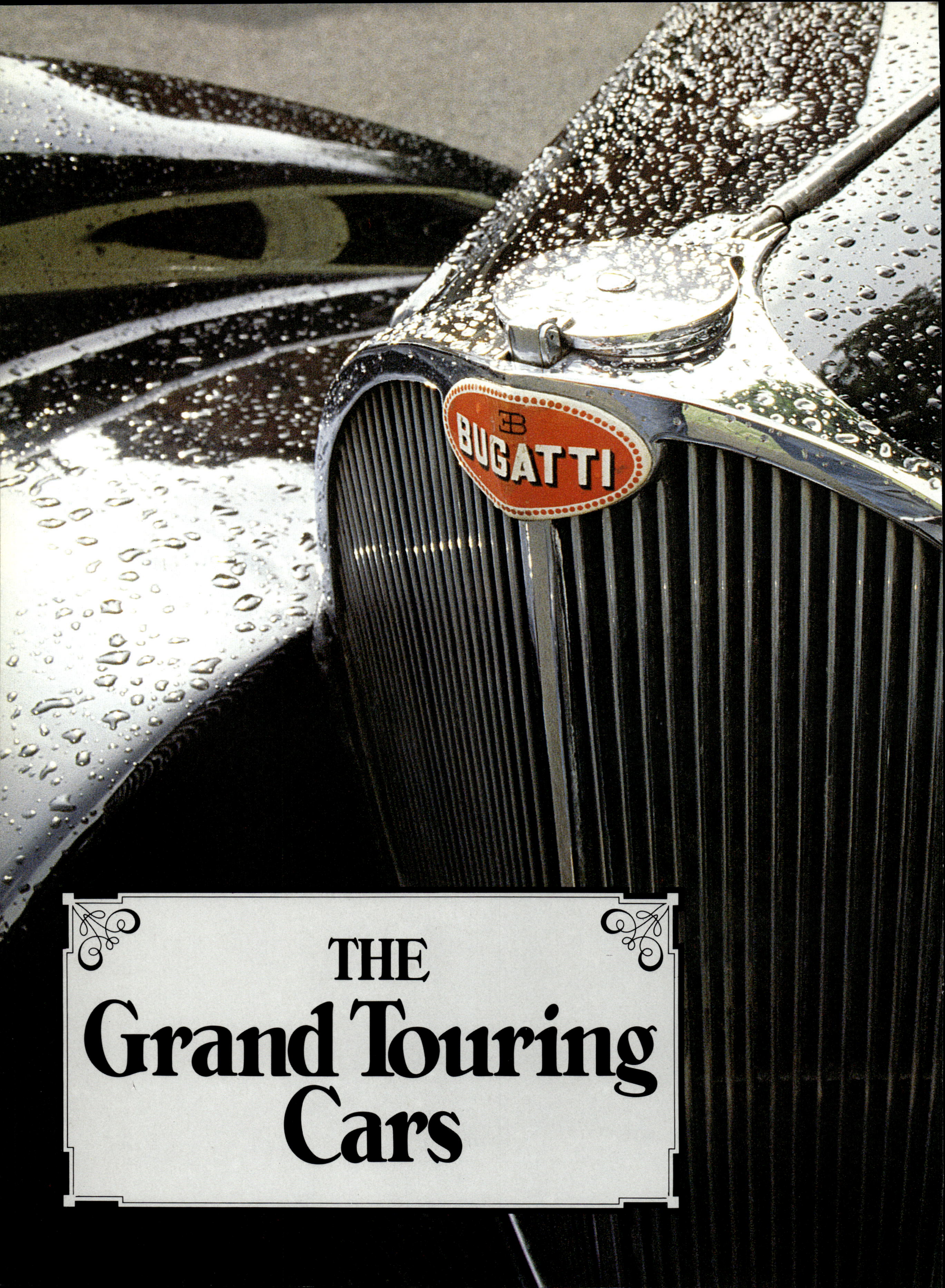

THE Grand Touring Cars

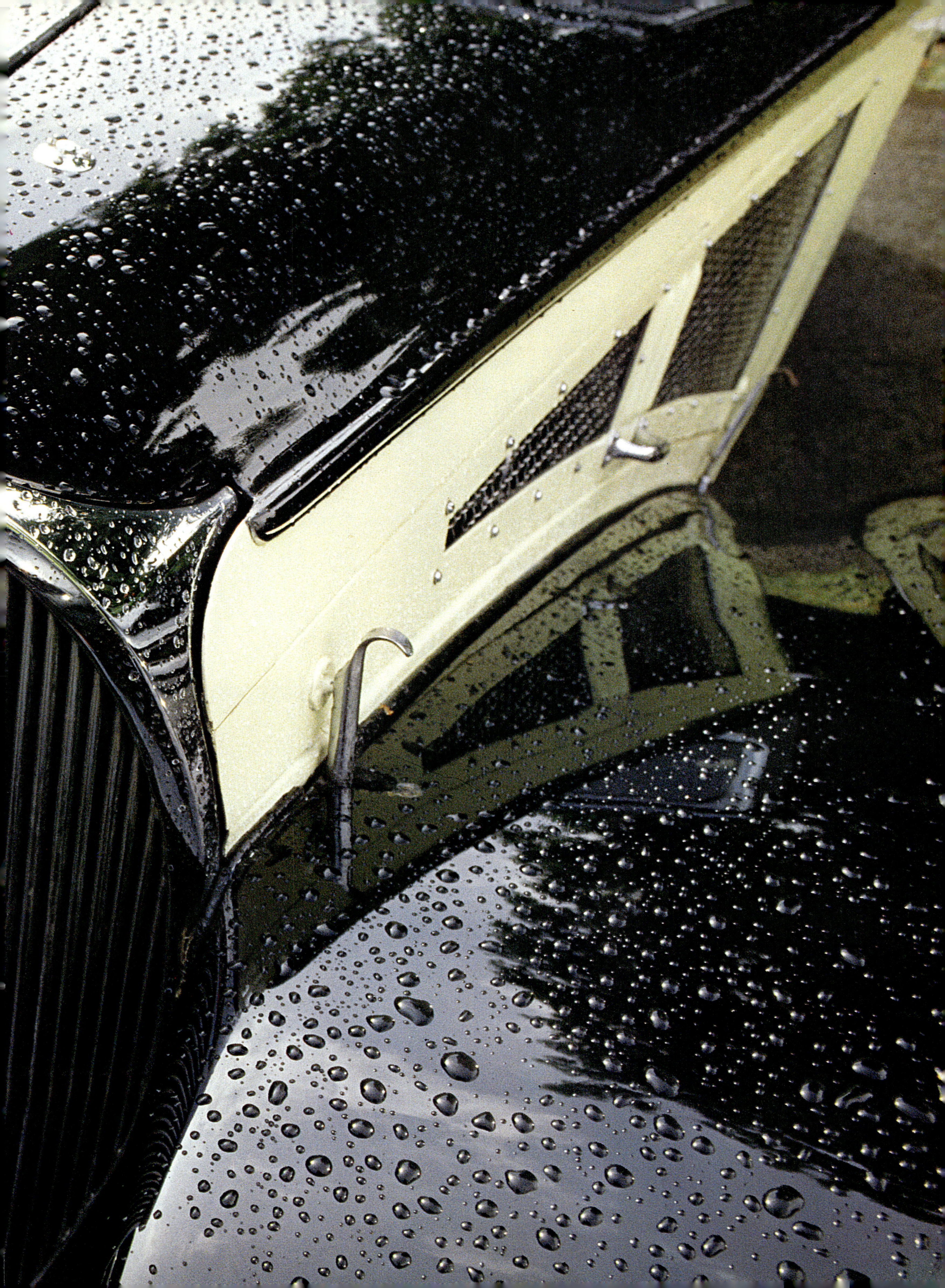

WE know from a letter Bugatti wrote to his friend and later colleague Dr G. Espanet in 1913 that even then he contemplated building a large car to match the Hispano-Suiza or Rolls-Royce. It was not, however, until success came in 1926 that he could think of fulfilling his ambition.

What happened then was typical of the man with his mixture of creative ability and commercial intemperance, which his frequent success did nothing to moderate! He began to make his monster 12.7-litre Royale for kings who did not buy it, then produced a more sensible 5.3-litre T46 super-car, which was successful until the world recession hit sales. Next he converted this car's engine into a supercharged twin-cam T50 whose sales also suffered, and eventually allowed Jean to design the final and successful 3.3-litre Type 57, which was the backbone of production at Molsheim from 1932 to 1939, when war and invasion closed the factory once more.

The Type 41 Royale

For the French Government Bugatti had produced a paper study of a 125 mm bore eight-cylinder aero engine in 1923, under his type number 34. Although this was never made he used the layout as the basis of the engine for his large project in 1926. This design used the interesting concept of a one-piece cylinder block with integral head, and Bugatti's normal three-valve layout, with webs between the bores extending down to form the main bearing housings so that explosion loads were dealt with on the same piece. The crankcase proper now became an oil-retaining casing only without primary loading. A 'minor' snag with this construction was that the crankshaft had to be removed, and thus the engine, to change or grind a valve!

The crank had nine main bearings and was now fitted with counterweights. The prototype Type 41 engine had a stroke of 150 mm to give 14.7 litres, but production versions had a shorter stroke at 130 mm with 12.7 litres displacement – by any standard large enough! This enormous engine was the largest ever to be offered on a production car, larger even than several 12-cylinder vehicles produced in the United States or by Hispano-Suiza in France. Under the pre-war British RAC rating system, the Royale was listed as 77 hp; the V12 Hispano-Suiza was 75, the Marmon V12 63, and the 16-cylinder Cadillac a mere 58 hp!

The chassis dimensions matched the engine size, with a track of 1.6 m (5 ft 3 in) and a wheelbase of 4.3 m (14 ft 1¼ in), half a metre longer than the biggest Rolls-Royce of the period. The chassis layout was conventional Bugatti, from polished circular front axle to reversed quarter elliptics at the rear, but Bugatti reverted to a three-speed gearbox in the back axle, and now put the clutch in a separate casing behind the engine. The 24 in wheels were handsome castings with enormous 6.75 × 36 in tyres. Notwithstanding the dimensions of the car Bugatti was able to claim that it was docile and could 'easily be driven by a lady in spite of its size'!

The prototype was first fitted with a body from a Packard touring car Bugatti had bought for test purposes. This chassis then carried two experimental stagecoach bodies successively, finally being fitted with a fine-looking Weymann coach. Bugatti crashed this version on the way back to Molsheim from Paris – he is said to have fallen asleep after lunch! The car was then rebuilt on a new frame with a Molsheim-constructed 'Coupé Napoléon', a small passenger coupé with an open compartment for the chauffeur, who sat behind an enormously long engine compartment. This car remained for many years in the family use and is now in the Musée National (Schlumpf collection) at Mulhouse. (Fritz Schlumpf bought the whole of the Molsheim collection of historic cars during a period of financial difficulty at the factory in the 1960s.)

Sales (at three times the price of a Rolls-Royce!) were slow, and the first delivery to a customer was not until April 1932, when the clothing manufacturer Armand Esders received his handsome roadster designed by Jean Bugatti – surely the smallest possible body for so large a chassis. Mr Esders did not drive at night, so no headlamps were fitted to the car! Later this chassis was rebodied with a coupé by Binder (now in the Harrah Museum at Reno, Nevada). In May 1932 the German Dr J. Fuchs took delivery of a chassis, to which Weinberger of Munich fitted a drophead coupé (now in the Ford Museum at Dearborn, Michigan). The third and last delivery was made a year later in June 1933 to Britain for Captain Cuthbert Foster; a sedate Park Ward limousine body was fitted to this chassis, modelled on a 1920 Rolls-Royce he had owned. This car is also in the Musée National.

The final two chassis that were built remained unsold, one having a Kellner sedan body (on display today in the Briggs Cunningham Museum

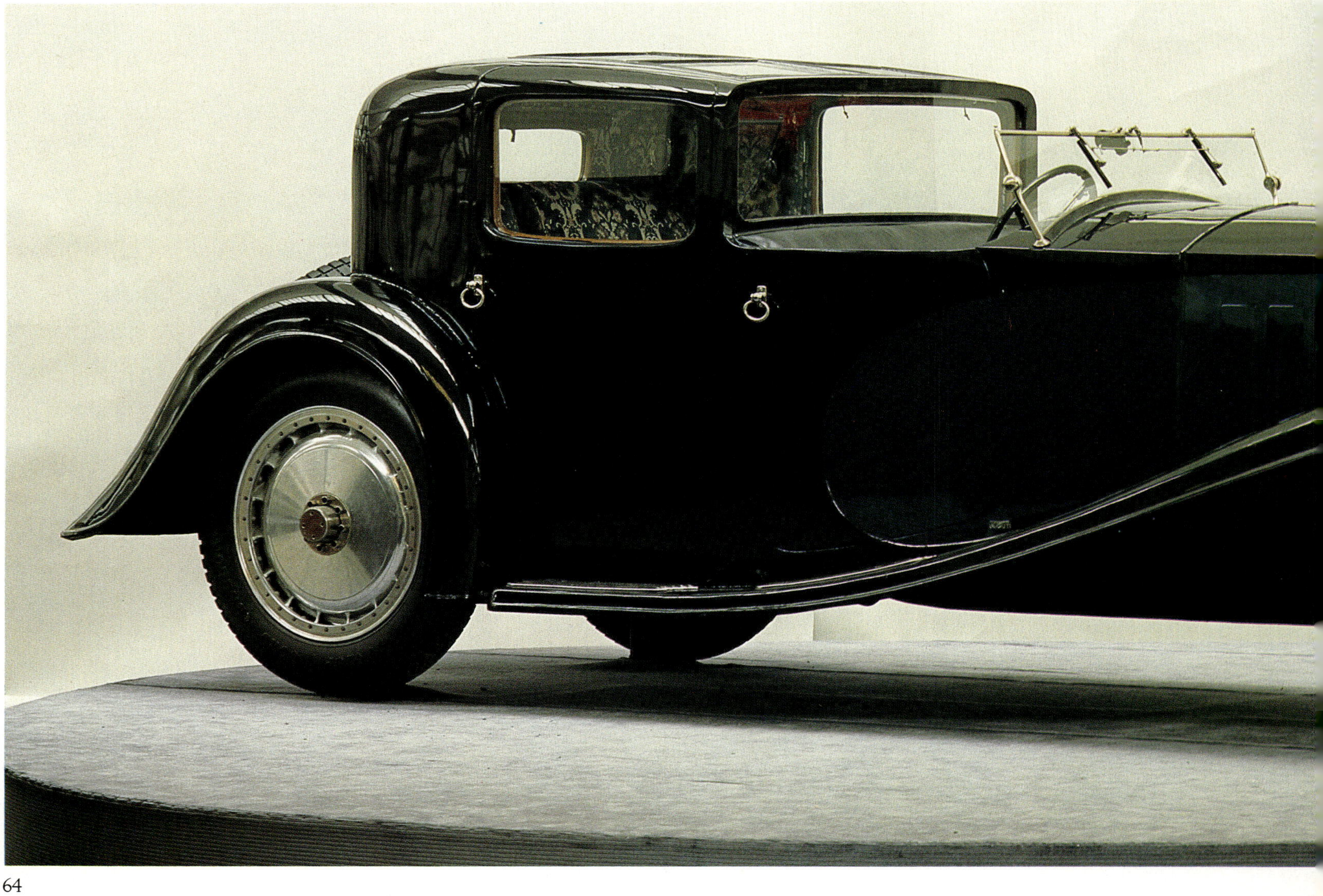

RIGHT The Royale prototype was fitted initially with a body from an American Packard touring car Bugatti had bought for testing. This car had a stroke of 150 mm, larger than was later used, giving a capacity of 14.7 litres! The wheels, too, were different. The car did many miles in Ettore's hands and was seen in Paris, Milan and at San Sebastián in Spain, where King Alfonso was lobbied for an order, which might have materialized if the monarch had not lost his throne. The chassis was subsequently fitted with experimental closed coachwork built at Molsheim.

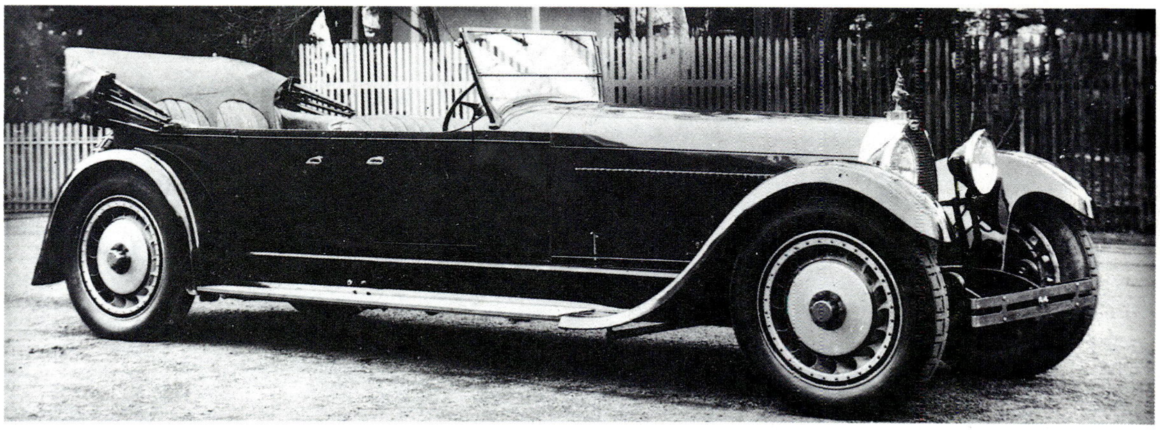

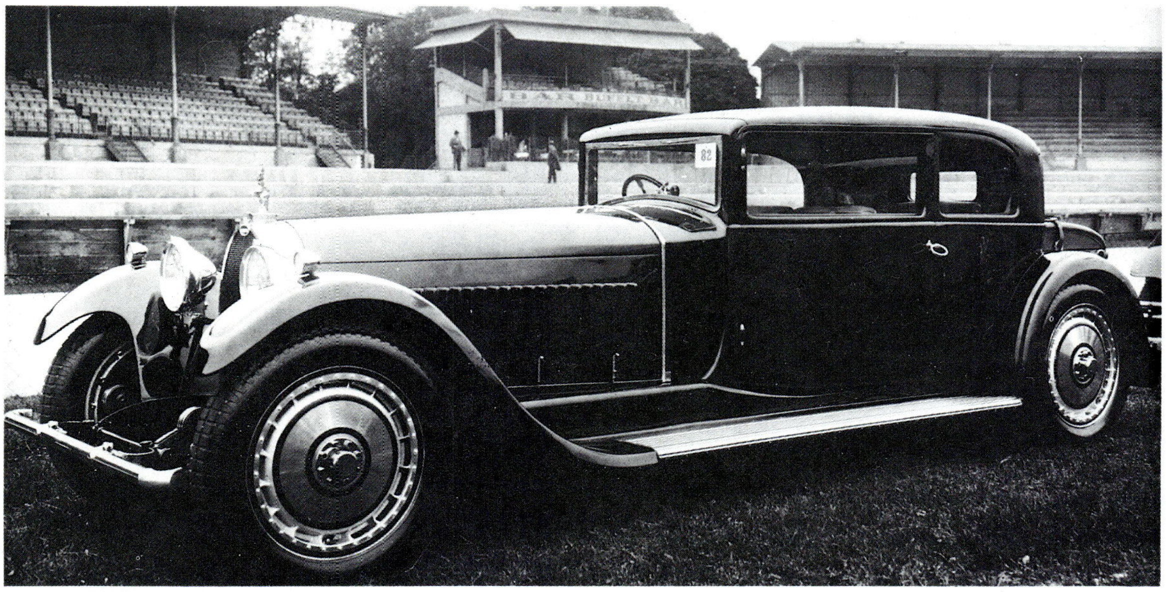

LEFT The prototype chassis was next fitted with a superb two-door coach by Weymann of Paris, and won a prize at a concours d'élégance. Bugatti crashed the car on the way back from Paris to Molsheim – falling asleep after a good lunch, it is said. The car was then rebuilt on a new frame, but preserving the original chassis number (41100), and a new body was produced for it at Molsheim.

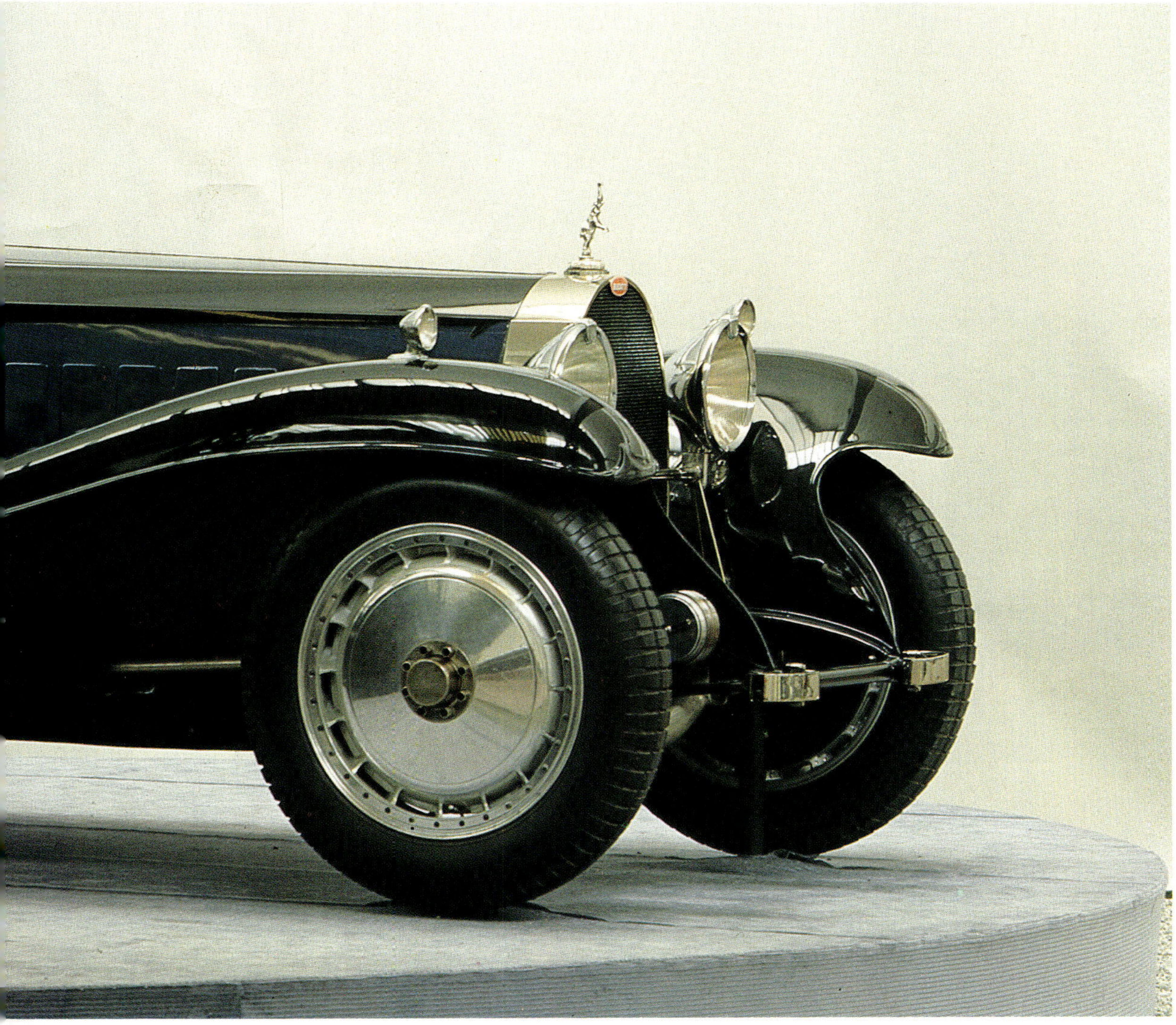

Type 41 Royale	
Years made	1929–32
No. made	6
ENGINE	
Type	Monobloc, integral main bearings
No. of cylinders	8
Bore/stroke mm	125 × 130
Displacement cc	12,763
Valve operation	2 inlet, 1 exhaust per cylinder
Sparkplugs/cyl.	2
Supercharged	No
Carburettor	1 Bugatti-type
BHP approx.	275
DRIVE TRAIN	
Clutch	Multi-plate, dry
Transmission	3-speed and reverse, in rear axle
CHASSIS	
Wheelbase	4.3 m (14 ft 1¼ in)
Track	1.6 m (5 ft 3 in)
Suspension – front	½ elliptic
Suspension – rear	Reversed ¼ elliptic
Brakes	Cable
Tyre size	6.75 × 36
Wheels	Cast aluminium alloy
PERFORMANCE	
Maximum speed	160+ km/h (100+ mph)

LEFT The final body on the prototype chassis built at the Molsheim factory was a 'Coupé Napoléon'; this was a two- or three-seat coupé with the driver in the open. This style was derived from equivalent horse-drawn vehicles of an earlier age. At the time Ettore was much preoccupied with the shapes and lines of horse-drawn carriages, or hippomobiles. This car was used by the Bugatti family for many years and was bought with the rest of the Molsheim collection by Fritz Schlumpf in the 1960s. Provided by the Musée National de l'Automobile, Mulhouse.

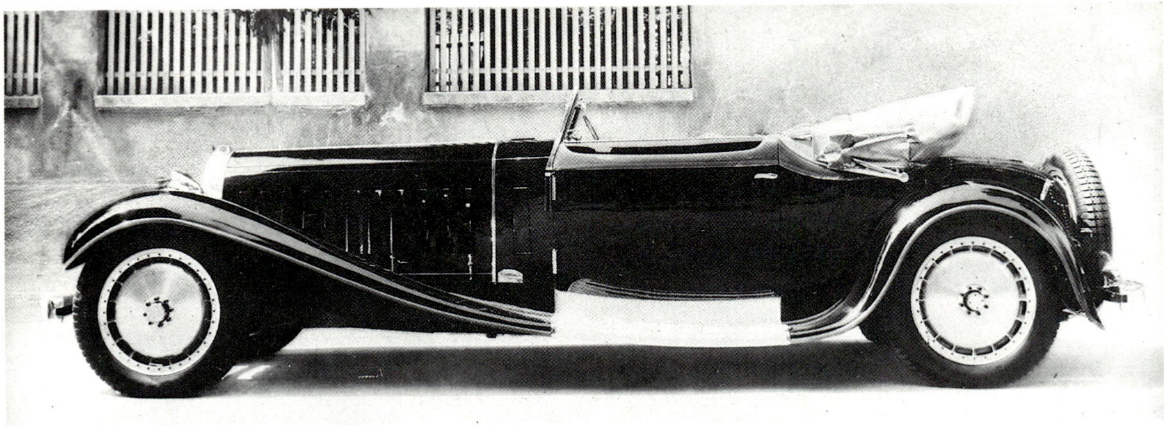

LEFT, *ABOVE* Dr J. Fuchs ordered a drophead coupé from Weinberger of Munich and took it to Shanghai, then to the United States. This T41 is now in the Ford Museum at Dearborn.
LEFT, *BELOW* The final Molsheim-built body, a 'Berline de Voyage', remained unsold before World War 2, but went to the United States afterwards. It is now in the Harrah Museum, Reno.
BELOW This Park Ward body on Capt C. Foster's Royale is a replica of one the firm had fitted to his Rolls-Royce. Provided by the Musée National de l'Automobile, Mulhouse.

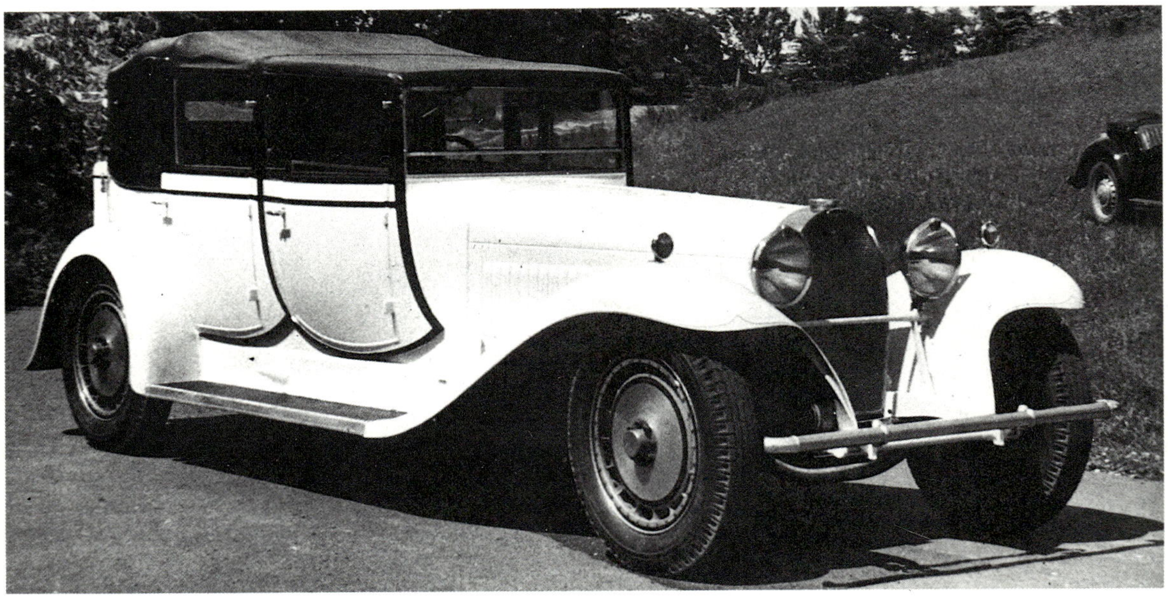

RIGHT, *ABOVE* Extravagant perhaps – but the engine of the Royale is a thing of beauty. The double carburettor is by Bugatti, and each cylinder has two sparkplugs.
FAR RIGHT, *ABOVE* This Binder coachwork is the second body on the Esders car (right, below), replacing that attractive if impractical roadster. This car is in the Harrah Museum, Reno.
FAR RIGHT, *BELOW* Kellner built this fine-looking coachwork on another chassis that was not sold until after World War 2 – to Briggs Cunningham, in whose Californian museum it remains.
RIGHT, *BELOW* The first Royale sale was to the clothing manufacturer Armand Esders, who never drove at night – so the beautiful roadster body by Jean Bugatti had no lamps.

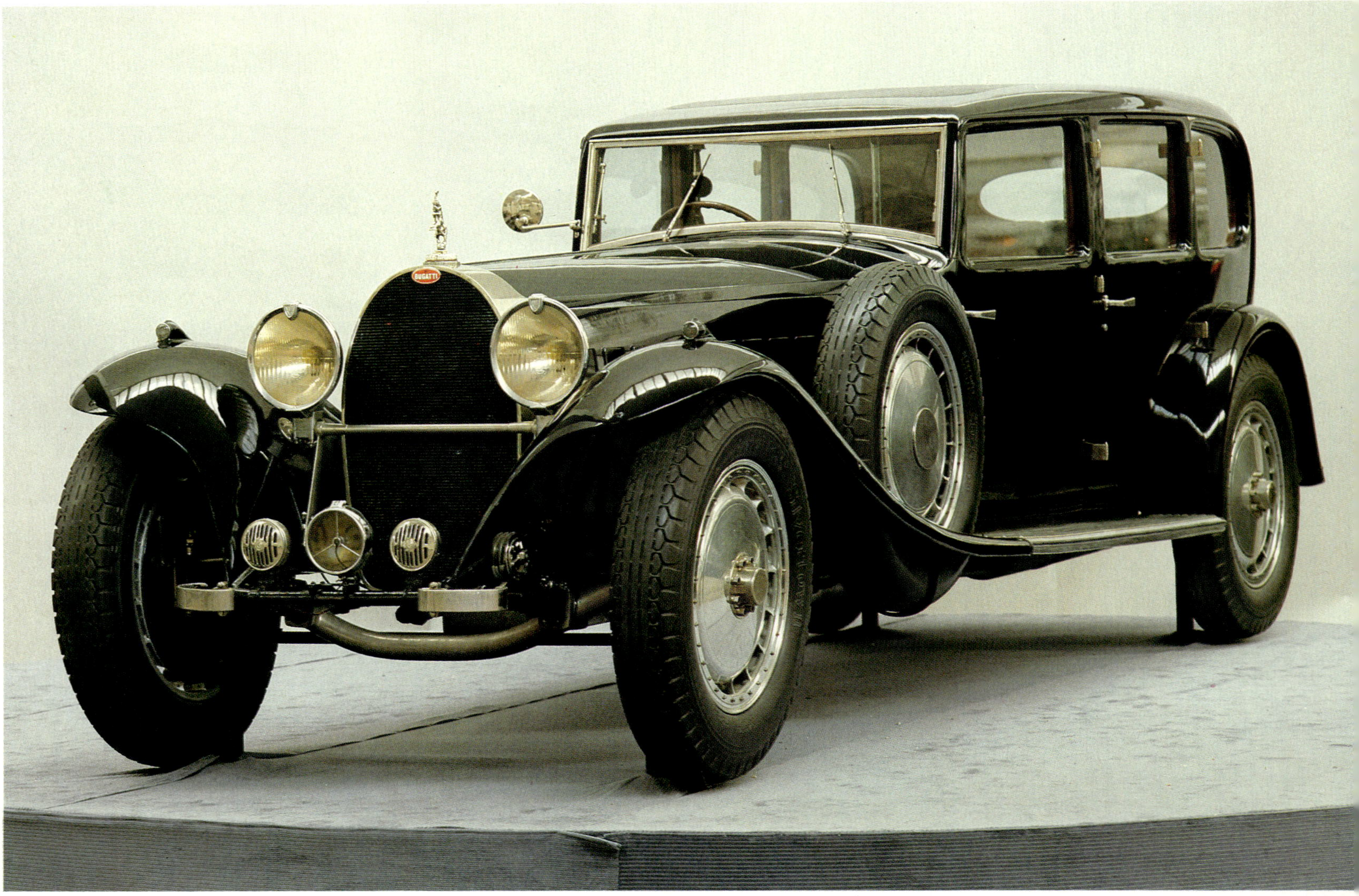

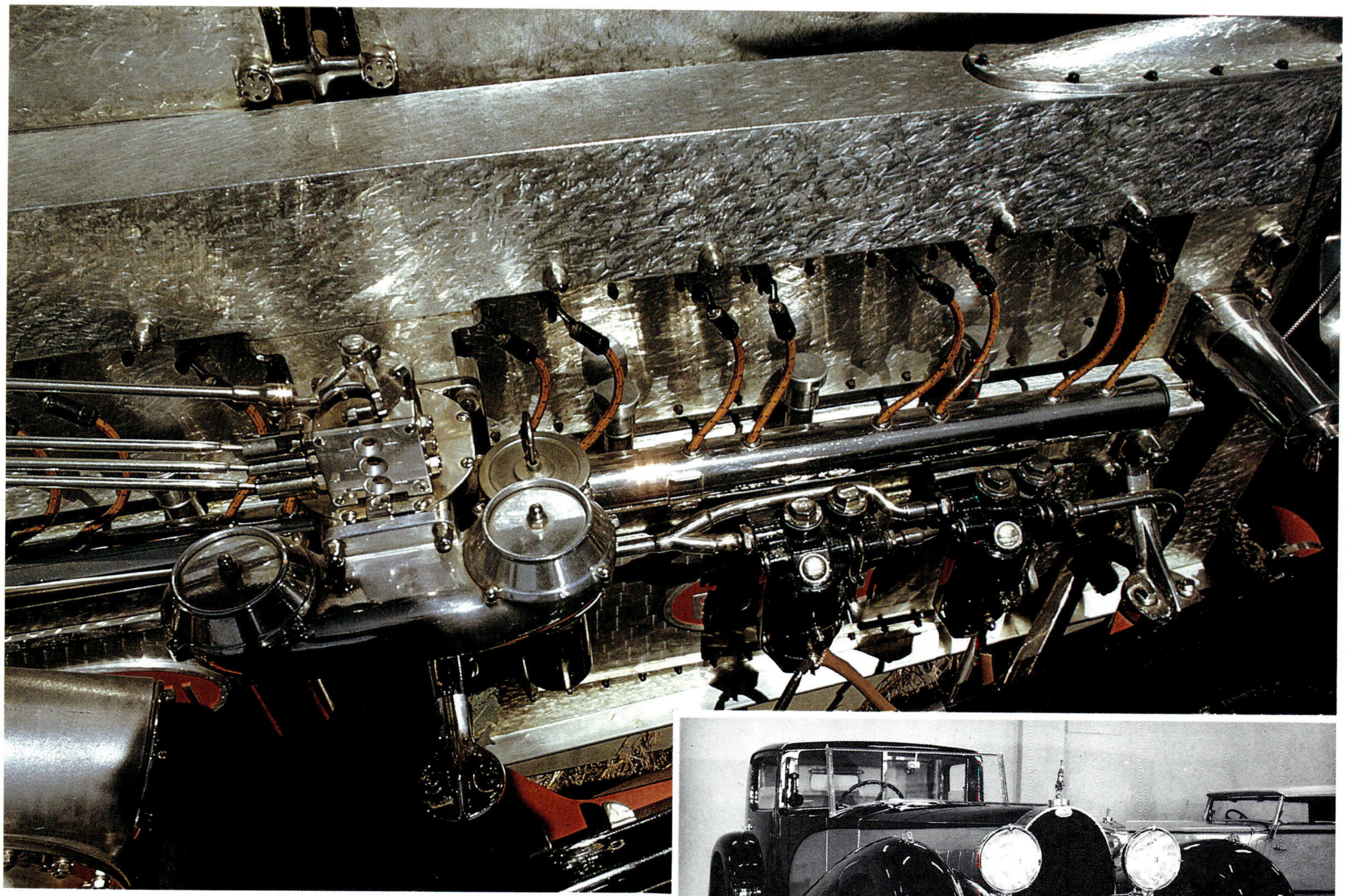

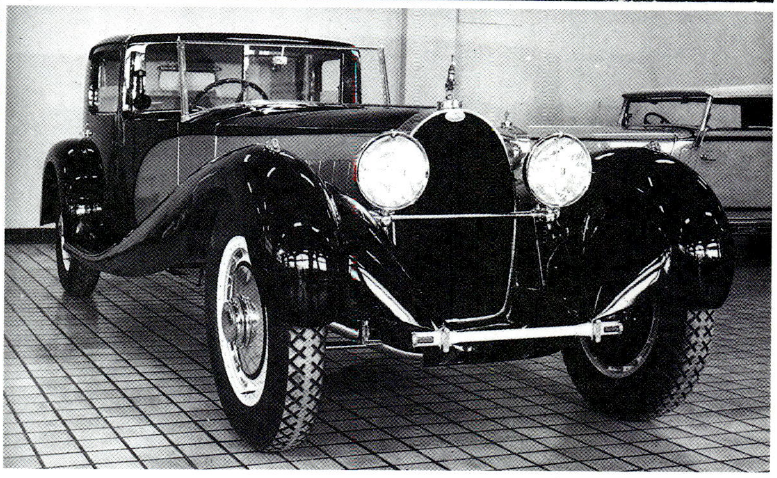

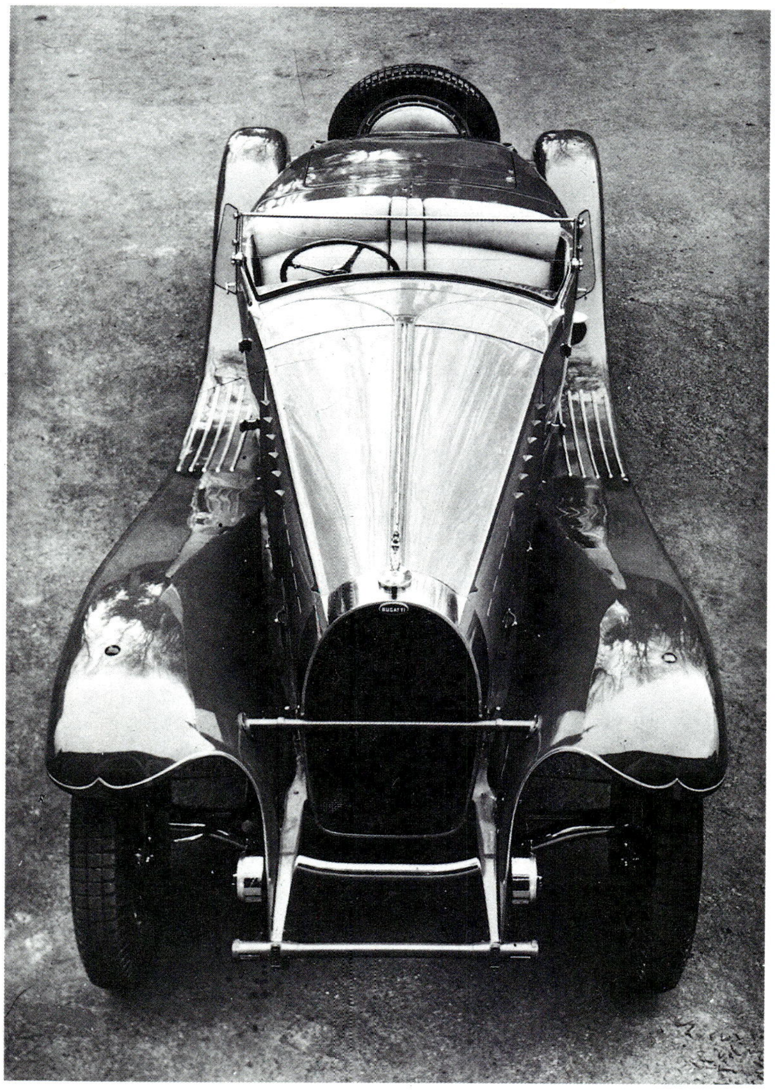

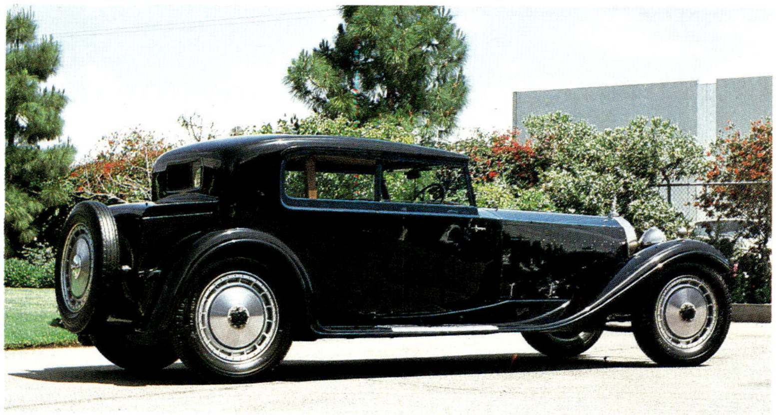

in Costa Mesa, California), the other a Bugatti-built 'Berline de Voyage', modelled on a horse-drawn coach (now in the Harrah Museum). Both of these cars were sold by the Bugatti family after the war. The total is therefore six chassis, allowing for one rebuild and 11 bodies in all.

Bugatti had hoped to sell this large car to 'top people'. He had called it the Royale after King Alfonso of Spain had shown an interest, and King Carol of Romania had nibbled. However, its absurd size and cost was out of touch with a world in financial difficulty, as it was in the early 1930s and with war clouds overhead at the end of the decade. Today its proper place can only be in museums, but at least one (the Briggs Cunningham car) is taken out for exercise regularly at Costa Mesa! Happily, the excellent large engine later found a home in Bugatti's successful railcars of the mid-1930s and performed well in these for many years.

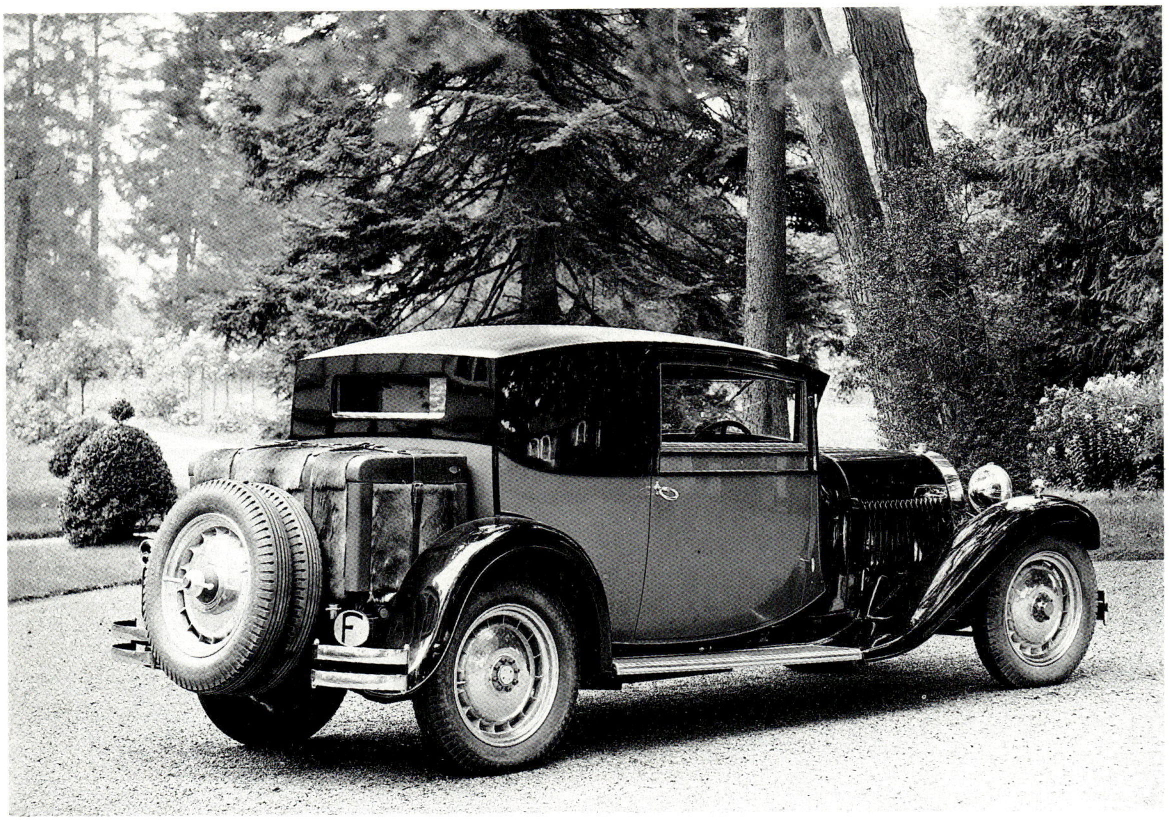

Type 46/46S Tourer	
Years made	T46: 1929–36/T46S: 1930–6
No. made	400
ENGINE	
Type	Monobloc, overhead camshaft, plain bearings, dry sump
No. of cylinders	8
Bore/stroke mm	81 × 130
Displacement cc	5359
Valve operation	2 inlet, 1 exhaust per cylinder
Sparkplugs/cyl.	2
Supercharged	46S only
Carburettor(s)	T46: 1 Smith T46S: 2 Zenith
BHP approx.	T46: 140/T46S: 160
DRIVE TRAIN	
Clutch	Multi-disc, dry
Transmission	3-speed and reverse in rear axle, ball change
CHASSIS	
Wheelbase	3.5 m (11 ft 5¾ in)
Track	1.4 m (4 ft 7 in)
Suspension – front	½ elliptic
Suspension – rear	Reversed ¼ elliptic
Brakes	Cable, auto adjustment
Tyre size	(modern) 6.00 × 20
Wheels	Rudge wire, or cast aluminium alloy
PERFORMANCE	
Maximum speed	145 km/h (90 mph)

ABOVE A fine example of Bugatti coachwork on the 5.3-litre Type 46. The square-edged coach-style body, the calfskin-covered trunk at the rear, even the old-style door handles, blend well with 'Royale'-type aluminium wheels and the Bugatti radiator. This is a contemporary picture, taken at Molsheim, of a car that is not known to have survived, although a significant number of the few hundred of the type that were produced are still about. This square-edged body style has reappeared from time to time and is generally designated as 'razor edge', and will no doubt do so again.

RIGHT Bugatti, probably at the instigation of his son Jean, made a few profilée (streamlined) bodies on his Type 49 and 50 chassis – the latter is illustrated here. The style perhaps anticipated the modern concept of a clean penetrating front, with a sharper rear to separate the air flow cleanly, but the drag coefficient would be severely influenced by the projecting headlamps and square-edged radiator. Clean separation at the rear would not be assisted by the exposed spare wheels. Nevertheless, this is a striking and dramatic body style. Provided by Mr M. Seydoux.

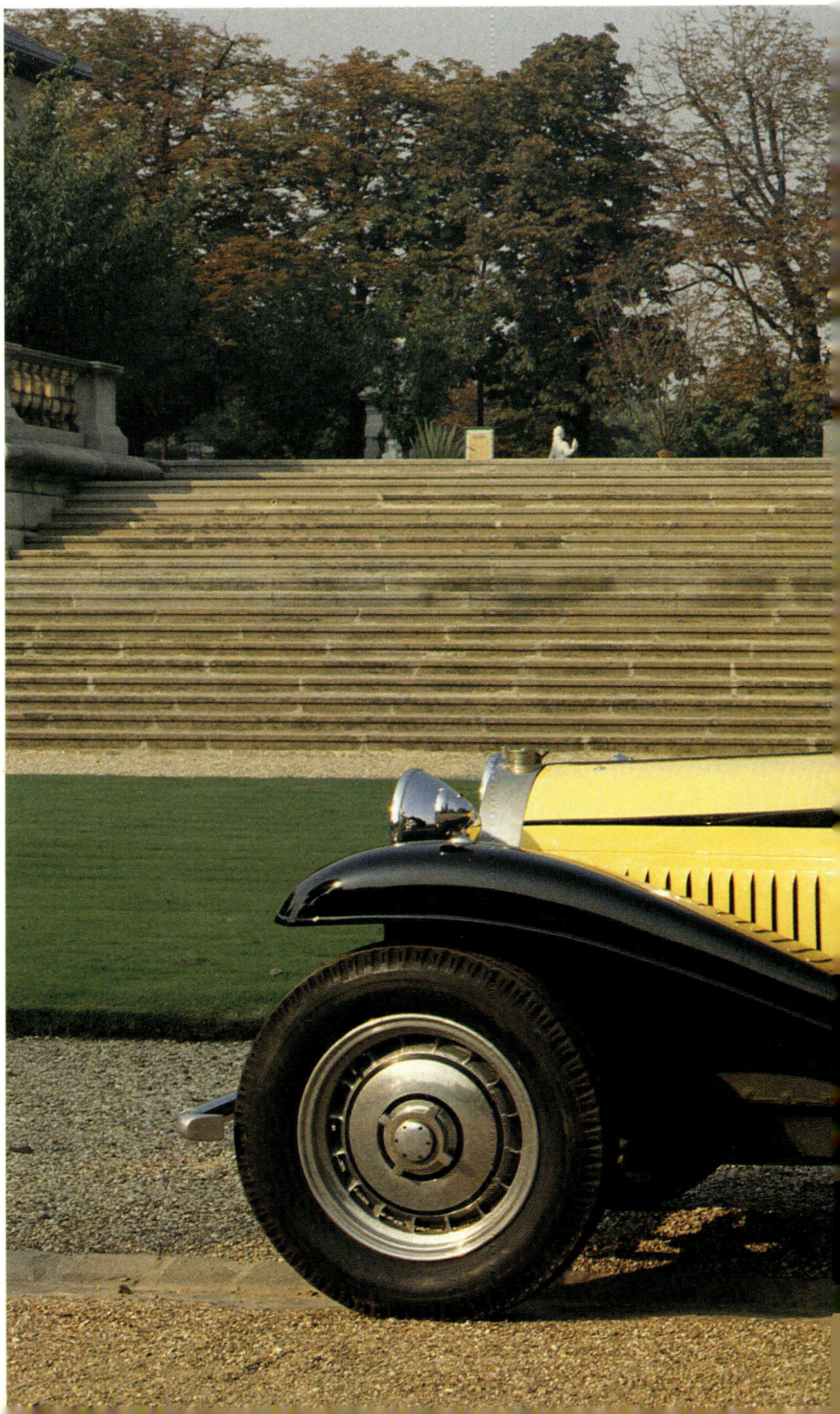

The Type 46: luxury and elegance

In 1929 Bugatti realized he would probably not be able to sell many of the large Royales and turned his attention to a 'petit Royale', a 5.3-litre model along similar but more modest lines, known as the Type 46. Now the eight-cylinder engine had a more sensible bore of 81 mm, retaining the same stroke of 130 mm as the Royale. The cylinder block construction was similar with extensions to support the crankshaft on nine bearings, and the traditional three-valve, single camshaft top end. The chassis layout was like the Royale with the three-speed gearbox in the back axle, but the clutch was at the rear of the engine rather than separate. Suspension, axles and brakes were as on the Royale but smaller, and the wheels were 20 in wire initially but later cast aluminium alloy. The overall chassis dimensions were a modest enough 1.4 m (4 ft 7 in) track and 3.5 m (11 ft 5¾ in) wheelbase, rather less than the large Rolls-Royce of the period.

The car first appeared at the Paris and London motor shows in October 1929 and was immediately received favourably by the press. Orders came in well and the chassis was fitted with fine coachwork from all the best European coachbuilders – Labourdette, Weymann, Mulliner, d'Ieteren, Freestone and Webb, Saoutchik, James Young – and by Bugatti. Road tests praised its flexibility, silence and comfort – a real top-gear car: 'rock steady on corners . . . can be steered to an inch'. *The Autocar* concluded a road test: 'Altogether a most remarkable motor car highly satisfying in the easy purposeful manner of the performance and with a charm and individuality it is impossible to appreciate adequately without actually going out in the car.'

At the end of 1931 Bugatti added a supercharger to the engine to make the 46S ('S' for 'Sport'), but only about 20 of these were produced. The Roots blower was operated by a bevel drive off the vertical gear train driving the camshaft at the front of the engine, and produced only a modest boost.

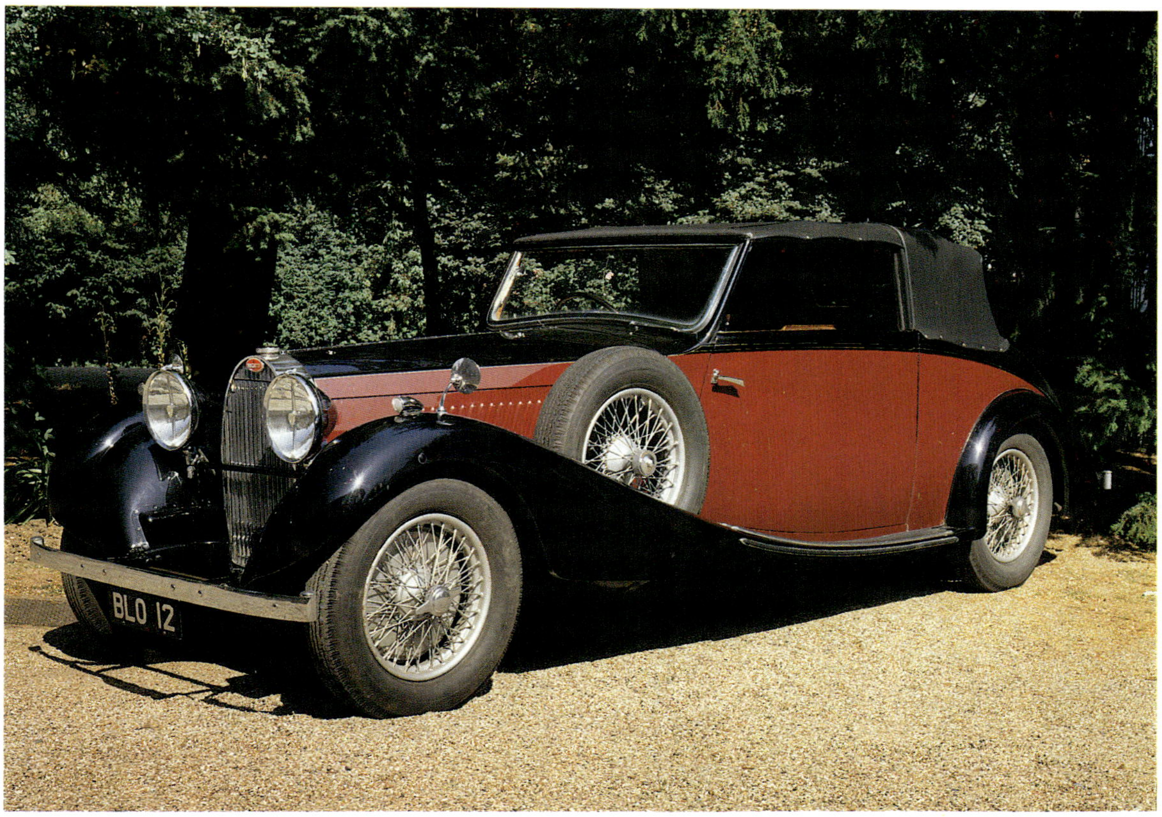

LEFT Many Type 57 chassis were imported into the United Kingdom to be fitted with bodies from the best British coachbuilders. The one illustrated is a drophead coupé by James Young of Bromley, on a 1936 chassis. The Type 57 had a performance of around 150 km/h (95 mph). Provided by Mr J. Marks.

Type 50 Grand Sport
Years made 1930–4
No. made 65

ENGINE	
Type	Monobloc, twin overhead camshafts, plain bearings, dry sump
No. of cylinders	8
Bore/stroke mm	86 × 107
Displacement cc	4972
Valve operation	1 inlet, 1 exhaust per cylinder
Sparkplugs/cyl.	1
Supercharged	Yes
Carburettors	2 Zenith
BHP approx.	225
DRIVE TRAIN	
Clutch	Multi-disc, dry
Transmission	3-speed and reverse in rear axle, ball change
CHASSIS	
Wheelbase	3.1 m (10 ft 2 in), 3.5 m (11 ft 5¾ in)
Track	1.4 m (4 ft 7 in)
Suspension – front	½ elliptic
Suspension – rear	Reversed ¼ elliptic
Brakes	Cable, auto adjustment
Tyre size	6.50 × 20
Wheels	Cast aluminium alloy
PERFORMANCE	
Maximum speed	170+ km/h (105+ mph)

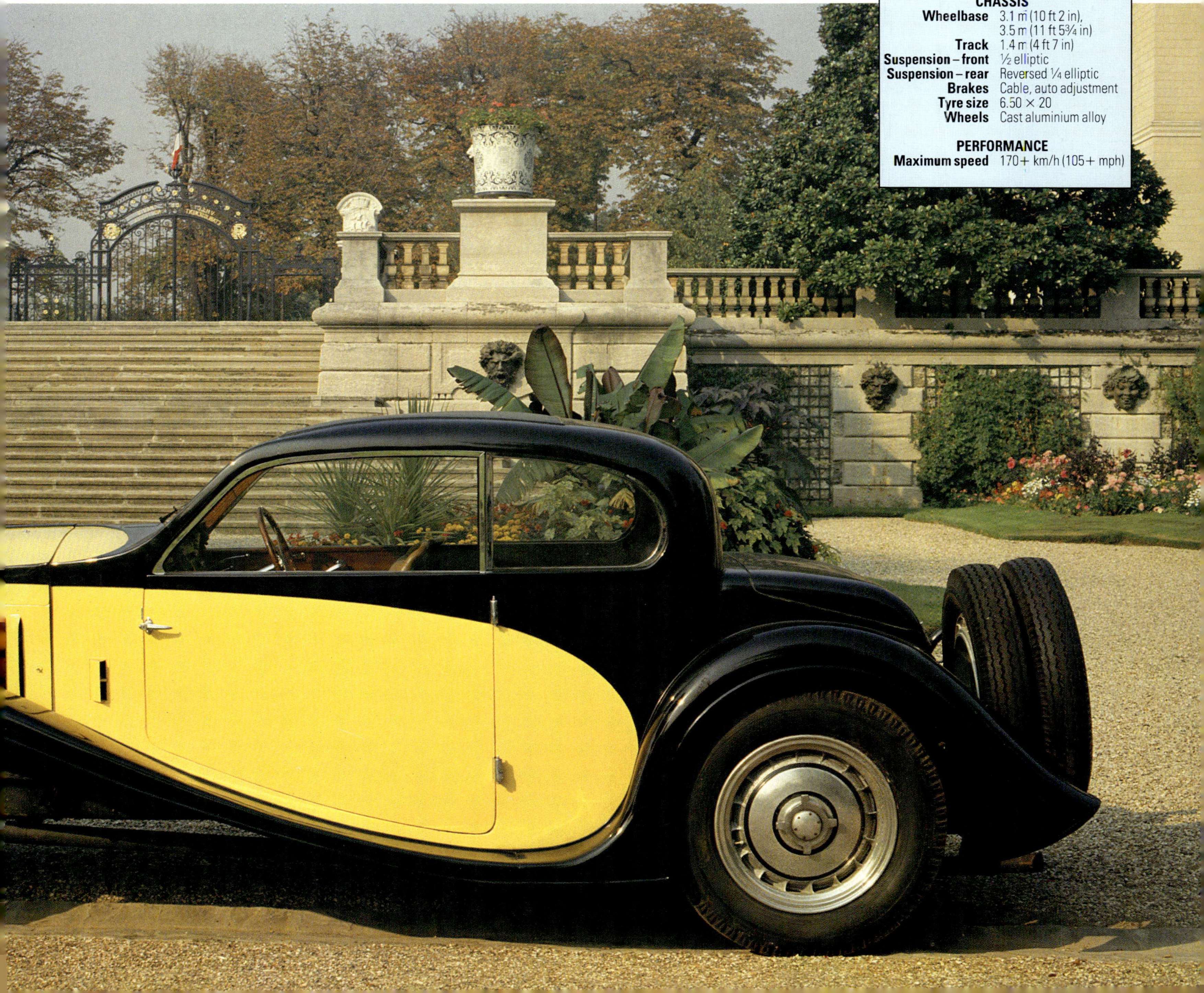

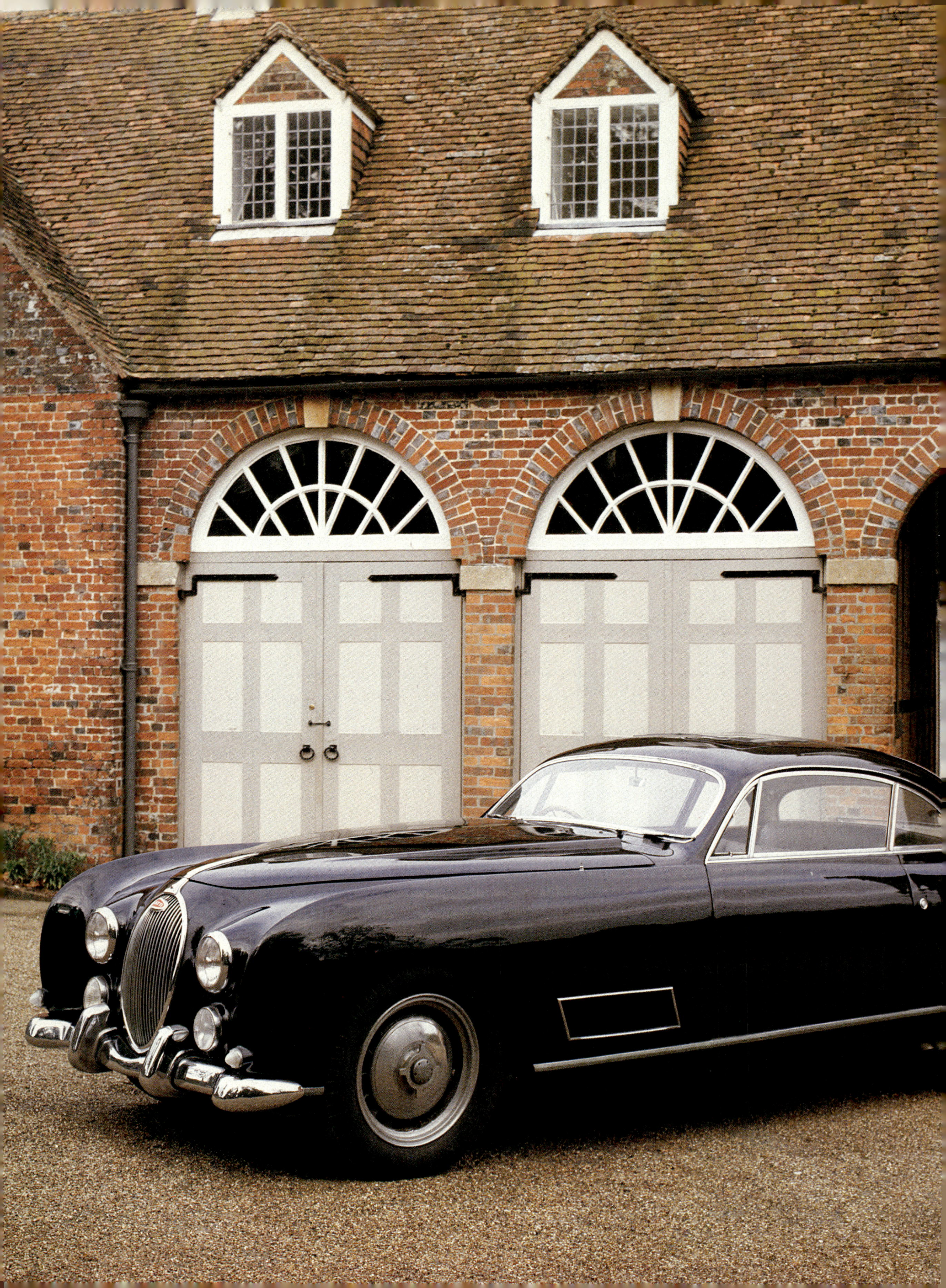

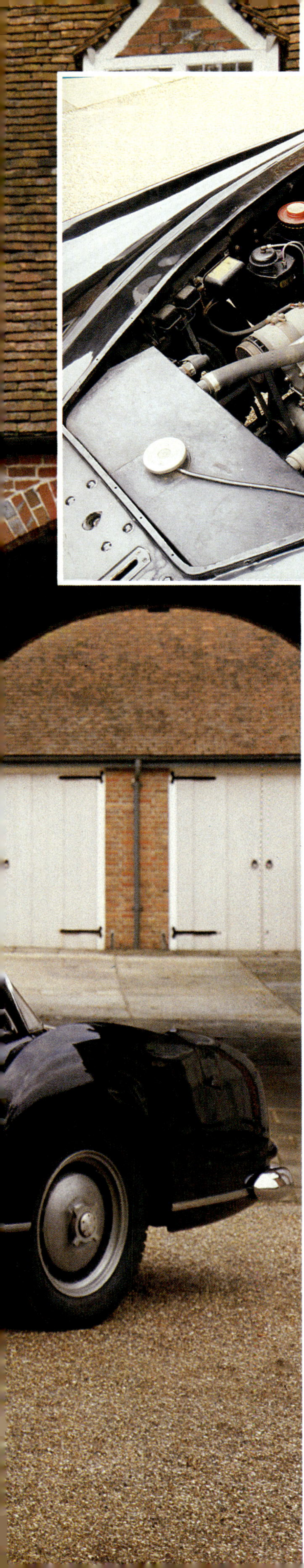

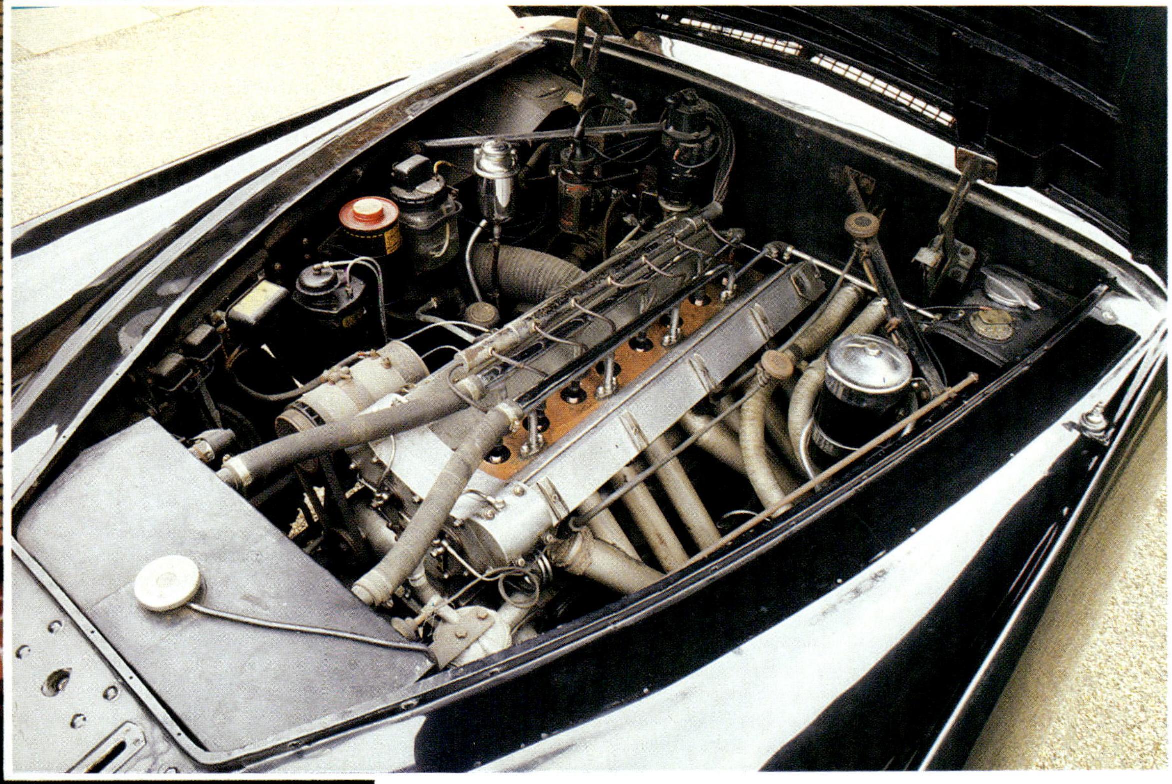

LEFT AND FACING PAGE *Few Bugattis have been successfully modernized. An exception is this fine Type 50, originally produced in 1932, bought by an Englishman in Paris after the war, and rebodied to his requirements in the 1950s by Saoutchik of Paris: it is said in time for his honeymoon! Today heads will turn in admiration as it passes. The powerful twin-cam 4.9-litre engine gives the car a top speed well over 160 km/h (100 mph), and the Cotal electro-mechanical gearbox makes gear changing easy. Sun roof and electric windows add to the comforts of a unique example that would have pleased Ettore had he lived to see it. From a private collection in England.*

BELOW *One of the best-known and most effective factory bodies on the Type 57 was the Ventoux 'coach', modelled on the profilée Type 50, a two-door 2 + 2 seater with raked windscreen and cut-off tail. This particular car is from the final 1939 series with hydraulic brakes; it was in stock in the London depot when war broke out in September. Provided by Mr G. Perfect.*

Type 57/57C Tourer
Years made T57: 1934–40/T 57C: 1937–40
No. made T57: 546/T57C: 96

ENGINE		**CHASSIS**	
Type	Monobloc, twin overhead camshafts, plain bearings	**Wheelbase**	3.3 m (10 ft 10 in)
No. of cylinders	8	**Track**	1.35 m (4 ft 5 in)
Bore/stroke mm	72 × 100	**Suspension – front**	½ elliptic
Displacement cc	3257	**Suspension – rear**	Reversed ¼ elliptic
Valve operation	1 inlet, 1 exhaust per cylinder	**Brakes**	1934–7 cable, 1938–40 Lockheed hydraulic
Sparkplugs/cyl.	1	**Tyre size**	5.50 × 18
Supercharged	57C only	**Wheels**	Rudge wire
Carburettor	1 Stromberg	**PERFORMANCE**	
BHP approx.	T57: 135/T57C: 160	**Maximum speed**	Approx. 150 km/h (95 mph)
DRIVE TRAIN			
Clutch	Single plate, dry		
Transmission	4-speed and reverse, constant mesh gears, central ball change		

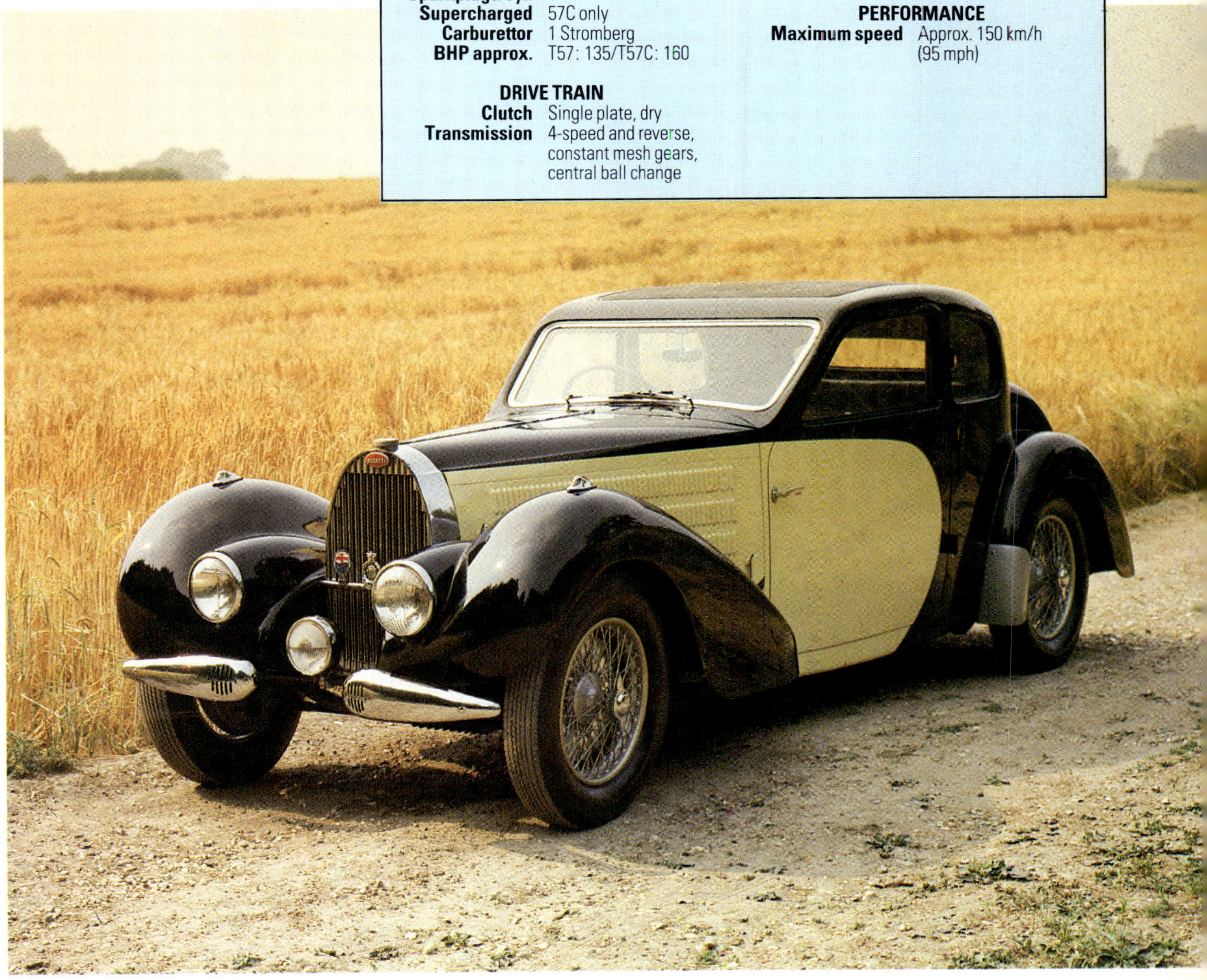

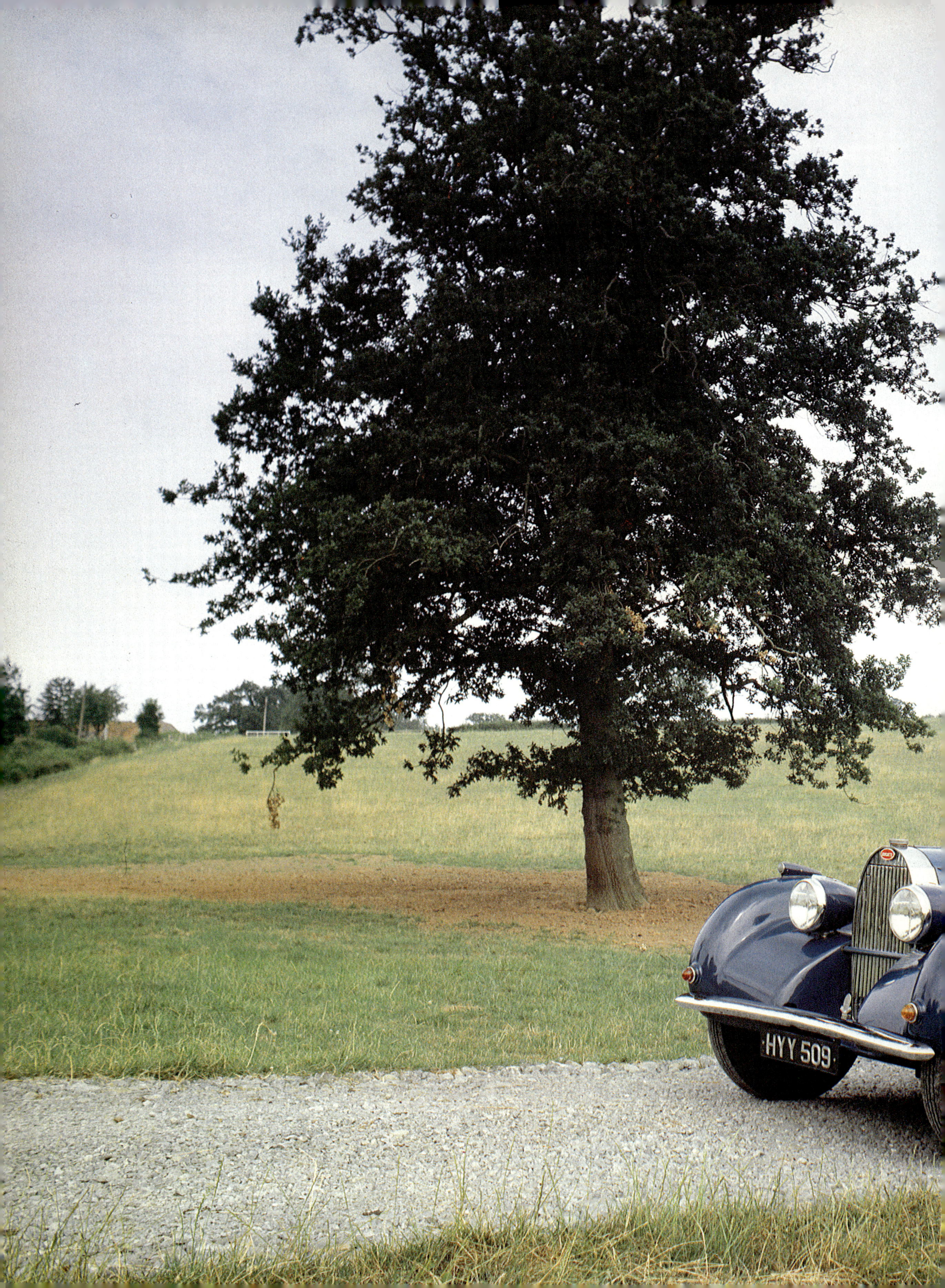
HYY 509

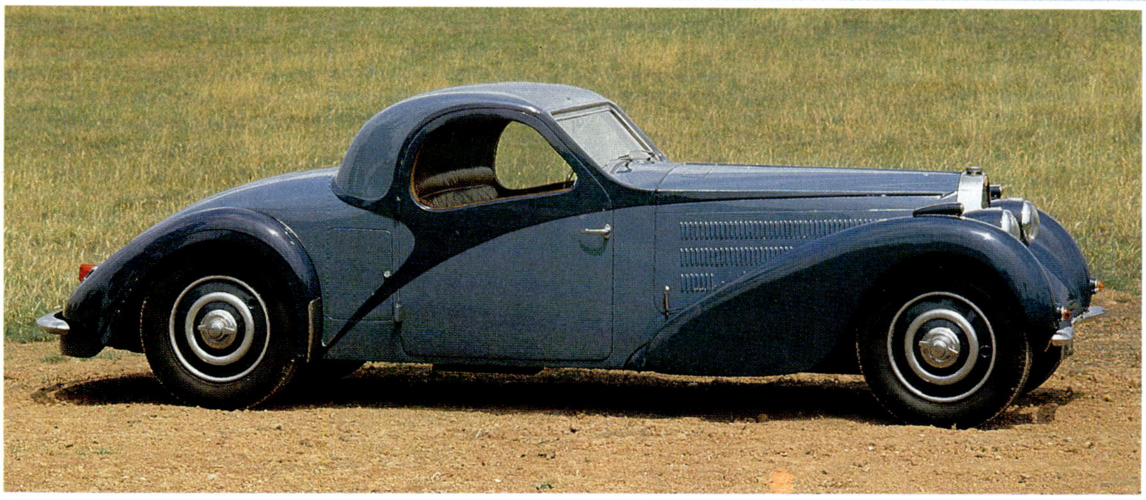

To many an eye the most handsome Type 57 body is the two-seat Atalante fixed-head coupé; the flowing lines, long tail and adequate but small passenger compartment suit the elegant front end very well. The body is light and rigid, and ideal for taking two people across France to Monte Carlo! This 1936 car has been well looked after by its engineer-owner, and has been modernized with the 1939 series hydraulic brakes – much to be preferred to the earlier mechanical type. A Bugatti of this quality needs the kind of attention that a normal garage cannot give, but it rewards the diligent owner with superb manners and a 'long-legged' performance. Provided by Mr I.L. Merryfield.

Production of the Type 46 was about 400 chassis in 1930-2 but, because of shortage of work at the factory at Molsheim, Bugatti made many for stock which remained unsold for some years. Indeed, a few brand-new, unused chassis turned up after the Second World War. Nevertheless, it can be said that the Type 46 was the best de luxe chassis that Bugatti produced, and well worthy of his name.

The twin-cam Type 50

As already recounted, Bugatti copied the twin overhead camshaft layout of the American Miller racing engine when he produced the Type 51. In fact, the first engine to be produced on these lines was the Type 50, a 4.9-litre conversion of the Type 46 engine. A new block and crankshaft were made to use much of the rest of the engine, but with a bore and stroke of 86 × 107 mm, rather than the long stroke 81 × 130 mm of the earlier model (bore/stroke ratio 1.25 rather than 1.6), and the blower and drive from the 46S were fitted. The engine produced over 200 hp and, fitted to a short wheelbase Type 46 chassis, using the same gearbox in the rear axle and other details, it clearly had a considerable performance.

Three T50 chassis with regulation Le Mans touring bodies were entered in the 24-hour race in 1931 but were withdrawn after Maurice Rost left the road when a tyre burst at 185 km/h (115 mph), the car hitting a tree and being wrecked. Unhappily, a spectator who should not have been in the area was killed, but Rost was thrown clear. The car acquired a reputation for being dangerous, which it probably deserved when not in skilled hands. Only some 65 were produced between 1931 and 1933, but the engine was also used in the 4.9-litre Grand Prix Type 54. Most Type 50s were fitted with as fine coachwork as its sister car, the Type 46, but the customer had to pay dearly for the extra power of the Type 50; the chassis price in 1932 in Britain was quoted as £1725 compared with £975 for the simpler model, an interesting example of Bugatti's sales technique.

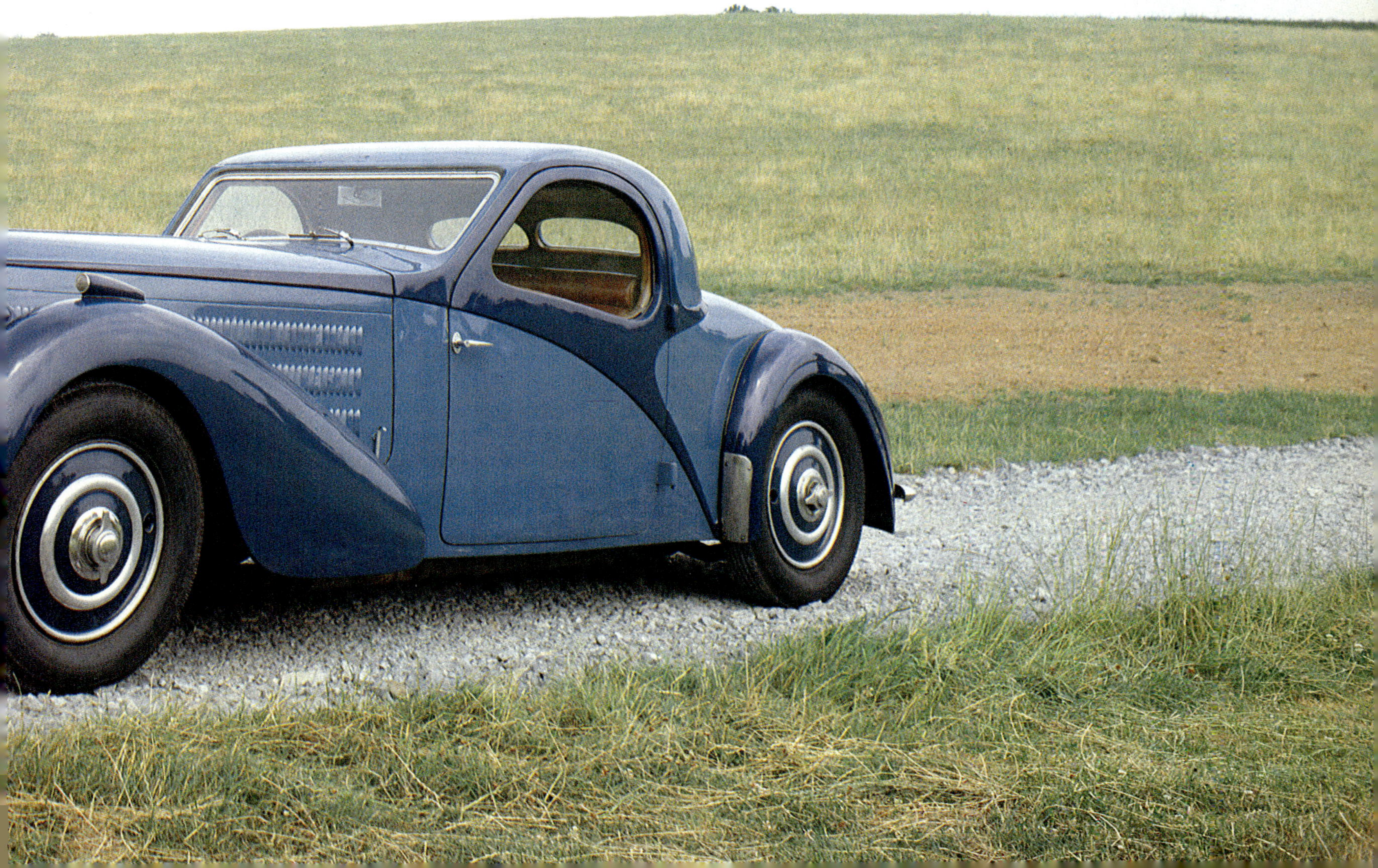

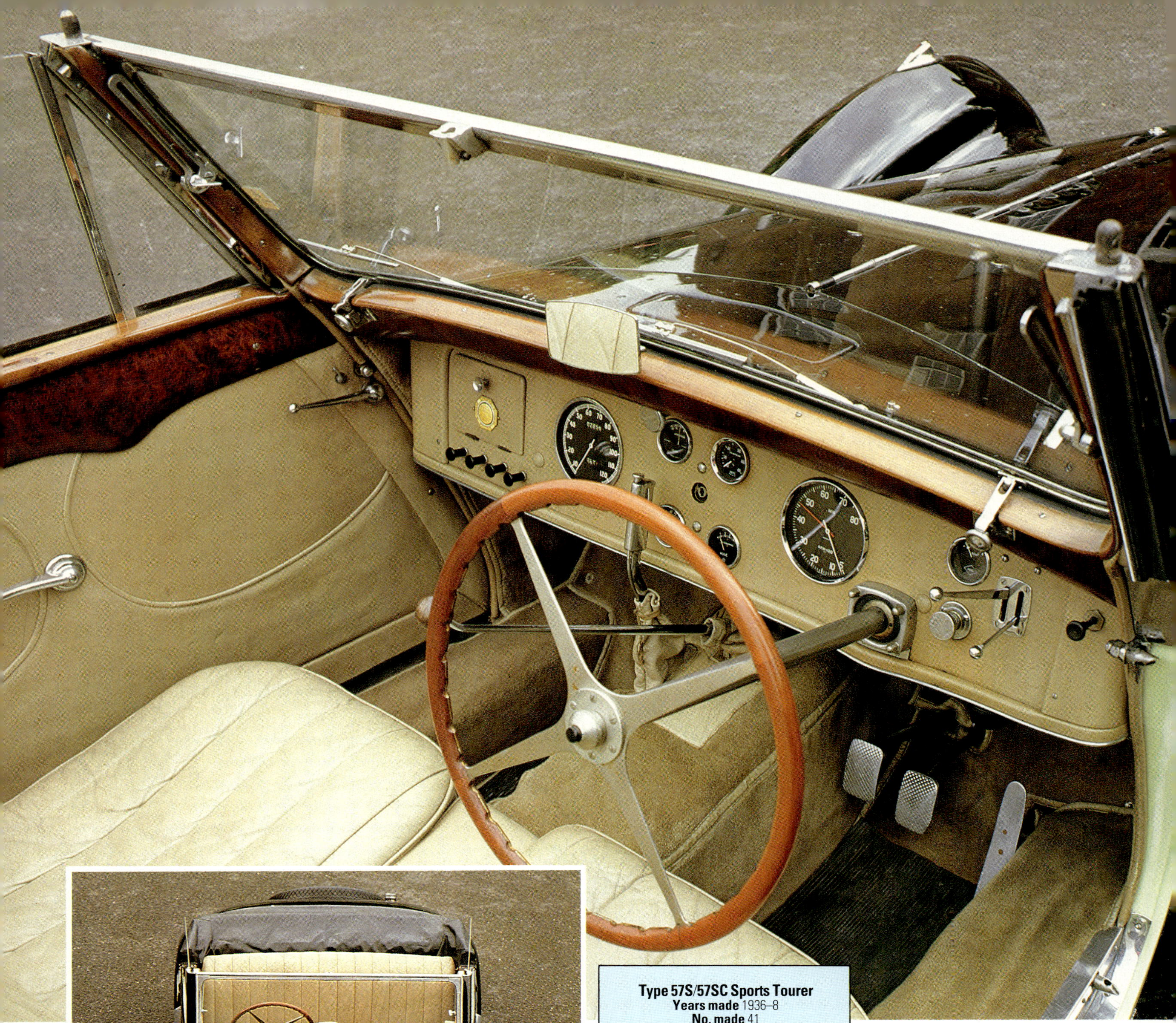

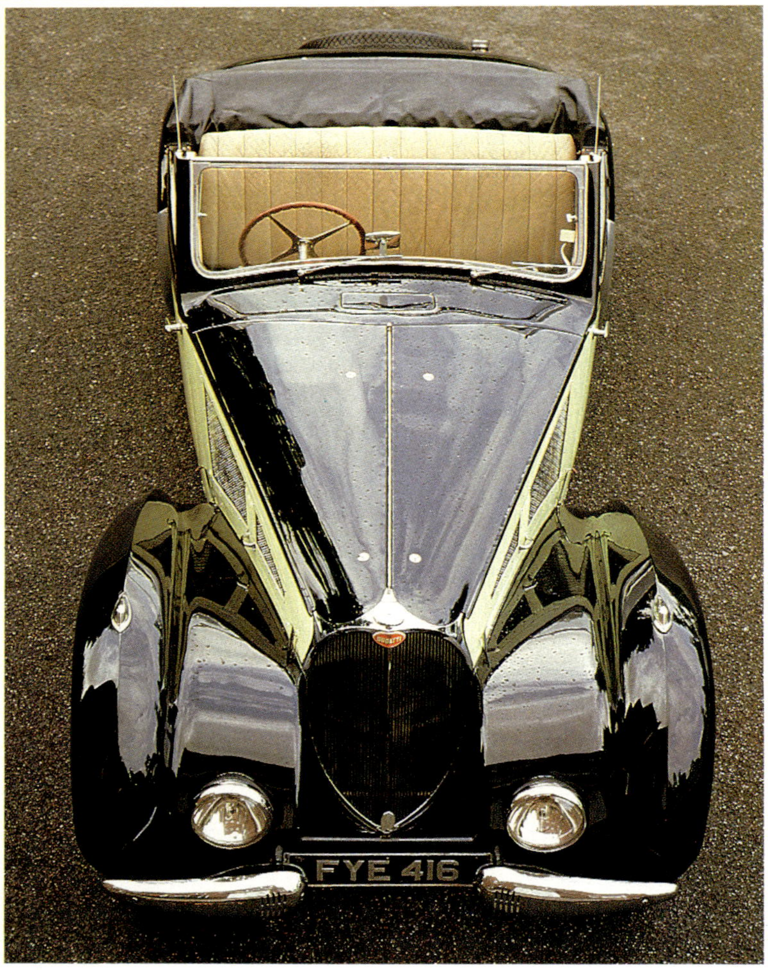

Type 57S/57SC Sports Tourer
Years made 1936–8
No. made 41

ENGINE

Type	Monobloc, twin overhead camshafts, plain bearings
No. of cylinders	8
Bore/stroke mm	72 × 100
Displacement cc	3257
Valve operation	1 inlet, 1 exhaust per cylinder
Sparkplugs/cyl.	1
Supercharged	57SC only
Carburettor	1 Stromberg
BHP approx.	T57S: 170/T57SC: 200

DRIVE TRAIN

Clutch	Twin plate, dry
Transmission	4-speed and reverse, constant mesh gears central ball change

CHASSIS

Wheelbase	2.98 m (9 ft 1 in)
Track	1.35 m (4 ft 5 in)
Suspension – front	½ elliptic
Suspension – rear	Reversed ¼ elliptic
Brakes	Cable
Tyre size	Front 5.50 × 18, rear 6.00 × 18
Wheels	Rudge wire

PERFORMANCE

Maximum speed	180 km/h (112 mph)

LEFT AND ABOVE The Type 57S chassis was the ultimate roadgoing Bugatti, invariably fitted with superb coachwork: in this case a splendid Van Vooren convertible coupé. This particular car was first registered in 1939. Provided by Mr T.A. Roberts.

RIGHT This Type 57C supercharged model, fitted with a drophead coupé by Gangloff, was supplied direct from the factory to the well-known Bentley driver, Woolf Barnato, in April 1939. The engine seized at high speed after 2580 km (1600 miles) in his hands. A new engine was ordered but the outbreak of World War 2 prevented its being fitted. After Barnato's death, the car passed to David Porter in 1949, then to the present owner in the 1950s. Provided by Mr G. Dunn, CBE.

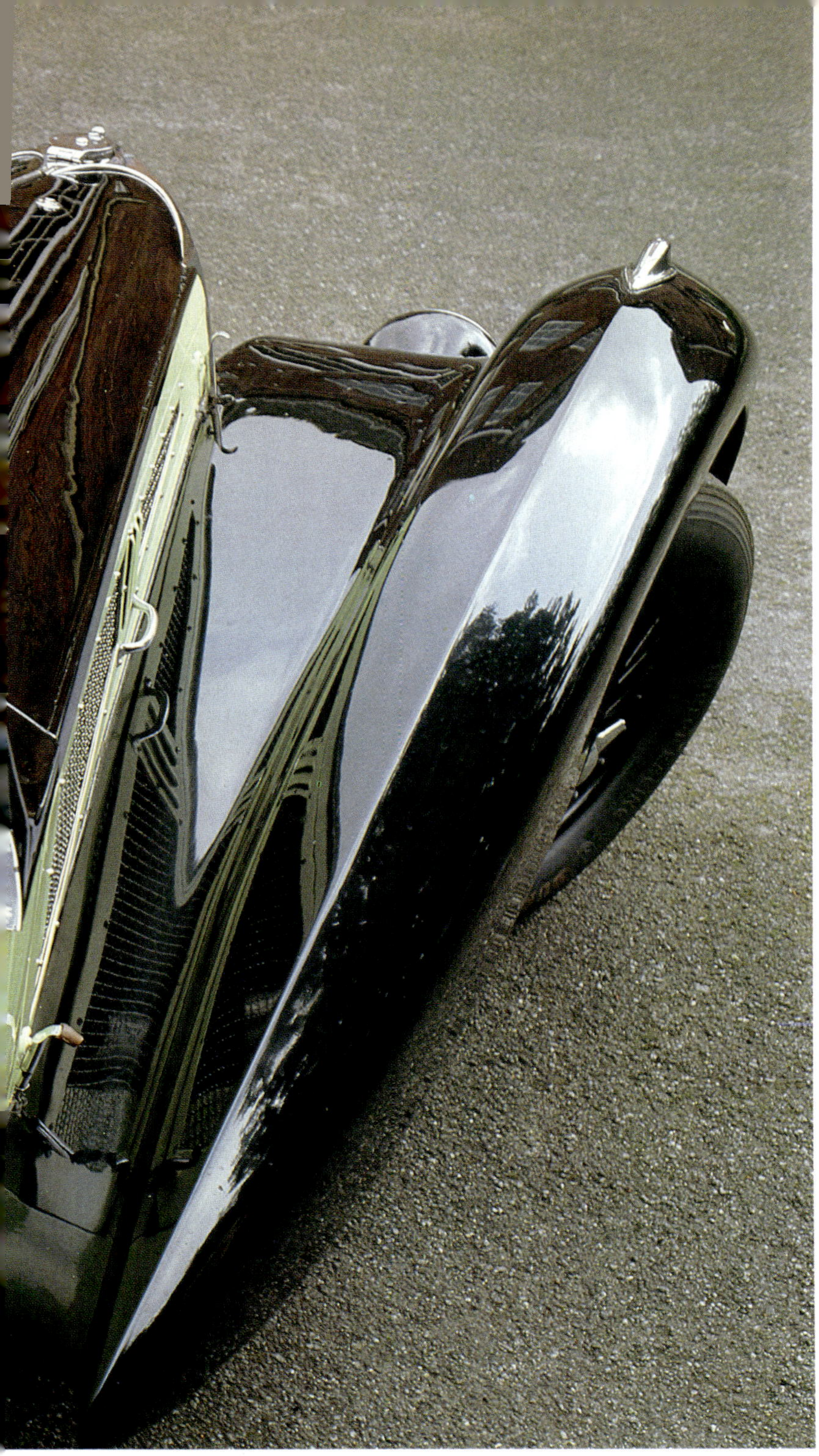

A few examples of this model remain today, including one of the surviving Le Mans cars.

The 3.3-litre Type 57

We now come to an important point in Bugatti's history where Ettore's son Jean was able to get the company to change direction into a simpler, indeed more sensible policy of concentrating on a single production model able to carry a variety of body styles.

In this period Ettore was spending a great deal of time in Paris on railcar work. In 1932 the design office at Molsheim was largely under the direction of Jean, then 23 years old – but Ettore probably remembered how much responsibility he himself had carried at that age in 1904. The design office was not large: seven or eight men of great ability well steeped in the ways of the *Patron* and capable of producing design drawings of the required standard, well led by Antoine Pichetto, who had joined Bugatti from Italy originally to design the four-wheel-drive Type 53. In those days a design was expected to be right first time and, if a prototype was made, it too would eventually be sold.

An almost completely new chassis was laid out, the Type 57. It was an eight-cylinder of course but, like the Type 59 racing car, with a six-bearing crank, a one-piece cylinder block and two valves per cylinder operated by a pair of camshafts, driven by a gear train at the back of the engine. The prototype engine was 72 × 88 mm, 2.8 litres, but all production engines were 72 × 100 mm, 3.3 litres. Rockers were used between cams and valve, rather than cups. The dynamos and water pump were gear driven on the left of the engine, and the oil pump in the sump was operated by vertical shaft and skew gears.

For the first time the gearbox was mounted integrally with the engine, with a single-plate clutch in the housing between. Helical constant mesh gears were used for quietness with sliding dog clutches for engagement. The rear axle was standard, initially based on that of the Type 44/49, but soon replaced with heavier gears from the T46. The chassis layout was normal Bugatti at the rear, with the usual reversed quarter elliptics, but initially two chassis were built with independent suspension by transverse springs at the front. The story has been recounted by Noël Domboy, one of the designers in the office at Molsheim, how Ettore on a visit saw the design of the independent suspension and immediately gave instruction that a Bugatti must have a 'proper' Bugatti axle, which is what the car had when it went on the market!

A new development was the abandonment of the superb nickel-silver honeycomb radiator used on all roadgoing Bugattis to date, in favour of a cheaper dummy and plated shell – of Bugatti shape – with a separate core, and with thermostatically operated shutters.

Another important policy decision was to offer the car with standardized Bugatti-built coachwork in addition to selling bare chassis. The Gangloff company of Colmar produced a drophead coupé called the Stelvio, and Molsheim made various bodies under Jean's guiding eye: a four-door pillarless saloon, the Galibier; a coach, the Ventoux, a fixed-head coupé, the Atalante; and later the Aravis and the exotic Atlantic.

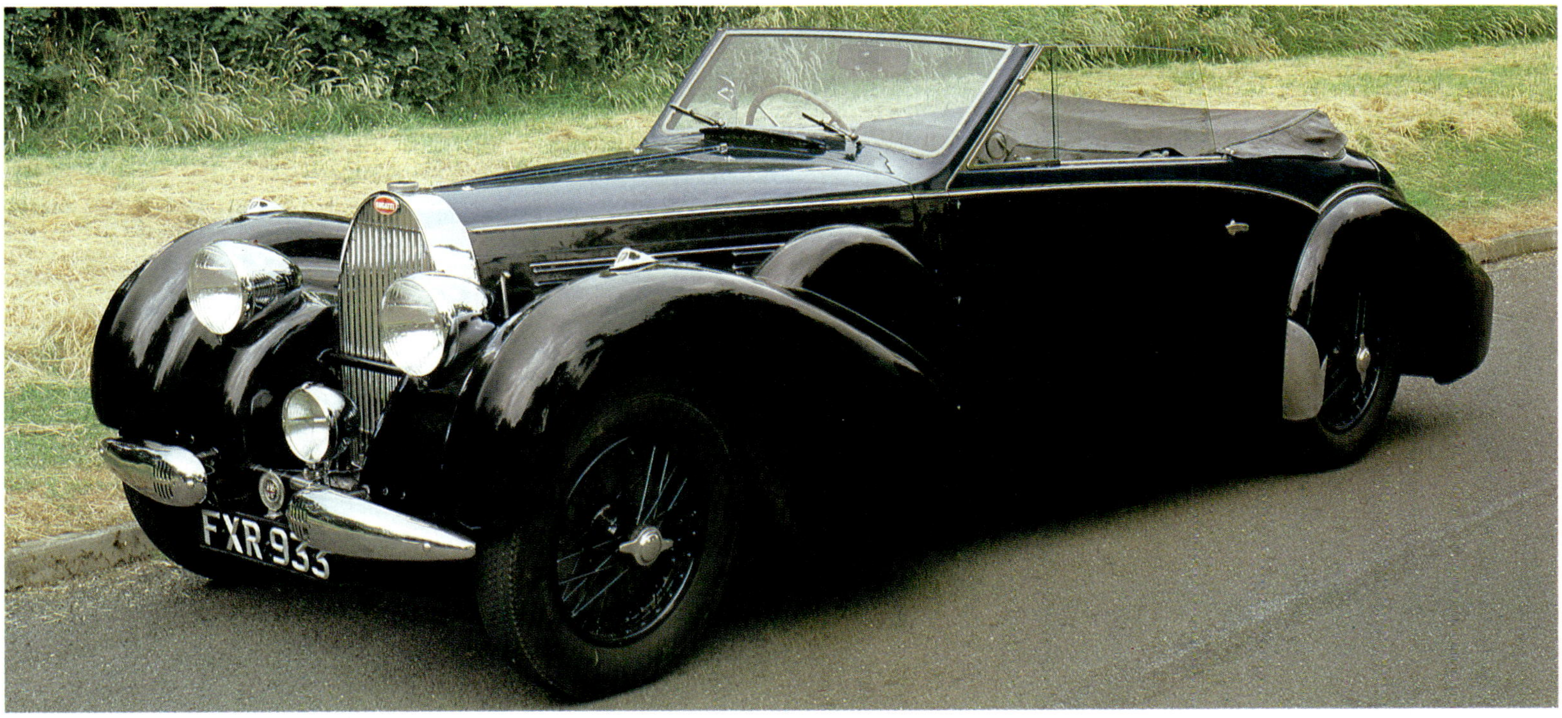

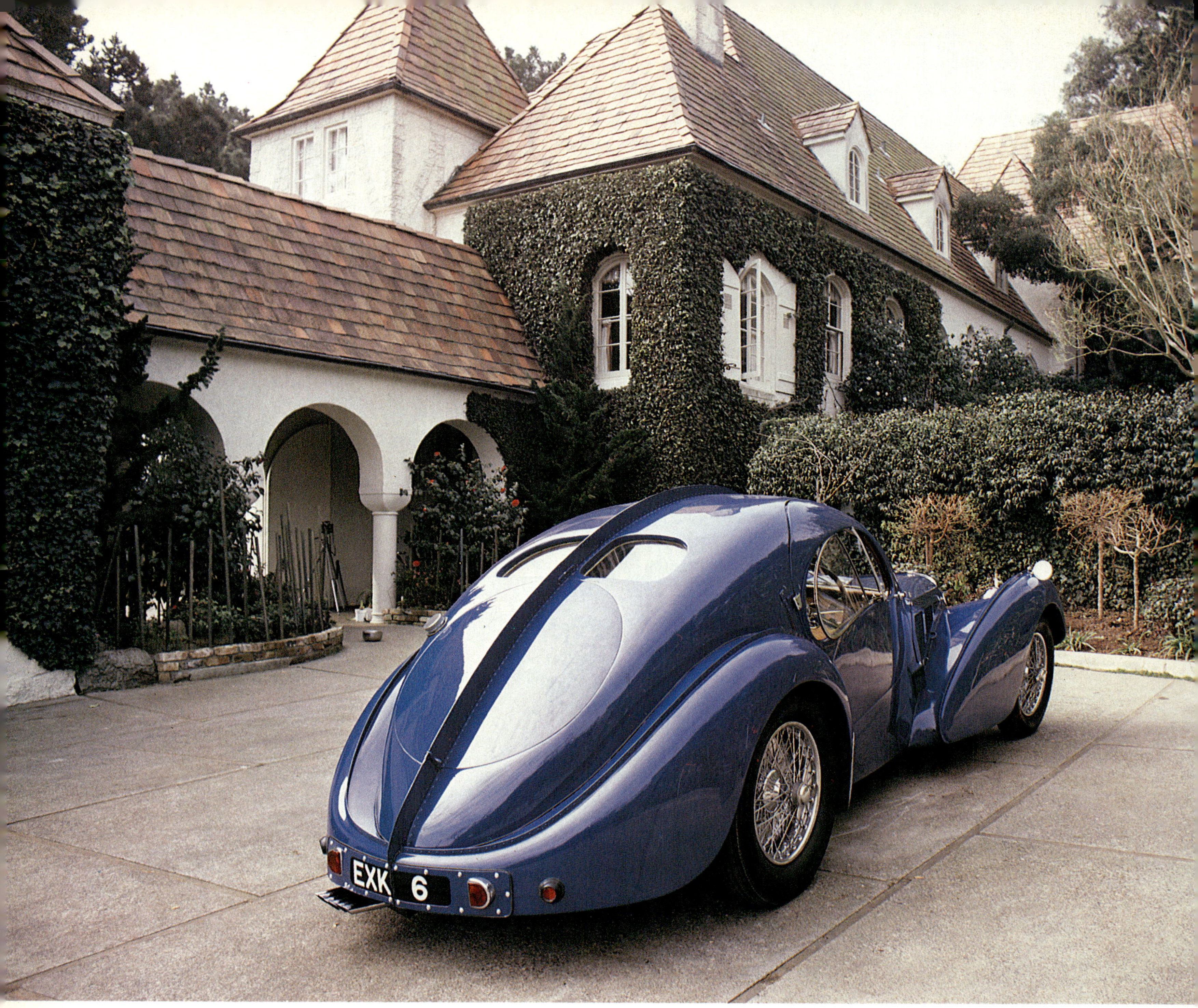
EXK 6

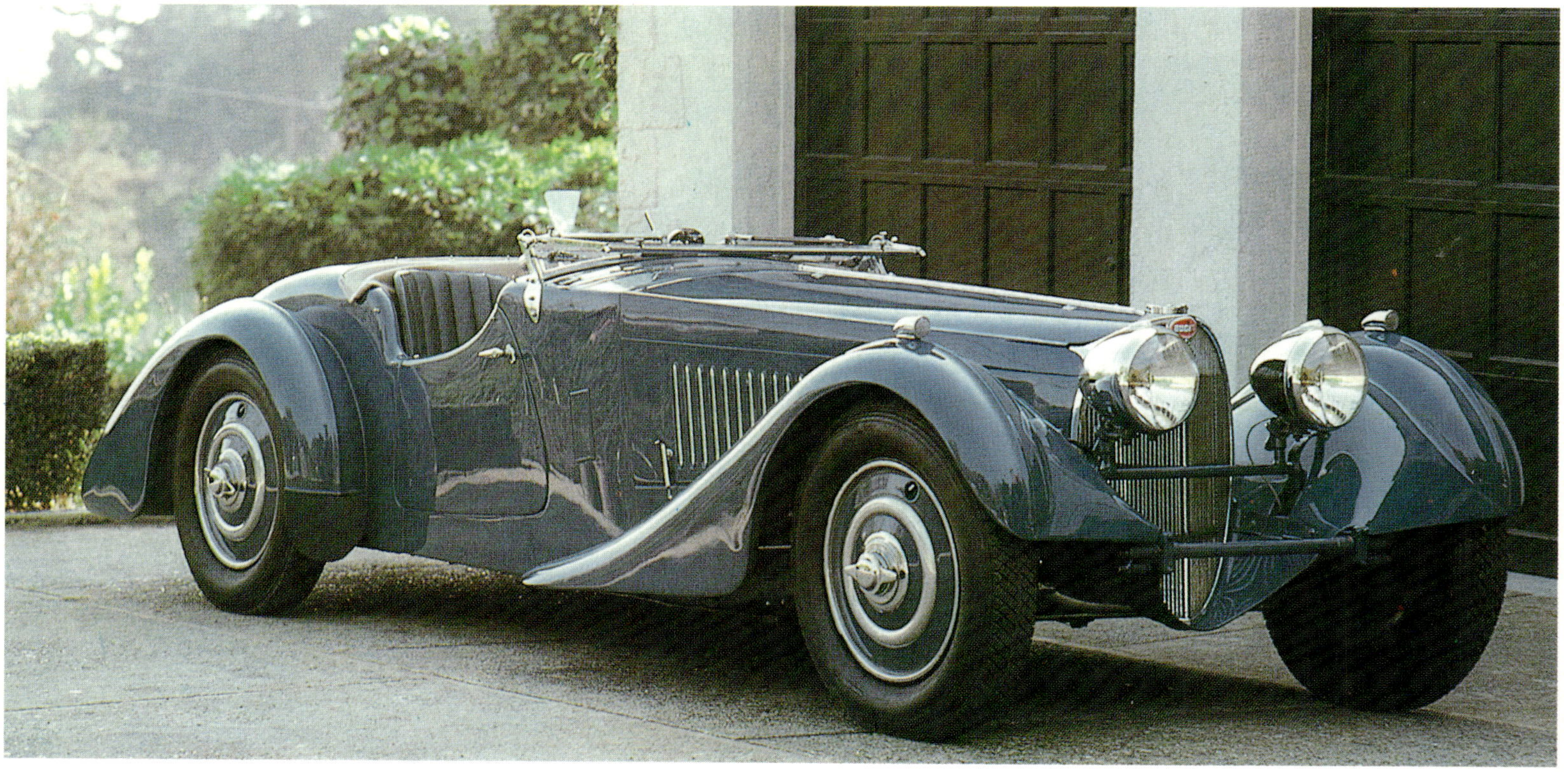

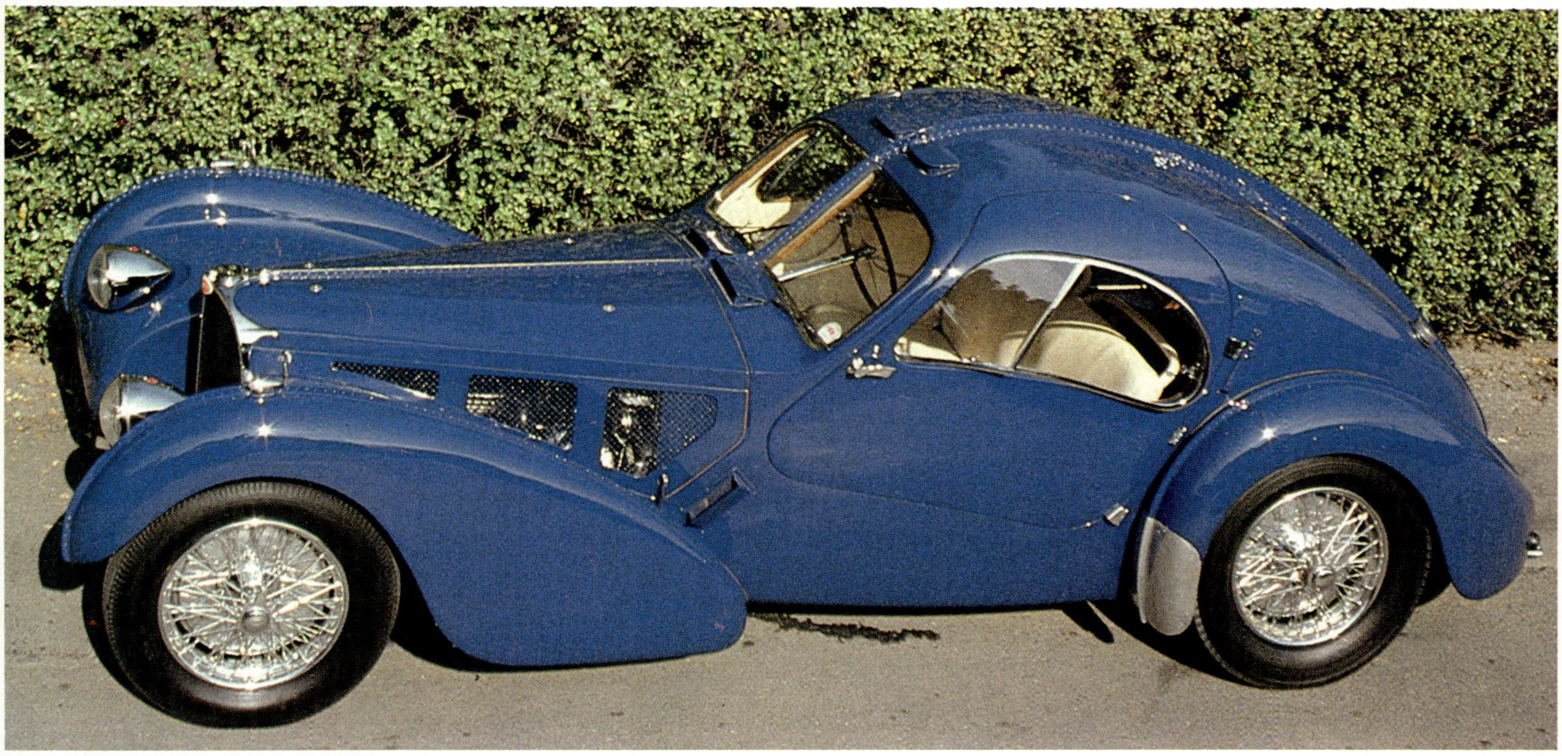

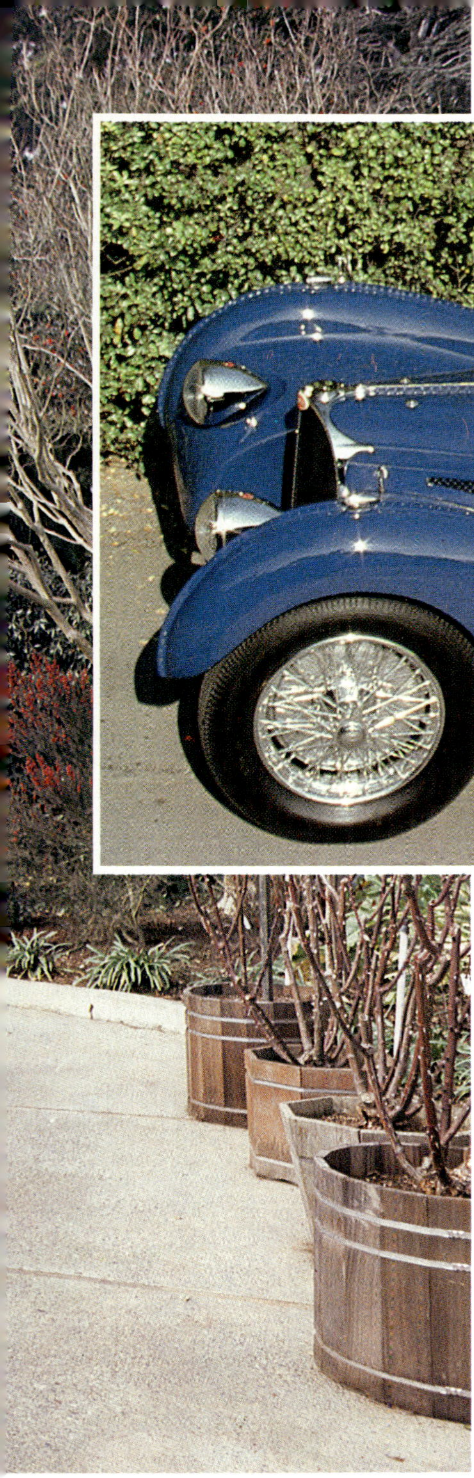

LEFT AND ABOVE The 57SC Atlantic coupé: perhaps the most exotic Bugatti ever made. Only three cars were delivered and all remain, two in the United States, one in France. The body panels are riveted together along a flanged spine, and the door penetrates the roof panel to improve access. This car was delivered new to R.B. Pope of Ascot (the supercharger was fitted later by the factory) and is now owned by Tom Perkins of California.

LEFT Sir Malcolm Campbell, the racing driver, took delivery in 1937 of a Type 57S chassis with a pretty two-seat body by the London coachbuilder Corsica. He only drove it some 1290 km (800 miles) before passing it on to R.E. Gardner, who kept it in perfect condition for 40 years! Owned by Tom Perkins, the car is now in California.

The first Type 57 was not delivered until the spring of 1934 but production was in full swing by the time of the Paris Salon in October. It had probably originally been intended to be displayed at the Salon the year before. About 830 of all versions were produced by the time war came in September 1939 and production was halted. The first batch of some 200 had solidly mounted engines and more or less normal and flexible Bugatti chassis frames. Then a stiff, cross-braced frame was introduced with a rubber-mounted engine with limited flexibility. Finally in 1938 a much-needed improvement came in the shape of hydraulic brakes, and telescopic shock absorbers replaced the earlier de Ram or friction types.

Meanwhile, in October 1936 came the inevitable supercharged version the Type 57C (C for *compresseur*), with a Roots blower driven by a pair of gears at the rear, and with a carburettor underneath the blower, not above as had been used in the racing T59 with a similar engine layout. The blower enhanced the performance and improved flexibility making the 57C the most attractive model. By 1939, after hydraulic brakes had been added, almost all production was of the C model; about 105 of these were made.

The normal Type 57 had an excellent performance and could reach about 150 km/h (nearly 95 mph) easily enough. The Type 57C was considerably faster. Indeed Robert Benoist, the racing driver, completed a standing start hour at 182.6 km/h (113.5 mph) at Montlhéry, in May 1939 on ordinary pump fuel in a 57C Galibier saloon, with a best lap of 195 km/h (121 mph) although the car must have been considerably 'tuned' to reach this speed, whatever the works may have claimed!

Some of the cars were fitted with Cotal electro-mechanical gearboxes, with gear change effected by a switch on the steering column; this was an attractive addition as the standard constant mesh 'box had a slow change, and no synchromesh (although this feature was in fact used on the 57G racing 'tank' cars).

The 57 itself was not raced by the factory except for one occasion in 1935, when two cars were entered in the Ulster Tourist Trophy and Lord Howe managed a third place. The cars had lightweight bodies and higher compression ratio, but were not really suitable for road racing.

The Type 57S: 'the best all-round super-sports car'

In August 1936 Molsheim launched a new sports version of the Type 57 under the designation 57S, initially unsupercharged but soon to have a blower added to become the 57SC. The chassis had a shorter wheelbase and, by arranging for the rear axle to pass through large holes in the rear of the frame, the whole frame line was lowered. Much of the car was standard, but the engine, with a higher compression ratio, now had a dry sump with a double oil pump, and a twin disc clutch to handle additional torque. Ignition was by Scintilla Vertex magneto lying in a cradle in the dash, driven by the left-hand camshaft, similar to the mounting of a normal Scintilla magneto in the racing Type 51. De Ram shock absorbers were standard.

Appearance was enhanced by a V-shaped radiator, and factory fitted bodies included the Atalante coupé, either fixed head or convertible, or the remarkable Atlantic coupé with a riveted spine down the centre line of the body joining two halves, and doors cutting into the roof to improve access. However, only three Atlantics were made.

Several bare chassis were supplied and fitted with special coachwork, including very pretty Corsica roadster bodies on chassis coming to Britain. One of these was owned by Sir Malcolm Campbell who wrote of its virtues as 'the best all-round super-sports car which is available on the market today' (1937) and also believed it to be the fastest obtainable.

The low build of the car improved the appearance and with the blower added the performance was as startling as Sir Malcolm indicated. The factory cost was high, however, as the small numbers produced had to be hand-built; after some 42 cars had been turned out the last deliveries were made in May 1938, before the type could receive the hydraulic brake improvement applied to the standard model.

The Type 64 prototypes

In mid-1938 Jean started to plan a new touring car to replace the Type 57. On the Type 57 engine he had been experimenting with chain drive for the camshafts, to quieten the gear noise of the existing drive – the prototype had suffered a disastrous engine breakdown when the chain

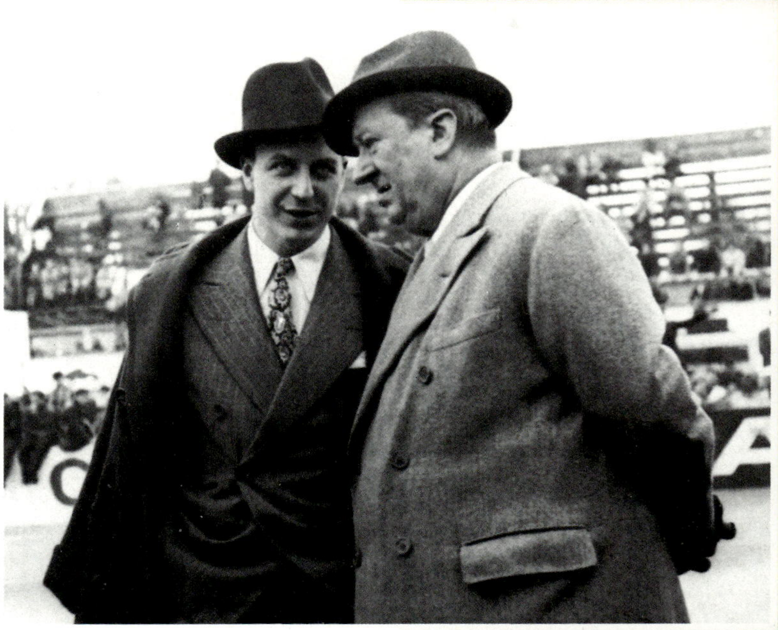

RIGHT Ettore Bugatti and his son Jean. Born into an artistic family (Carlo, Ettore's father, was a furniture designer and silversmith), Ettore and his brother Rembrandt inherited a creative talent. In Rembrandt it turned successfully to animal sculpture (tragically he died young in 1916). The talent passed to Jean, effectively in charge of all automobile design after 1932.

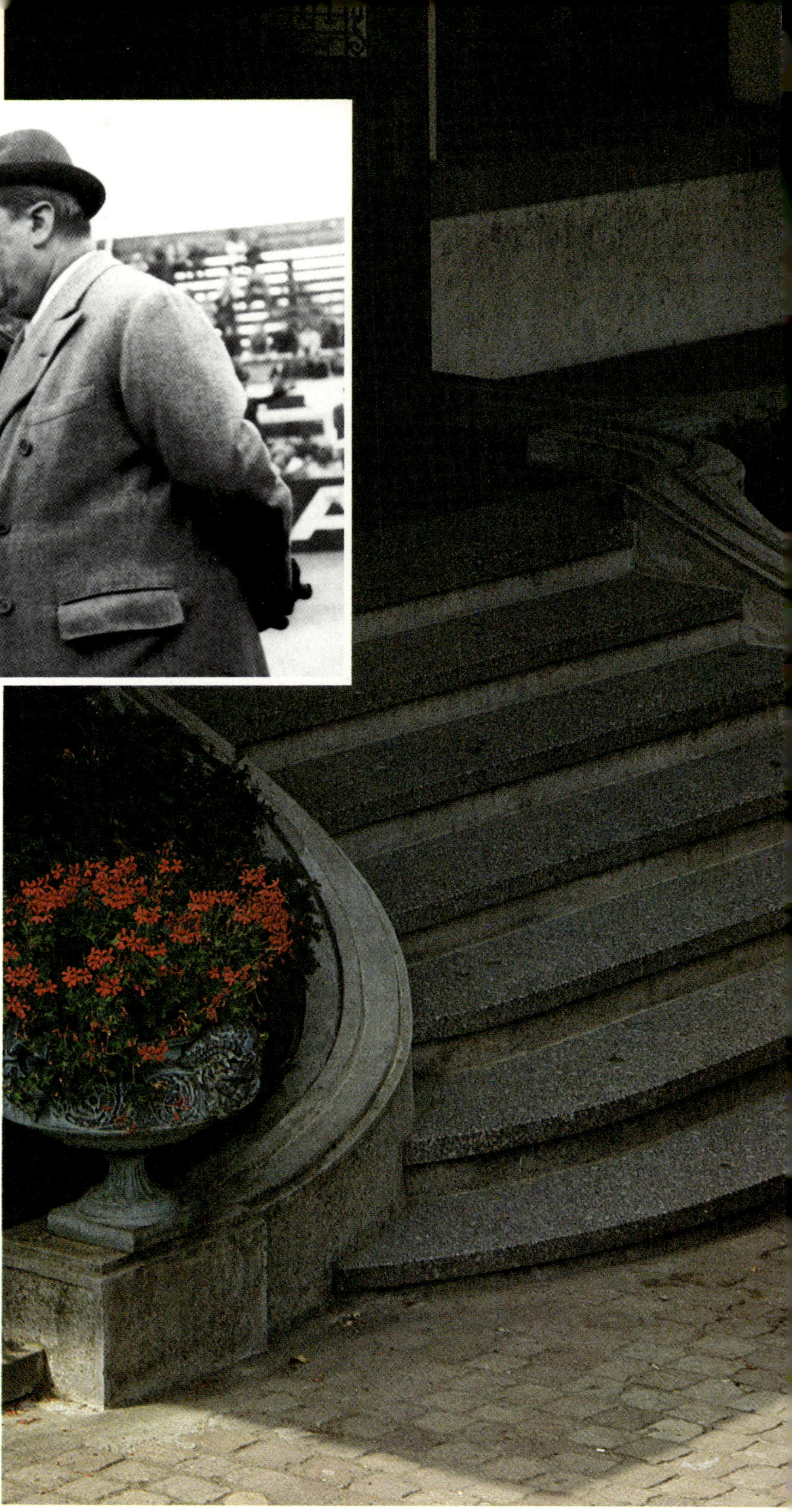

FAR RIGHT The post-war Type 101 with a drophead coupé by Gangloff of Colmar. The chassis was in all respects similar to the last Type 57 cars built in 1939, and no attempt was made to replace the solid front axle. Only six cars were completed. This particular car remained at the factory until acquired by Fritz Schlumpf, along with other cars retained there in the family collection. Provided by the Musée National de l'Automobile, Mulhouse.

failed! The new model, to be known as Type 64, was planned for the 1939 Paris Show and was to have the 4½-litre Type 50B engine, 84 × 100 mm bore and stroke. The chassis was similar to the Type 57, with the normal solid front axle, and usual reversed quarter elliptic springs at the rear. Four frames were built but only one or two cars seem to have been made and tested in 1939. One is now in the Musée National. Another was finished off from stock parts after the war and is in California.

Of historical interest is a recent revelation from a former coachbuilder from the factory that a prototype body was built to the designs of Jean Bugatti making use of 'gull-wing' doors, thus anticipating by a number of years the celebrated Mercedes-Benz 300SL with this feature – and indeed its problems of door clearance! This design was not proceeded with and the car intended for the Paris Salon had a more normal two-door body with good flowing lines.

Had not the Second World War intervened it is certain that the T64 with its greater power, and thus an ability to cruise fast at part throttle, would have been a worthy model in the best tradition of Bugatti Grand Touring cars, eventually to replace the Type 57.

Bugatti's plans for the 1947 Salon

A few weeks before his death Ettore Bugatti issued a brief statement to the press outlining his plans to resume car production, and listed what he would show at the Paris Salon in October. He had just recovered his factory at Molsheim, after its occupation by the Germans during the war, and a battle with the French authorities occasioned by his Italian nationality. He announced that no fewer than 800 employees were at work at Molsheim, mainly overhauling Bugatti railcars.

Three cars were in the programme: the 73A, 'with or without compressor', 1500 cc, normal Bugatti leaf springs and carrying a two-door, four-seat saloon body; the racing 73C mentioned on page 52; and an interesting

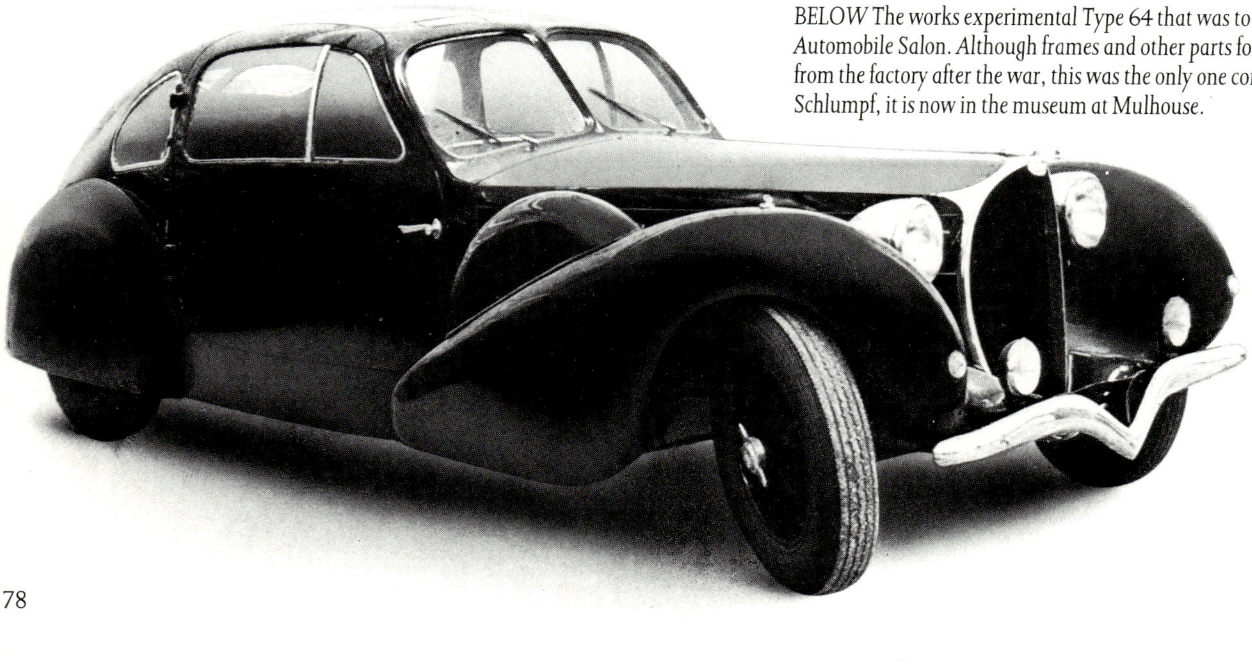

BELOW The works experimental Type 64 that was to have been shown at the 1939 Paris Automobile Salon. Although frames and other parts for two or three more cars 'escaped' from the factory after the war, this was the only one completed. Acquired by Fritz Schlumpf, it is now in the museum at Mulhouse.

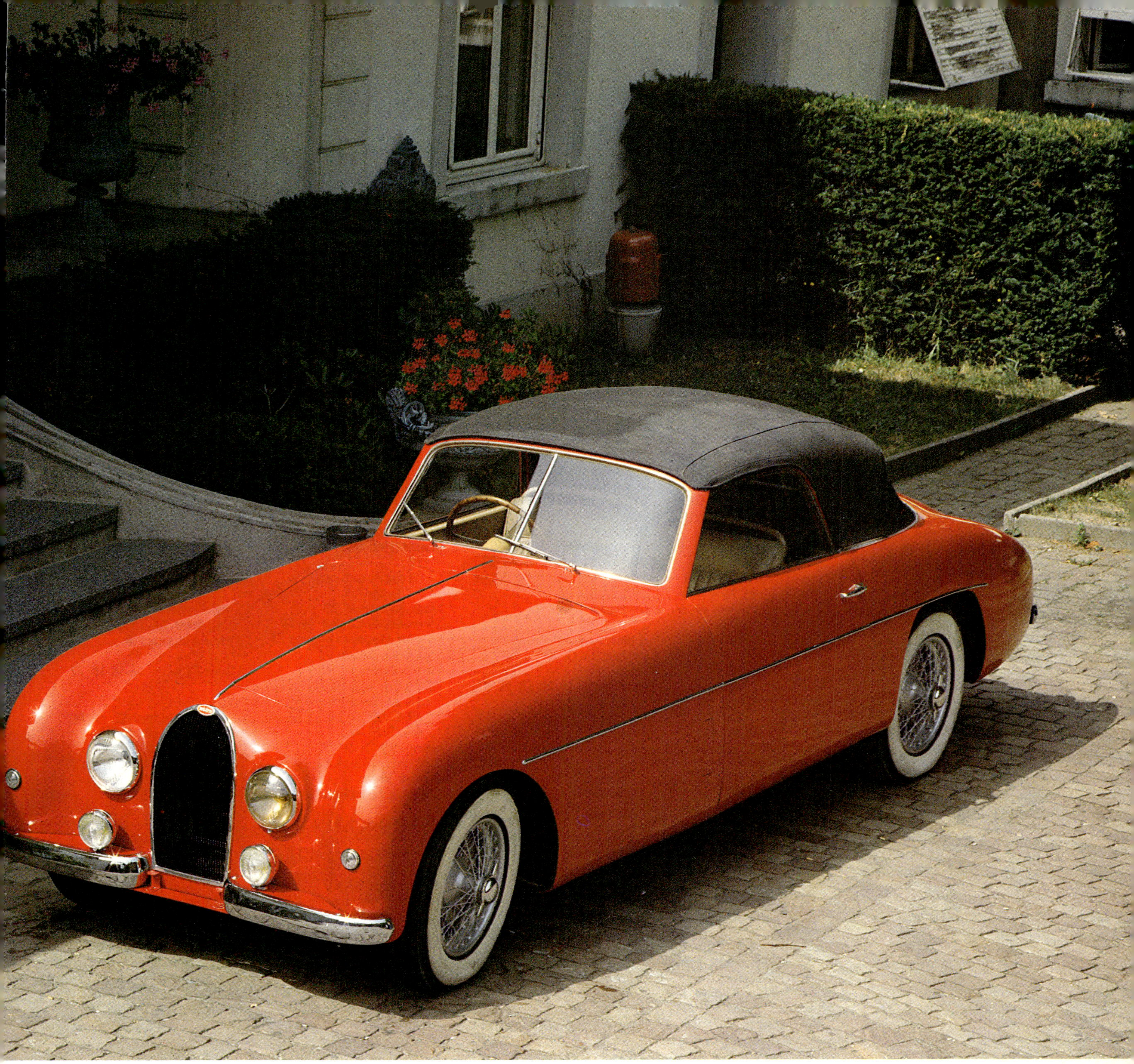

project, the Type 68, a little car of only 350 cc, with twin overhead camshafts and a compressor. The prototype of this remarkable and expensive project, which was not completed at the time of Bugatti's death, lies with other prototype cars in the museum at Mulhouse.

The press statement also mentioned that the programme included production of a fishing boat, and a small dinghy with inboard single-cylinder Bugatti engine, to be produced at a shipyard Bugatti owned on the Seine near Paris, the Chantiers Navals de Maisons-Laffitte.

None of these plans came to fruition after Ettore's death.

The Type 101: a revival of the T57

Four years after the death of Ettore Bugatti in August 1947 the works, under the direction of his son Roland and Bugatti's former racing driver, Pierre Marco, now factory manager, made an attempt to revive the Type 57 under the designation Type 101. This was virtually a standard 1939 Type 57, with Cotal electro-mechanical gearbox, and new inlet manifolding to take a Weber carburettor, and available with or without supercharger. The solid front axle was retained understandably, but probably unreasonably, for 1951: a major development programme for an independently sprung chassis was out of the question.

The car was shown at the Paris Salon in 1951, with coachwork by Gangloff of Colmar, but there were few orders. Only six cars were completed before lack of finance brought Bugatti's car-building activity to an end.

Epilogue

The demise of Bugatti as a car manufacturer had begun on Ettore's death on 21 August 1947, but it came finally at the end of July 1963. The company was absorbed by Hispano-Suiza who by then was a manufacturer of jet engines, having ceased making cars before the war. Hispano-Suiza in turn has been absorbed into the empire of the French national aero-engine company, SNECMA, and an association created with the Messier company, the principal French manufacturer of aircraft landing gear, hydraulics and wheels. Now Bugatti is part of Messier-Hispano-Bugatti, and the elliptical Bugatti badge has been replaced on the factory wall at Molsheim with an overlay of a Messier eagle, a Hispano stork and the dotted ellipse.

All vestiges of Bugatti's car production finally left Molsheim in 1979 when the Bugatti Owners Club of Britain took over all remaining spare parts (some dating back to 1914!). Now only memories remain.

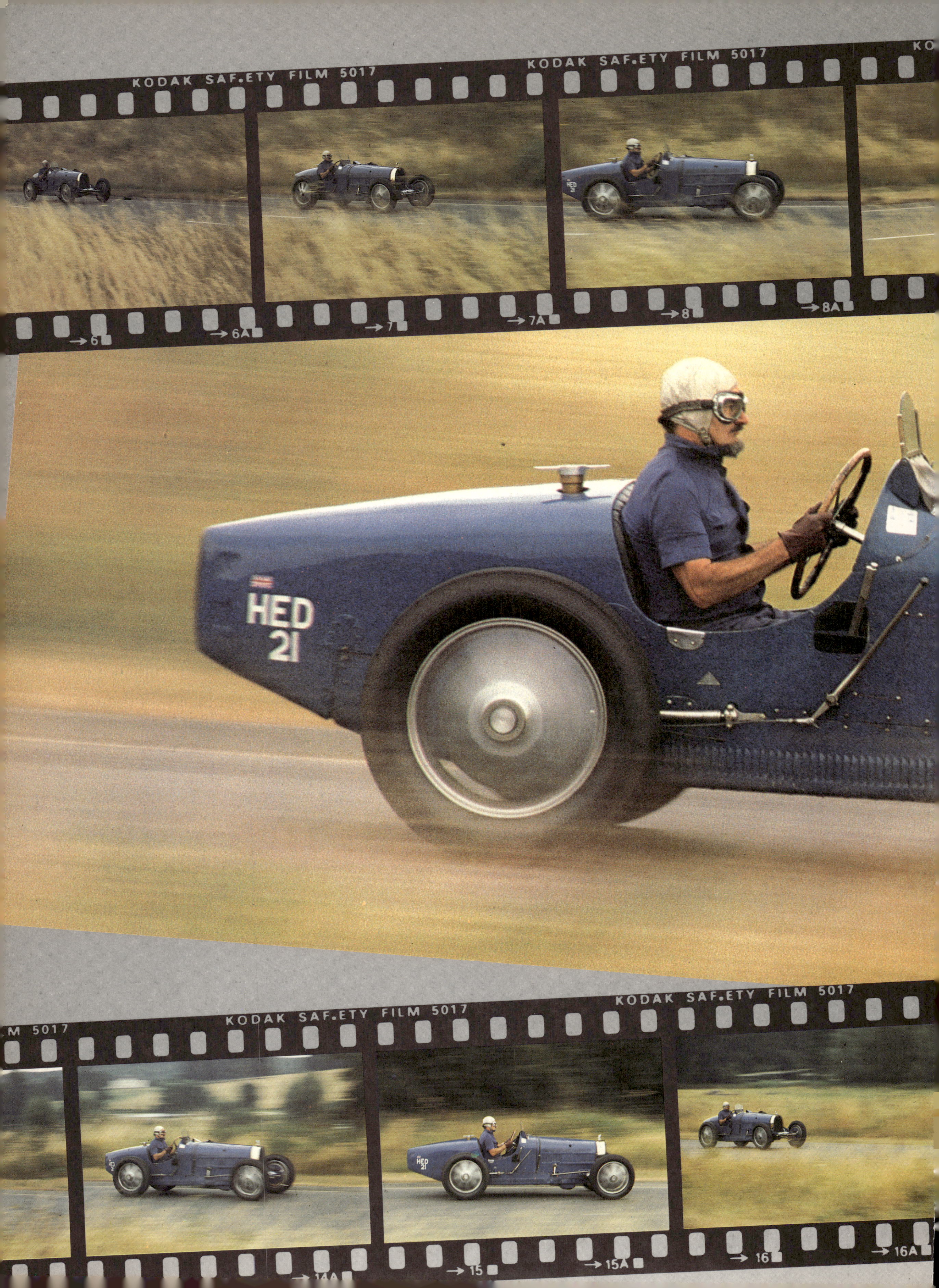
KODAK SAF.ETY FILM 5017
KODAK SAF.ETY FILM 5017
→6
→6A
→7
→7A
→8
→8A
HED
21
KODAK SAF.ETY FILM 5017
KODAK SAF.ETY FILM 5017
→15
→15A
→16
→16A